Spiritual Discourses

Volume II

MAHARAJ CHARAN SINGH

Spiritual Discourses

Volume II

(translated from the original Punjabi)

Maharaj Charan Singh

RADHA SOAMI SATSANG BEAS

Published by:
Sewa Singh, Secretary
Radha Soami Satsang Beas
P.O. Dera Baba Jaimal Singh
Dist. Amritsar 143204
Punjab, India

First Edition   1997   5,000 copies
Second Edition   1997   5,000 copies

Printed by: Baba Barkha Nath Printers, New Delhi 110 015

But for the presence of saints on earth,
the world would burn to death.

Sant na hote jagat me^n jal martaa sa^{n}saar.
Tulsi Sahib

Contents

Foreword

If we want to discover the nature of the truth, where in the world do we go? If we want to know who we are, whom can we go to? There are practically infinite resources available to us if we want to understand our bodies. We have all sorts of options if we need to explore the workings of the mind. But is there anyone who knows who we really are, who understands the truth of our spirit, the soul?

Modern times are dominated by the physical sciences, by materialism and technology. For many, even the very notion of the spirit is an idea we have outgrown.

What if we think that we are more than mind and body? What if our hearts tell us, somehow, that we are something more than the reality described by the physical sciences?

In the past, we would go to the religions of our parents, our cultures, for answers to these questions. In this Information Age things are different: we meet people, both physically and electronically, from all over the world. We soon discover that the absolute unqualified Truth of our parents' religion is often contradictory with the absolute unqualified Truth told to the people we meet from neighbouring cultures. But surely—if we are all human beings, equal in every fundamental, with the same needs and aspirations—the Truth must be the same for all of us?

Instead of a universal Reality, a Truth that is the same wherever and whenever we are, we have been given a God that is dependent on the culture we live in. The characteristics of our God depend on our time and place in the pageant of human history. His nature reflects our condition in this physical, material world.

As a global perspective emerges in this Information Age, it allows us to transcend our national, cultural and regional perspectives. We see how humanity, to help achieve worldly ends, has manipulated the natural and fundamental human longing towards the spirit. Misunderstanding the nature of the spirit, we have failed to make contact with it. Indeed, far from making contact with it, we have been deluded to the point that we misuse religion to justify slaughter and oppression.

Where, then, can we go to find that truth of the spirit? If it could be expressed or understood through the use of mere words, then surely such constant disagreement as to the nature of God would be impossible? Is there any similar disagreement about the nature of electricity, or about the components of water or of blood, from one culture to another, from one language group to another? It is precisely because the spirit cannot be known through the mind and senses—because it cannot be rendered or expressed in symbols—that there is this endless disagreement amongst human beings as to what the spirit really is.

Again we ask: where can we go? Whenever we want to study a subject, we look for a teacher who has practical knowledge and experience of that subject. Whether it is dancing, particle physics, football or medicine, only someone who has explored the subject thoroughly, who has worked with it and loves it, who can communicate it and teach others how to learn it for themselves, only such a person will make a proper teacher. We enrol in a class; we attach ourselves to our teacher; we study and practise—only in this way do we learn.

It is no different with spirituality. To find the spiritual Truth, we attend a spiritual discourse. It is the forum in which one who knows the truth of the spirit—a spiritual Master—

bears witness to that truth, so that others may catch a glimpse of it also.

Imagine for a moment that you are in a wilderness, without any shelter, and it is bitterly cold. As your body gets colder and colder, you put on more and more layers of protective clothing. The sun may be shining, but its warmth is not reaching you. You dare not take off even one layer, even though other people keep telling you that the sun is, in fact, warm. You can't feel it yourself. You don't trust them. You are chilled to the bone from the biting cold.

But then you happen upon a sheltered spot where, for a moment, the sun's warmth does penetrate. Enjoying the relief, you stay there for a while. Eventually you cautiously remove one layer of clothing. You allow yourself to feel the warmth of the sun. Your confidence builds and you take off still further layers as you delight in the power of the sun to revive your frozen limbs.

The discourse of a spiritual Master is that shelter where the warmth of God's truth first touches our hearts. Swathed as we are in the layers of the mind, only the truth, spoken by an adept who knows that truth, has the power and authority to penetrate the thick layers covering our souls.

When we attend such a discourse, our souls, lying petrified within us, come to life. They respond to the vibrant ring of the truth. They hear their own language. They hear themselves spoken of. They recognize their friend. If the time is right, just one word, one phrase, can strike us with such force that from that day on our entire lives are transformed.

As long as we focus primarily on the material, the world of mind and matter, the soul's power remains subdued, latent and unknown. Like a child in a large gathering, the soul is inward and shy. But give it company of its own kind and it revives—our hearts gladden. Then we say with conviction,

"Yes! That is who I am!" We had been confused for so long!
The core of us, our very heart, the wellspring of our being,
had been ignored, unrecognized, neglected and in exile.

Then our soul is able to shout out in joy, "This is me! This
is I. This is you. We are all one." From that day we see everything in a new light. We understand, we see, that spirit is the
prime reality—eternal and unchanging. The spirit is our life:
it unites us in its power. Our minds and bodies are suits of
clothes in which our spirits live in this world. These outer shells
are transient and perishable. But our souls never die.

The true spiritual discourse gives us this certainty. It is
the key that unlocks the door to our spiritual hearts. Self-
realization must come before God-realization. If we do not
even know what we are, what hope is there for us to understand what God is?

Through a spiritual discourse, we associate with those
that know and love the world of the spirit. We associate with
the spiritual adept who has explored this world, who knows
how to realize it, who speaks with the authority that only
practical experience can bring. For us this encounter is a
means to an end, for ultimately, to know the truth, we have
to experience it ourselves. Until that day, the discourse is our
lifeline, securing us to the reality that is the fulcrum of our
lives. We are reminded of what is real. We remember who
we are. Gradually, we begin to understand the true order of
the world.

The eight discourses in this book were given by one of the
greatest teachers of spirituality of the twentieth century. From
1951 until 1990, Maharaj Charan Singh carried the mantle of
spiritual Master of the Radha Soami Satsang Beas. He travelled ceaselessly the length and breadth of India and to every
corner of the globe, to spread the universal message of spiritual truth.

Born into a Sikh family, he supported himself from his agricultural property throughout the forty years of his ministry, neither taking nor receiving so much as a pin or a penny from his disciples. Like all great lovers of God, he never spared himself in his service of God's one family, maintaining, year in, year out, a schedule that most would have found impossible to sustain for even a few days. During the years of his Mastership, he initiated over a million souls into the practice of realizing the spirit that is central to all mystic experience, irrespective of the religion or culture in which it takes place.

Maharaj Charan Singh was a lawyer by profession before being appointed spiritual Master of the Radha Soami line. He said that his way of speaking reflected his lawyer's training. When giving a discourse, he spoke quietly and slowly at the beginning. Without notes, he quoted extensively from the Sikh scriptures and from the writings of many Indian saints. His concern was always to remind his audience that all saints and God-realized souls teach the same truth.

As the discourse progressed, his speed increased, and he built around his core text an unassailable and overwhelming case for the inner way to God. The discourse could last anything from one to two hours. He followed the traditional style of India, where a text is sung verse by verse and the speaker explains the text after each verse is sung.

These discourses are gifts of inestimable value that Maharaj Charan Singh bequeathed to the world. When reflecting on the potential of the spoken word, as uttered to a seeker of truth by one who has travelled the spiritual road, we may do well to recall a story told of one of the Desert Fathers in the early years of Christianity.

A monk went to his spiritual guide and said, "Speak a word, Father."

The Father spoke: "Thou shalt love the Lord with all thy heart."

The monk went away.

Twenty years later he returned to his guide and said, "Father, I have struggled to keep your word. Now give me another word."

The Father said: "Thou shalt love thy neighbour as thyself."

The monk returned to his cell.

Just a few words from a living God-realized soul can tell us everything we need to know at the level of the mind. We may search no further for the whys and wherefores of life. If, by God's grace, we are blessed with contact with those who know—if we absorb their words into our hearts and they lead us to the practice that transmutes words into the gold of practical experience, then we have started on our journey home.

Sat means 'truth' and *sang* means 'association with'. The Indian term for a spiritual discourse, *satsang*, means 'association with the truth'. Truth is simple. It is our minds that are complex. To retain control, they will do everything within their power to stop us from knowing anything other than themselves.

We give thanks to our Maker that to awaken and to guide us, He gives us, on this earth, precious souls that embody the truth of the spirit, and who can teach us that Truth.

Margaret Faith Singh

Preface

For forty years, Maharaj Charan Singh spoke to gatherings of seekers of spiritual truth, from all parts of India and the world. Now, six years after his passing from the physical plane, this book reminds us, once again, of the fundamentals of the path he taught.

He always began his discourses saying that the essential teachings of every saint are one and the same. The eight discourses or satsangs in this volume reflect that truth. The texts on which they are based are drawn from the writings of three great saints of Uttar Pradesh, who lived in the eighteenth and nineteenth centuries, and two of the Gurus in the line of Guru Nanak of Punjab, who lived in the sixteenth century. He illustrated his teachings with dozens of quotations from a wide range of saints, so the universality of their message became very clear.

This universality is offset by the particular focus Maharaj Charan Singh drew from each text. In the first discourse, "My Friend, Why Stay Caught in This World?", he explains why we experience so much stress in our modern lives. In "O Friend, Observe the Law of This Age", he clarifies the one effective way of true worship for the present age. He emphasizes the primary importance of love on the spiritual path, through Paltu Sahib's text, "In the Court of the Lord", and the universal nature of human suffering and its remedy, through Tulsi Sahib's poem, "Cleanse the Chamber of Your Heart".

The fifth discourse, "Among Your Companions, None Is Your Friend", warns us of our ignorance of our true condition. And in the sixth, "Hold Fast Your Mind", he explains the importance of the spiritual teacher and gives details of the technique for controlling the mind and turning it towards devotion for the Lord. "Come, My Friend, to Your True Home" is again a warning, alerting us to the way we lose sight of who we really are. The last satsang, "He Is the True Creator, the Only Giver", is a great celebration of the oneness of the creation, the one family of God, calling us all to raise our consciousness so that we can understand this truth.

Satsang is the primary instrument of the Masters to reach out to the world. Through their satsangs, they communicate the simple message of the inner path of the Word. This path has been known over the centuries by many names. The Beas Masters generally refer to it as *Sant Mat* (the path or teachings of the saints), *Surat Shabd Yog* (the yoga or union of soul and Word) and *Radha Soami Mat* (the teachings of Radha Soami, the supreme Lord of the soul).

They repeatedly explain that Radha Soami is not the name of a religion, and the teachings it represents are not new. The message of the saints is age-old, and rather than letting ourselves be distracted by the difference in words and outward forms, the saints always guide us to seek the spiritual essence itself, by putting into practice their words.

Sewa Singh
Secretary

Radha Soami Satsang Beas
May 27th 1996

Translators' Note

Whenever Maharaj Charan Singh gave discourses abroad or addressed the overseas sangat in India, he would speak in English and often base the discourse on the Bible. When he spoke in India, he based his talks on the Indian scriptures and drew his examples and metaphors largely from the rural culture of Punjab, which was his background and which he loved. Wherever he spoke, his language and explanations were always simple and direct. Like many others of his generation and culture, his mother tongue was Punjabi, his preferred language and that of his education was Urdu, and since the official language of India is Hindi, he used all three. This enabled him to reach the widest range of people, and in the process, he created his own distinctive patina by repeating words and concepts in strings of three.

The discourses in this book were given in different locations in India, to crowds as large as several hundred thousand people coming from all walks of life. He addressed himself to everyone—to the uneducated shepherds of the western desert, high-court judges and scholars from the great cities, the farmers of Punjab, the village folk of the central plateau, to merchants, shopkeepers and business people from towns and villages far and wide, uneducated women, professional women, mothers, daughters, sons, the old and young, rich and poor—he spoke to all.

No translation can ever truly match its original. The translator's work is threefold: to carry meaning accurately from one culture and language to another; to mirror the style and linguistic flavour of the original; to achieve a text that sounds natural and true. The closer the two languages and cultures are to each other, the easier it is to fulfil all three concerns. The further apart they are, the more certain it is that one or other will have to be compromised.

In this book, our absolute priority has been to convey the meaning of Maharaj Charan Singh's words accurately. Working both from transcripts and tape recordings of the discourses, we have taken note also of the emphases and modulations of his voice. Sometimes, where we felt it necessary to convey the meaning, we have added words. Where frequently used words or terms have several nuances of meaning, we have used different words in different contexts to convey the meaning as a whole.

Secondly, we have tried to convey Maharaj Charan Singh's particular manner of speech. Rather than rendering the discourses in a literary form, we have specifically tried to retain the spoken style—his frequent use of rhetorical questions to draw the listener into his line of thought, and the direct form of address when explaining quotations, speaking as though on behalf of the saint whose words he had quoted. Working with his words, we became aware that any effort to transform the text into a written style ran the danger of compromising nuances of meaning.

When speaking of the dynamic power of God that is the essence of the teachings, he rarely used the word 'Shabd' without linking it with the word 'Nam'. Shabd or Nam, the Word and the Name, were linked in his speech as one. These two terms occur together so frequently in every discourse that we have chosen sometimes to give both, sometimes to give one only, and in places, to give them in the original Punjabi juxtaposed to the English forms. The Word and the Name point to one reality, to one, single, limitless power. To convey this correctly would mean that no conjunction should ever be used between the terms, for the moment we say 'this *or* that', or 'this *and* that', we are saying that there are two. At a practical level, we found this impossible, so we have interspersed both these forms among the philosophically correct one: the Word, the Name.

Language expresses the way we live in the world and how we understand our place in it. We rejoiced to discover that in the Indian scriptures, most terms used to designate the individual and the supreme reality, the human and God, demonstrate a common root. For example:

aatmaa (soul),	
mahaatmaa (great soul, saint)	*parmaatmaa* (supreme soul)
nar (human)	*naraayan* (God)
purush (human being)	*param* **purush** (supreme being)
eeshwar (lord)	*parameshwar* (supreme lord)
purakh (human being)	*akaal* **purakh** (timeless being)
purakh (human being)	*sat* **purakh** (true being)
purakh (human being)	*kartaa* **purakh** (creator being)
dhanee (provider)	*pooran* **dhanee** (absolute provider)

The terms themselves reflect the mystic understanding that the relationship between the individual and God is that of a part to its whole, that God-realization is an expansion from the partial or incomplete to the perfect, the complete. This understanding is not generally shared by the Western scientific mind, which grew out of the Judaeo-Christian world-view that was first formalized when the Greek and Roman cultures dominated the world. In the Western world-view, God, the supreme reality, is perceived as transcendent rather than immanent, apart from and other than the human being—separate from the entire world. This fundamental

perception of both the individual and the world as intrinsically godless and profane may underlie the abject conditions
we have reached today.

In his discourses, Maharaj Charan Singh mostly used two
terms for God: *parmaatmaa* and *maalik.* The latter we have
always translated as 'Lord', and for *parmaatmaa* we have generally used 'Supreme Being'. In specific instances we have
chosen to use the more literal translation 'supreme soul', to
communicate to the reader the mystic relationship embedded in the language.

When speaking of the role of the spiritual Master, he always used the term *gurmukhaa*[n] (literally, those whose face is
turned towards the Guru), which we have translated as 'the
lovers of the Lord', 'God's lovers', 'devotees' and 'saints'.
Never did he say anything which would indicate that he himself was a spiritual Master, loved and revered by many. At
such times, his language was reserved in the extreme. We have
therefore used the term 'Master' sparingly, to avoid giving the
reader the impression that Maharaj Charan Singh referred
directly to himself with such a term.

He saw himself simply as being in the service of his
Master, living in the Lord's will by obedience to his Master's
command that he should continue his work. In the entire
book, representing approximately fourteen hours of speech,
he makes statements in the first person on three occasions
only, other than when introducing the discourses or reminding his audience of something he had already said. He uses
the first person once when recalling his own Master, and
twice when stating that those who have hatred in their hearts
for others have not yet developed love for the Lord, and are,
in truth, hating Him.

It is not possible in translation to convey the restraint,
respect and humility that is present in the way he used the

Indian language. This inherent deference within language reflects a cultural tradition that is still present in traditional India. Human relationships, and the relationship of the individual to his or her Guru or spiritual Master—that person who leads us to the divine—are defined within recognized parameters. The well-being of the individual is perceived in specific relation to the context—be it the family, the society or the divine. Fulfilling the relationship is paramount, and respect for the relationship is fundamental, since acknowledging interdependence enables each to be fulfilled and safeguards the whole. Even within a family, personal names are rarely used except by an elder or senior when speaking to one younger or junior within the family structure.

Thus, when speaking of one's Master it would be inconceivable for a disciple to use the Master's personal name. This sensibility is reflected in the discourses when Maharaj Ji speaks of his Master, Maharaj Sawan Singh, using the honorific 'Hazur'. It is also reflected in his use of honorifics when referring to other saints and Masters, and in the way he refers to the Gurus in the line of Guru Nanak, which was his own cultural background and that of a large proportion of his audience.

The reader will note that he always observed the tradition of his own Sikh culture—dating back to the days when the Gurus themselves taught—of referring to all the Gurus by the name of the first Guru, Guru Nanak, or simply by an honorific, without any name at all (e.g., Guru Sahib, the first Padshahi, etc.). When identifying the writings of the different Gurus, the practice in the Adi Granth is to refer to them as 'M1' (the first Guru, Guru Nanak Dev), 'M2' (the second Guru, Guru Angad Dev), etc., a custom we have followed in this book. These traditions arose from the understanding that the true spiritual Master becomes a Master by surrendering his identity—only then can he fulfil his role of absolute service.

We have included in the text certain words, phrases and scriptural quotations in the vernacular (Punjabi, Hindi, Urdu, Sanskrit, Persian, Arabic) where we felt the reader might like to know the original. In other cases, certain Punjabi words have been retained and absorbed into the English text. These are either terms that are already familiar to English-speaking readers of Sant Mat literature, such as simran and satsang, or because the word has no satisfactory cultural equivalent, such as tattva (vital element) and chaurasi (the cycle of transmigration, the wheel of eighty-four). All such words may be found in the Glossary, with further clarification and discussion of their meaning. For ease of reading, we have used the most simple, popular system of transliteration, and have indicated nasalization with a small, superscript 'n'.

We take this opportunity to acknowledge our debt to those scholars whose earlier translations contributed to our understanding of the Adi Granth: Gopal Singh, Manmohan Singh, Gurbachan Singh Talib and P. S. Chahil. Without their work, our own task would have been much greater. We are also beholden to the late K. S. Narang, former Vice Chancellor of Punjabi University, Patiala, and the late J. R. Puri, both of whom patiently shared their scholarly wisdom with us at the beginning of the project.

Publications Department
Radha Soami Satsang Beas

Discourses

1

My Friend, Why Stay Caught in This World:
A Warning

Atak too kyo^n rahaa jag me^n:
Chitaavanee

My friend, why stay caught in this world?
By wandering aimlessly, what will you gain?
Now let one thought haunt your mind:
for your quest, keep the company of saints.
When the fire of longing begins to blaze,
you will cast off the moss of the world.
Give your heart to the perfect Master;
you will then gain the Word by true love.
You will escape from birth and death;
the state of immortality will be yours.
Your dormant fate will awaken;
you will find both the Name and your home.
What shall I say? Kal has crushed the world
and encircled all creatures with delusion.
No one is frightened of death;
Death's henchmen evoke dread in none.
The noose of attachment strangles all;
all are struck down and consumed by greed.
How will you become aware of your condition?
You have not fled to take refuge with the Master.
First into lust, and then into anger,
life's creatures are hurled out to burn.
Apart from the Master, no one is ours;
who can sever this entangling web?
Family and relations act from self-interest;
none come near if we have no wealth.
What words will persuade the mind:
it is our loved ones who gnaw on our flesh.
Masters and saints tell in so many ways,
but we never take note of their words.
Without grace, can anyone believe them?
This is what Radha Soami proclaims.

Soami Ji, *Sar Bachan* 15:12, p. 121

Atak too kyo[n] rahaa jag me[n],
bhatak me[n] kyaa mile bhaaee.
Khatak too dhaar ab man me[n],
khoj satsang me[n] jaaee.
Virah kee aag jab bharke,
door kar jagat kee kaaee.
Lagaa lo lagan satgur se,
mile phir shabd lau laaee.
Chhutegaa janm aur marnaa,
amar pad jaay too paaee.
Bhaag teraa jaage sotaa,
naam aur dhaam mil jaaee.
Kahoo[n] kyaa kaal jag maaraa,
jeev sab gher bharmaaee.
Nahee[n] koi maut se dartaa,
khauf jam kaa nahee[n] laaee.
Pare sab moh kee phaa[n]see,
lobh ne maar dhar khaaee.
Chet kaho hoy ab kaise,
guroo ke sang nahi[n] dhaaee.
Kaam aur krodh bich bich me[n],
jeev se bhaar jho[n]kvaaee.
Guroo bin koi nahee[n] apnaa,
jaal yaha kaun turvaaee.
Kutumb parivaar matlab kaa,
binaa dhan paas nahi[n] aaee.
Kahaa[n] lag kahoo[n] is man ko,
unhee[n] se maas nuchvaaee.
Guroo aur saadh kahe[n] bahu vidhi,
kahan unkee na patiyaaee.
Mehar bin kyaa koee maane,
kahee raadhaaswaamee yaha gaaee.

Soami Ji, *Sar Bachan Radhaswami, Chhand Band*
(Beas: Radha Soami Satsang Beas), p. 121:15:12

～

My friend, why stay caught in this world?
By wandering aimlessly, what will you gain?

Atak too kyo^n rahaa jag me^n, bhatak me^n kyaa mile bhaaee.[*]

𝐼n my satsang[**] yesterday, I submitted to you that all saints
and Masters come into the world with one message and
teaching, regardless of the country, society, religion or time
in which they are born. They never come to found sects or
religions, nor do they come to put weapons in anyone's hands
or incite strife between different races, religions or countries.

Saints come with the sole purpose of awakening within
us the desire to meet and love the Lord, and to explain the
method by which we can find Him. They do this so that we,
the creatures of this world, may escape forever from our bodies and the endless pain of death and rebirth, by worshipping
the Lord.

All the various religions have their own particular rules
of conduct, their rituals and ceremonies and guidelines for
daily living, because they have been devised by human beings
according to their needs. But the spiritual base, the reality and
essence of truth that is at the heart of each religion, is the same
in all.

Until we are dyed in the hue of this spirituality—regardless of what race, religion or country we belong to—there is
simply no way that we can escape from the prison of our
body.

---

[*] The small, superscript 'n' indicates a nasalized sound.
[**] *See* Glossary and Translators' Note for explanations of unusual usage, and technical or Indian-language terms, such as: satsang, the Word.

7

Different saints of different races, religions and countries have tried to describe this spirituality to us using different terms. If we read the Vedas and Shastras, we find that sages and holy men call it the Voice from the skies *(aakaash vaanee)*, the Name of God *(raam naam)*, the Melody of God *(raam dhun)*, the pure Sound *(nirmal naad)*, the divine Melody *(divya dhuni)*, and by many other names. When we read the Christian scriptures, we find the same spirituality is called the Word, Logos, Spirit, Holy Ghost, Name, and by various other terms. When we read the Muslim scriptures and mystic literature, we find it described as the Word *(kalmaa)*, the Call from the skies *(baang-e-aasmaanee)*, the Word of God *(kalaam-e-ilaahee)*, the imperial Sound *(nidaa-e-sultaanee)*, and by many other terms. Guru Nanak Sahib and his successors call it the Guru's Voice *(gur kee baanee)*, the Voice from the highest *(dhur kee baanee)*, the true Voice *(sachee baanee)*, the Order *(amar)*, the Command *(hukam)*, the unutterable Lore *(akath kathaa)*, and God's Song of praise *(hari keertan)*. Generally, saints describe it using the terms Word *(shabd)* and Name *(naam)*. Only when our attention is linked to this Word or Name will we be able to escape from the prison of the body and the pain of death and rebirth.

The relationship between the spiritual reality and the code of conduct of a religion may be compared to that of a very beautiful photograph, picture or painting and its frame. The value and beauty lie in the photo, picture or painting, not in the frame. Similarly with a piece of diamond jewellery and a jewellery box—the value and beauty lie in the jewellery, not in the box. Without the jewellery, no one would lock the box in a safe. Again, it is a sword, not a scabbard on its own, that is useful. Whatever we are to gain will come through that spiritual essence. But we drift away from spirituality and little by little become tied down by codes of conduct, prisoners of our outward practices.

These codes of conduct lie in the hands of the priests: the Hindu *pujari,* the Christian clergy, the Muslim mullah, the Sikh *bhai,* and so on. They guide us into performing outward rites and rituals. They neither understand the spiritual reality nor do they see any need to explain it to us. They make us so narrow-minded about these outward practices that we then give a particular social, religious or national character to the teachings of the saints and start quarrelling and fighting among ourselves. Why do we do this? To fill our stomachs or to win honour and prestige. For them it is a means of livelihood; for us, because of our lack of understanding, it makes us their prisoners.

The teachings of the saints are meant for the entire world—for everyone, everywhere. They are not meant for a particular race or a particular religion. Guru Nanak Sahib says:

> For all the four castes,
> the teachings are one and the same.
> *Updes chah warnaa kao saajhaa.*
> Adi Granth, M5,* p. 747[1]

By this, Guru Sahib means that his teachings are universal, since the 'four castes' includes the entire human race. Just note how the practice of external ritual has, in present times, confined these elevated, pure teachings to a dozen or so districts of Punjab. The fault is not Guru Nanak Sahib's. It lies

---

* When identifying the writings of the different Gurus, the practice in the Adi Granth is to refer to them as 'M1' (the first Guru, Guru Nanak), 'M5' (the fifth Guru, Guru Arjan), etc., a custom we have followed in this book. *See also* Translators' Note.

with those whose sole concern is to uphold the code. If, with an open mind and heart, we search within the writings of any saint, we will discover that they all come with just one message and teaching.

Today I am taking my text from the writings of Shri Hazur Soami Ji Maharaj. He explains—and this he says with reference to the whole world—that we have forgotten the Lord and become entangled in our earthly loves and attachments. And what is the result? We are now caught in the prison of chaurasi.

Our souls are particles of the Lord, the supreme soul; we are drops of the ocean of the true Name:

> Says Kabir, the soul is a particle of the Lord.
> *Kahu kabeer ihu raam kee ans.*
>> Kabir, Adi Granth, p. 871

And Guru Nanak Sahib says the same:

> God abides in the soul, the soul in God.
> *Aatam mah raam, raam mah aatam.*
>> Adi Granth, M1, p. 1153

God, the supreme soul, exists within each soul, and our soul *(aatmaa)* exists within the supreme soul *(parmaatmaa)*. By separating from God, we have become enmeshed in this web of illusion (maya). When we came into this world, our soul took the company of the mind, and the mind loves all manner of perversions, the sense pleasures, and social, religious and political controversies.

Each and every action we do under the sway of the mind, whether good or bad, brings us back into the prison of chaurasi in order to undergo its reaction. This world is a region of

karmas, a field of actions.[2] It is the seeds we sow that determine the harvest we reap. If we sow chillis, we will gather a
harvest of chillis; if we plant mango saplings, we will naturally eat mango fruits. Soami Ji says:

> For everything you do,
> you will have to experience the consequence.
> *Karam jo jo karengaa too vohee phir bhognaa bharnaa.*
>
> Soami Ji, *Sar Bachan* 19:2, p. 143[3]

Neither can our good deeds make us free from the limitations
of the body, nor can our bad deeds save us from the suffering
of death and rebirth.

Even if we do virtuous deeds, what will happen? We will
be born as rich and successful people, as leaders and kings,
or as people of power in our communities, religions or nations. The broom will be taken from our hands and replaced
by the reins of authority. Instead of making our bed in a small
hut, we will make it in a palace. At best, we may go to a paradise or one of the lower heavens—but even there we will be
given a form of life with no free will *(bhog jooniaa^n)*, and for
a certain time only. And then again we will have to return to
the prison of chaurasi. If we do bad deeds, hell and chaurasi
stand ever in wait.

Whether king or subject, rich or poor, woman or man,
all of us are working out our karmic accounts in this world.
In settling those accounts—whatever form we take—we have
always to put up with suffering and pain, as everyone knows.

Every day thousands of animals of different kinds are
slaughtered just to fill our stomachs. How they screech and
squawk, bleat and cry, those chickens, sheep and goats, as day
and night their throats are cut. Have we ever paused to consider what state we would be in if we had to take birth in those

bodies on account of our actions, if they were the ones with the knives and axes in their hands? When a doctor gives us an injection, he has only to sterilize the finest of needles, and in spite of our sturdy bodies we begin to tremble with fear. Yet how mercilessly the slaughterhouse blades go on striking down those poor creatures. One shudders to think of the plight of these lower forms of life. Words simply fail us.

Just research carefully the subject of the human being, that form we refer to [in Urdu] as *ashraf-ul-makhluqaat,* the top of the creation, and which the ancient sages and seers describe as *nar-naraayani deh,* the human form divine. What peace and happiness can we find, living in this body? Ask anyone, and you will find that some people are suffering from sickness and disease, while others are troubled by unemployment. Some have no offspring and are therefore miserable, while others are distressed on account of their offspring. Some have to collect dues, while others have debts to pay. In this cold weather, just look at the condition of poor people living on the streets. Visit a jail and listen to the stories of some of the innocent people imprisoned there. Go to a hospital and listen to the groans of the sick.

In this world, wherever one looks one sees pain and suffering, trouble and misery. One need only open a newspaper or listen to the radio to be reminded how much strife there is between the different races, religions and nations—how many poor people are slaughtered, how many women widowed, how many children orphaned. When, in this hamlet of the world, people have to suffer and struggle simply to find food and clothing, how can anyone expect to find peace and happiness in the human form? And if one cannot find happiness in the human form, then just ask yourself: is there any form in which happiness is likely to be found? Soami Ji says:

Listen to me, dear soul,
your Husband lives in the regions above.
Surat sun baat ree, teraa dhanee base aakaash.

Soami Ji, *Sar Bachan* 19:6, p. 145

Soul, your husband is the supreme soul. He exists in the realm of truth, Sach Khand, while you are caught in the web of illusion. Until you go back to your true home, you will never fulfil your destiny as a wife, you will always feel dissatisfied, and you will never escape from the painful cycle of death and rebirth.

Saints generally explain that it is in the very nature of the relationship between the soul and the Lord that the soul will only attain happiness by devoting itself to the Lord and losing itself in Him. If a wife goes far away from her beloved, she will never be happy or enjoy peace of mind, though you may regale her with the luxuries of the world. She wants only to be with her husband, to be united with him. Even if the Lord gives us the wealth and sovereignty of the whole world, our minds will never be content or at peace.

Soami Ji tells us that by forgetting the Lord, we have become entangled in the web of illusion, we have grown to love the creation and become attached to it, so now we are stuck here in the world.

Everything we see is, in fact, the vast, formidable prison of chaurasi. The Lord has provided just one door to escape from this prison. And what is it? It is the human life. He graces us with it for this very purpose—giving us the opportunity to benefit from it by searching for Him and worshipping Him, so that we can escape from the imprisonment of the body.

But, as Soami Ji explains, whenever the Lord provides us with this opportunity, we get caught up in the pleasures of the senses, in racial, religious and political issues, in our love for our children, and in accumulating wealth. This is because we are trying to find peace and happiness through these things. Our constant search for happiness, he says, drives us day and night from place to place, and day and night we go on being dissatisfied. Such things have never brought anyone peace or happiness, nor will they ever do so. Without exception, everything we see is transient and perishable, and whatever little happiness we glimpse is inevitably transformed with the passage of time into sorrow.

People often think that perhaps there was a great deal more suffering in the world in the days when the scriptures were written than in present times. Nowadays, when we have made so much progress in every walk of life, perhaps the world is a happier place than it was before. Imagine, Baba Farid came to the world eight hundred years ago and at that time he said:

> I thought I was the only one in pain, O Farid,
> but the whole world is suffering.
> When I reached up high,
> I found the fire of suffering in every house.
> *Fareedaa mai jaaniaa dukh mujh koo*
> *dukh sabaa-i-ai jag.*
> *Ooche char kai dekhiaa taa ghar ghar ehaa ag.*
>
> Farid, Adi Granth, p. 1382

Now what kind of suffering could a saint experience? It must have been some trouble in connection with his food, his clothing or his hut. But he says: When I went to the higher regions, I saw that everyone is being roasted day and night in the fires of countless desires and cravings. Guru Nanak Sahib came to the world five hundred years ago and said exactly the same thing:

O Nanak, the whole creation is miserable.
Naanak dukheeaa sabh sansaar.

Adi Granth, M1, p. 954

All living creatures, all in their different situations, have to undergo their full measure of sorrow and troubles. Some two hundred and fifty or three hundred years ago, Sehjo Bai commented:

All those who possess wealth are unhappy;
the poor are the very picture of misery.
Dhanvante sabahee dukhee, nirdhan hai[n] dukh roop.

Sehjo, *Sehjo Bai ki Bani*, Doha 39[4]

People who possess excessive wealth and property are all, poor things, discontent. And those who have nothing, not even enough to eat, are bound to be miserable.

It is now a hundred years since Soami Ji also said repeatedly that we go on feeling restless and dissatisfied because we keep looking for happiness in the world. We cannot help thinking that in the days when these saints were living, perhaps conditions were not so good in the world—but that now, in the last one hundred years, we have progressed in every field.

In previous times people lived in small huts, and whole families lived in just one or two such huts. The land was cultivated by hand or with oxen. Marriages took place within the community, and our whole world existed within the radius of fifteen to twenty miles where we lived out our lives and died. Now we have made such progress in everything, in every area of life. Look at the wonderful houses we have built, and at the quantities of foodgrain we grow—tractors and chemicals are used in agriculture everywhere. Similarly, in the medical field we have made great progress. Look how many good medicines there are and how many highly qualified doctors are available. In the judicial field, there are now so many courts and capable lawyers that we can take our cases right up to the Supreme Court. Nowadays we can also marry the person of our choice.

So why do saints say we are unhappy? Everything is available to us in every sphere of life—so when everything is available, why are we unhappy? Either something is wrong in our way of thinking or in the way the saints explain things.

You see, in the days when we used to live in small huts, the whole family lived together in one place. We worked all day, and in the evening sat together to eat, and we had love and regard for one another. We played the drums, sang and danced—and when we went to sleep at night we would be completely relaxed. Now we build huge houses of brick and stone, we have air-conditioners in every room, and televisions and telephones. Our beds have nine-inch springs with six-inch mattresses, yet we cannot sleep at night and have to take sleeping tablets and tranquillizers. When we get up in the morning we complain of aching bones and stiff joints.

Look how much respect parents enjoyed in earlier times and how much love they showered on their children. Now both mother and father come home from their parties at ten or eleven at night, whereas the poor children go to bed at eight or nine. In the morning, no one gets up before ten or eleven, whereas the children have to leave for school at seven or eight. And these children are expected to have the same respect for their parents! How can they later become a support for their parents, or develop the same degree of love for them?

In previous times, the doctor or healer in the village may have been quite ordinary, but everyone could be certain of getting medicine and some sort of treatment. Now, although there has been definite progress in medicine and science, just consider how many new diseases keep on appearing, because we have to use so many chemicals in our food production, and they naturally affect our bodies. Moreover, who has access to the doctors? Who gets a hospital bed? Even if one does, hospital treatment is so expensive that many patients, poor things, are left haunting the verandahs.

In spite of the quantities of foodgrains grown, half the world goes to sleep hungry at night because food is so expensive. As you know, sugar is sold at twelve or thirteen rupees a kilo, so how can the average person make ends meet? It is not that there is a shortage of foodgrains in the world, but there seems to be something wrong with our way of distribution. Those with understanding explain to us that the rich do not eat because they cannot digest their food; the poor have no food because it is too expensive—so who benefits from all this food?

In earlier times, if there was a quarrel in the village, a few of the village elders would get together in the evening and resolve the dispute. Now, take any legal case and see whether it is settled in less than twenty or twenty-five years. No matter how expert the judges and lawyers may be, no one reaches a decision or verdict.

In the field of medicine it is the same: there are many drugs and many intelligent doctors, yet how many people actually receive treatment? So many big houses are being built, yet how many people still have to sleep outside on the streets at night? Either there is something wrong with our progress or we do not know how to use it properly.

People marry the person of their choice, yet by the third or fourth year they are standing in court seeking a divorce. Earlier it was the parents who arranged the marriage. Every marriage inevitably experiences one or two storms, but the parents of both sides would get together, work out a solution, and the storm would pass. Nowadays parents do not even know when their children get divorced or when they remarry.

Who then has benefitted from all this development? Ask anyone, and you will find that no one has any free time. The labourer has no time, the engineer has no time, the doctor has no time, the businessman has no time. Who has time? No one at all. What is the point of progress if we do not get an hour to ourselves, or even half an hour to relax? Tension is written on everybody's face, no one appears relaxed, and even a handful of people cannot sit together and laugh and play. So what advantage are we getting from progress?

It is not that there is anything wrong with development in itself; what is wrong is that we have become slaves to these things. They were made for our benefit, not we for theirs. We have become like components in these machines; we have failed to be their masters.

We should take control of development. Everyone should have food, clothing and a place to live; our food and environment should be healthy. There should be leisure for us; we should lead a simple, relaxed life—no one should live in a state of tension. There should be unity and peace in the family; children should show respect to their parents, and parents should love their children. We should be sympathetic and helpful to others. These are the things in life that every person wants—development should lead us in this direction. At no cost should we compromise with the basic values of human life. When basic values are lost, how can material progress be of any benefit to us?

This is why the words of bygone saints were relevant then and are equally relevant now. Happiness was not possible then through these worldly things, nor is it possible now.

The Lord has made this world out of both pain and pleasure. That is why Soami Ji says:

Mind, renounce this dwelling of pain and pleasure!
Tajo man yaha dukh sukh kaa dhaam.

Soami Ji, *Sar Bachan* 15:9, p. 119

He says: This world, my friends, has been made from pain and pleasure. You will never find happiness in it because it is the habitation of good deeds and bad. We will have to come here to settle the account of our good deeds; we will have to come here to settle the account of the bad. For our good deeds, we will experience happiness, and for our sins, we will know sorrow. If happiness exists, it lies in devotion to the Lord and love for Him. That is why he says:

Rise above it and attach yourself to the true Name.
Lago tum charh kar ab satnaam.

Soami Ji, *Sar Bachan* 15:9, p. 119

If you want to achieve happiness, worship the Lord and merge with Him. It is when the soul unites with the Lord that happiness will be achieved. Yet we go further and further from the Lord and deeper and deeper into the creation. The more we allow our mind to spread into the world, the unhappier we become; the more we disengage our mind from the world, the happier we will be.

Soami Ji explains that because we are caught in the creation, we keep on wandering from place to place, restless and unhappy, searching for happiness sometimes through one thing, sometimes through another. The more we try to find happiness, the more we suffer.

Think for a moment about those people to whom the Lord has given everything in life—a good life-partner, plenty to eat and drink, a nice house to live in, money and respect. The Lord has not withheld anything, yet sitting alone they find that they are not at peace with themselves, that happiness still eludes them.

In spite of having everything, from where does this feeling of loneliness come to us? There is no question of anything lacking—so why do we not feel happy and at peace? This is the soul's yearning to return to its origin. Until we let it go in that direction, we will never find peace or happiness. Guru Nanak Sahib says:

> Immortally wedded is the soul bride
> who attains union with her true Lord.
> *Pir sache te sadaa suhaagan.*
>
> Adi Granth, M3, p. 754

The soul is the wife, and the Lord, the husband. Only when the wife reaches the shelter of her husband's embrace will she be happy *(suhaagan)*; she will never be content by staying away from him. Guru Sahib says:

> By returning to one's true home,
> happiness, my friend, is attained.
> *Jinee ghar jaataa aapnaa se sukhee-e bhaaee.*
>
> Adi Granth, M3, p. 425

By going back to our true home and reaching the Supreme Being, we will attain everlasting peace and happiness. Because we have forgotten the Lord, we have become entangled in our love for the creation and our attachment to it. We are involved in worshipping bricks and stones, and in the worship of paper and water—no one worships the Lord. And that is why all living beings are undergoing their full measure of pain and suffering, all in their own particular situations.

Where can we go to find peace and happiness? In the lines that follow, Soami Ji indicates the direction.

∾

Now let one thought haunt your mind:
for your quest, keep the company of saints.

Khatak too dhaar ab man me^n, khoj satsang me^n jaaee.

When we are extremely unhappy on account of the things of the world—our jobs, legal problems, financial problems, family and children—in what direction do our thoughts go for peace of mind?

Some of us run to temples, some to gurdwaras or mosques, some to churches or synagogues. But then the priest increases our suffering by directing our thoughts outwards so that our mind gets misled in external forms of worship.

If you go to a gurdwara, what will they tell you? To perform a continuous recitation of the scriptures, to go and immerse yourself in a sacred pool, to make a pilgrimage to the holy sites, and all your problems will disappear. Go to a temple and they will tell you to have the gayatri mantra recited, to offer oblations before the sacred fire, perform a prayer here and a recitation there, make obeisance to this goddess and that god. They will involve you in more and more rituals and ceremonies, to ensure their livelihood. It is the same in mosques, churches and synagogues.

Our attention is never directed to achieving the one thing that could give us happiness. Happiness lies in devotion to the Lord and in union with Him. And where is the Lord? He is within us, within the human form. The One we are seeking will only be found within. Anyone who has ever found Him, has found Him within. We can confirm this in the writings of any saint. Guru Nanak Sahib says:

> In the body dwells the bountiful Lord,
> the life of the world, who sustains all.
> *Kaa-i-aa andar jag jeevan daataa wasai*
> *sabhnaa kare pratipaalaa.*
>
> Adi Granth, M3, p. 754

God Almighty, who has given life to the whole world and is the benefactor and emperor of all, who takes care of everyone and guides everything, lives within our body, within our very being. Kabir Sahib says:

> As oil is in sesame seeds and fire in flintstone,
> so is your Beloved within you: wake up, if you can.
> *Jyo[n] til maahee[n] tel hai chakmak maahee[n] aagi,*
> *teraa preetam tujh me[n] jaagi sake to jaagi.*
>
> Kabir, *Kabir Sakhi Sangreh*[5]

Just as oil is present in the sesame seed and fire is latent in flint, so does the supreme Lord exist within you. Paltu Sahib says:

> Why are you crying out 'Lord, Lord'—
> the Lord is right there with you!
> *Saahib saahib kyaa karai saahib tere paas.*
>
> Paltu, *Paltu Sahib ki Bani*, I:39, Kundli[6]

Who is this God you are seeking in forests, mountains, bricks, stone and sacred waters? He goes around with you all twenty-four hours of the day—He lives inside you, inside the human frame. In the Bible, too, it is written that the kingdom of God lies within you—and that is why you must repent.[7] Whatever you did in your previous lives, you must repent for it now and close your account. The Lord is nowhere outside; He is inside you, within your body.

When something is lost inside the house, it may be found if people go inside and look for it there. If they go searching for it in the streets and markets, how will they ever find it? Guru Sahib says:

> True devotees seek within;
> all others wander in delusion.
> *Gurmukh hovai su kaa-i-aa khojai*
> *hor sabh bharam bhulaaee.*
>
> Adi Granth, M3, p. 754

People who love the Lord, who are his devotees and his beloved ones, always search for Him within themselves. The rest of humanity remain entangled in superstitions and illusion, and keep on looking for Him through outward rituals—some chasing in one direction, some in another.

When will we realize that whatever we are to find can only be found within? Where can we go to gain this understanding? If a laboratory exists where we can conduct research into this quest for the Lord, it is our body. How are we to turn inwards and conduct this research? Soami Ji says:

> For your quest, keep the company of saints.

Attend the satsang of saints and Masters, keep their company, spend time with them. They will detach you from external practices and free you from outward rituals. They will not tell you to treat idols as though they were real, to circumambulate a building or prostrate yourself at the tomb of a holy man, or that liberation is gained by touching a relic or some possession of a saint. Instead, they will explain how to search for the Lord and worship Him by turning inwards.

It is by attending the satsang of saints that our mind is freed from superstitions, illusions, misconceptions and rituals. The moment we are free, we are able to devote ourselves to the Lord.

Saints tell us that our minds are easily influenced by the company we keep. If we keep the company of thieves, we will soon develop the habit of stealing. If we keep the company of people who drink, we will develop the habit of drinking. If we keep the company of lovers and devotees of the Lord, by seeing them a desire to love and worship the Lord will automatically awaken in us too.

That is why the saints and Masters put so much emphasis on satsang. In actual fact, the same three or four themes are emphasized in the satsang of every saint. It is essential that someone keeps hammering away at our minds, explaining things to us, reminding us what is real in the world, extricating us from our superstitions, misconceptions, doubts, outward practices and rituals, and directing our attention inwards. Only then does the mind turn somewhat in an inner direction; otherwise it will immediately try to spread back into the creation. That is why Soami Ji says we must attend the satsang of the Masters, the lovers of God.

As I said yesterday, a gathering where one group of people abuses another, or where one religion criticizes another, will never be called a satsang by the saints. There is no question of slander and abuse in the satsang of a saint. It is a shallow, narrow-minded approach to frighten people by threatening them with violence just because they do not worship the Lord the way we think they should. Rather, we should explain lovingly to them: My friend, these are the benefits I have derived by following this path. If it makes sense to you, you too can enjoy these benefits by travelling the same path. Guru Nanak Sahib says:

> Know that as true satsang
> where the doctrine of the one Name is explained.
> *Satsangat kaisee jaaneeai.*
> *Jithai eko naam vakhaaneeai.*
>
> Adi Granth, M1, p. 72

Only that is satsang where the teachings of the one Word and Name are proclaimed, where the desire to find and love the Lord is awakened, and where the way or method of true worship is explained. This is why there is no question of there being any criticism in the satsang of a saint. What saints do through their satsangs is extricate us from outward practices and rituals, clarify our thinking, and teach us how to turn inwards, to enter into this human form.

Soami Ji says: If you want happiness, it lies in worshipping the Lord and merging with Him. The supreme Lord is nowhere outside—He is within you.

Where will you discover the way to go in? You will get to know it in the satsang of the Lord's lovers, and by keeping their company.

ᕆ

When the fire of longing begins to blaze,
you will cast off the moss of the world.
Virah kee aag jab bharke, door kar jagat kee kaaee.

Soami Ji is presenting his teachings in a very systematic way. When we attend a saint's satsang, we come to know what is real. We learn that we will gain nothing from external practices, that the Lord lives within us and it is there we must search for Him by turning within. By keeping the company of saints, true love for the Lord and the longing to find Him will be awakened within us.

It is then that a very big obstacle presents itself in our way. What is that? The obstacle of public opinion: What will my parents say? What will my community and the people of my religion say? What will my friends and relatives say? To what community does this saint belong? To what social background? I myself am a person of substance and reputation, a person of some importance. If I start running after this holy man, what will people say?

Soami Ji says that if we have true love and longing for the Lord in our heart, if we really yearn for Him, we should not be bothered by public opinion—by people's taunts, insults and criticisms. He says we must be wholehearted in our worship of the Lord, not have reservations about it.

If we are timid and ruled by public opinion, it means we consider the world to be very important and the Lord to be insignificant. When true love and longing awaken in us, then we see the Lord, and the Lord alone, as important above all else, and the world as of the least significance. Therefore Soami Ji lovingly explains that once we come into the company and presence of a Master, we should cease caring about what others think.

On previous occasions I have often given the example of Shri Hazur Rai Sahib Saligram Ji Maharaj. He was a beloved disciple of Soami Ji Maharaj and had abundant love for Soami Ji. In those days he held the position of Postmaster General of Uttar Pradesh, but still he used to fetch water for Soami

Ji's bath from the river Jamuna, filling a big brass waterpot and carrying it some two and a half kilometres to Soami Ji's house. The part of the town through which he had to pass was where his own community lived, and they began to ridicule him, saying: "Just look—such a high official! Has he lost his mind?" When Rai Sahib came to know about this, he started wearing anklets with bells, so that even those who did not know should come to hear of it. Once love for the Lord awakens in someone, what does he care for anyone's opinion?

Look at the third Padshahi, Shri Guru Amardas Ji—how people ridiculed him: "Amru is homeless, he has no place of his own. He is there in the Guru's free kitchen so he can get his food." But Guru Sahib did not pay any attention to their comments, for one who has real love and devotion for the Lord is not bothered by people's abuses and insults. That is why Soami Ji says that if we truly wish to worship the Lord, we should take no notice of criticism.

∾

Give your heart to the perfect Master;
you will then gain the Word by true love.
Lagaa lo lagan satgur se, mile phir shabd lau laaee.

Once the Master sees that true love and the longing to meet the Lord have awakened within us, he tells us the method to worship Him. What is that method?

Saints explain that our spiritual journey starts from the soles of the feet and ends at the crown of the head. There are two stages in the journey: one is up to the eyes, the other is above the eyes.

In each one of us, the seat of the soul and mind in the body is behind the eyes. Some call this place the eye of Shiva *(shiv netra)*, the divine eye *(divya chakshu)*, the door to our home *(ghar dar);* some call it the gateway to liberation *(mukti daa darvaazaa)*, the single eye or third eye. It is from here that our attention descends and spreads through the nine gateways of the body—the two eyes, ears and nostrils, the mouth and the two lower openings—out into the whole world.

In what sense does it spread into the world? Even while we are sitting here, thoughts come to us of our children, homes and families, of our professions and clients. Our mind never stays still. Even if we were to shut ourselves in the darkest of rooms in the very interior of a house, our mind would not stay there—it would be roaming around the whole creation.

The process by which thoughts keep on coming to the mind throughout the day is described by saints as *simran*. This repetitive thinking is a natural habit already developed in each one of us. And whatever we think about—the object of our simran—its form appears before our mind's eye. If we think about our children, it is their forms that come to us. If we think about our customers, their forms appear before our eyes. The saints describe this as doing *dhyan,* and it is certain that whatever we think about, we will begin to see its form.

When we keep on thinking about something and visualizing it, little by little we become attached to it and start loving it. We develop so much love and attachment for these images and forms that it is they that come to us in our dreams at night. It is their forms that come before our eyes, as though on a cinema screen, at the time of death. And, "Where our desires are, there we dwell."[8] In this world, the direction in which our attention goes in our last moments determines the course of our next life.

What is it, therefore, that brings us again and again to the prison of the body? Our love and attachments in the world. What created them? Simran and dhyan. What kind of simran and dhyan? The simran and dhyan of this world, which will perish and pass away.

Since we already have the habit of doing simran and dhyan, of thinking constantly and visualizing, saints tell us to take advantage of it. Only simran will release us from simran, only dhyan will release us from dhyan—but we must do the simran and dhyan of that which will never perish or pass away. And what is that? It is the absolute Lord.

The saints explain to us how to do simran of the Lord's Name and how to concentrate on his dhyan, in order to withdraw our scattered attention from the nine gateways of the body and focus it behind the eyes. Once it is concentrated at this point, we automatically become aware of a most sweet and melodious call that is emanating from the court of the Lord.

This sound is reverberating at the eye centre within everyone—thieves and swindlers, saints and enlightened beings. The question of race, religion or nationality does not arise. Those who are blessed with the good fortune of being able to make the attention one-pointed at the eye centre, whether Hindu, Sikh, Christian or of any other faith, will hear that sound within themselves and will see its brilliance and light within.

Indian sages refer to that sound as the Voice from the skies *(aakaash vaanee)*, the Melody of God *(raam dhun)*, the Name of God *(raam naam)*, the divine Sound *(divya dhuni)*. Saints in the Muslim tradition call the same sound the Word *(kalmaa)*, the Call from the skies *(baang-e-aasmaanee)*, the Word of God *(kalaam-e-ilaahee)*, the imperial Sound *(nidaa-e-sultaanee)*. Guru Nanak Sahib and his successors, referring to the same sound, call it the Guru's Voice *(gur kee baanee)*, the Voice from the highest *(dhur kee baanee)*, the true Voice *(sachee baanee)*, the Order *(amar)*, the Command *(hukam)*, the unutterable Lore *(akath kathaa)*. Generally, saints refer to it as the Word *(shabd)*, the Name *(naam)*. The same sound is referred to by Christ as the Word, the Spirit, the Holy Ghost.

There is no point in debating the various terms; rather, we have to gather our attention together and focus it there at the eye centre, where the Lord is bestowing his gifts and showering his mercy. This is where the elixir of the Name is flowing—the elixir that makes us immortal when we drink it. No one has ever attained this elixir outside. It is flowing within everyone twenty-four hours of the day at this place behind the eyes. This is why the fourth Padshahi says:

> Nine are the doors, all nine are insipid;
> the divine ambrosia flows from the tenth.
> *Nao darvaaj nave dar feeke ras amrit dasve chu-eejai.*
>
> Adi Granth, M4, p. 1323

Below the eyes, my friends, lie the pleasures of the senses, the mind's negative tendencies and the physical appetites. If you wish to drink the nectar that is saturated with sweetness, the nectar that will make you immortal, it is flowing within you at the point behind the eyes.

Unless we bring our attention to this point, how can we possibly drink the nectar? If we place a container upside-down in the rain, even if it rains day and night, how will even one drop of water fall into it? Once we put the container the right way up, however, if not with the first rainfall, it will certainly fill with the second or third rainfall. Our mind, which was to be purified by drinking the nectar at the eye centre, has instead gone down from this point and spread out into the whole world through the nine doors of the body. So first we have to gather it together and concentrate it at the eye centre.

Mystics call this elixir Shabd or Nam, the Word and the Name. Soami Ji says:

> The Master speaks out in clear terms:
> My friend, attach yourself to the unending music of
>   the Word.
> There is no way, other than the Word,
> to break out from this mortal vessel of clay.
> *Guru kahe khol kar bhaaee*
> *lag shabd anaahad jaaee,*
> *bin shabd upaao na doojaa*
> *kaayaa kaa chhute na koozaa.*
>
> Soami Ji, Sar Bachan 20:10, p. 161

If you want to be united with the Lord, come to the eye centre and catch hold of the unending Sound within. Apart from the practice of listening to the Shabd, of meditating on the Word, there is no method by which you can escape from the prison of the body. Guru Nanak Sahib says:

> Closing the nine doors and restraining the
>   wandering mind,
> in the tenth, one finds one's true abode.
> There the unending music of the Word plays
>   day and night.
> Through the Guru's guidance, the celestial Word
>   is heard.
> *Nao dar thaake dhaavat rahaae.*
> *Dasvai nijghar vaasaa paae.*

Othai anahad sabad vajah din raatee
gurmatee sabad sunaavaniaa.

Adi Granth, M3, p. 124

When you withdraw your attention from the nine doors of
the body and bring it to the eye centre, you will reach the door
to your home. You can recognize this entrance by one sign—
the sound of the unending music of the Word that reverberates there, day and night, within everyone.

Whenever we want to go into a house, we first have to
find the door. When we knock persistently, the door is
opened from within and we enter. Christ also says this:

Seek, and ye shall find;
knock, and it shall be opened unto you.

Matthew 7:7

Keep searching with a sincere heart and He will most certainly
shower his mercy and grace. Seek out that door, keep knock-
ing resolutely as though at the gate of a fortress, and the Lord
will definitely open it from within.

Saints say that the spiritual journey starts from this door
because it is here that we begin to enjoy the bliss of that nectar they call the Word, the Shabd. The joy we then experience is so great, so pure, that the mind automatically gives
up the pleasures of the senses and all its negative tendencies.
As I often say, one who finds diamonds and precious stones
does not put up with being driven from door to door, begging for worthless trinkets; young girls play with dolls only
until they get married. Only attachment can bring about detachment in the mind; detachment can never create attachment within anyone.

This is the difference between the teachings of the saints

and Vedanta. Practitioners of Vedanta try forcibly to detach the mind from the world and concentrate it at the eye centre. The saints, on the other hand, teach that the mind is a lover of pleasure, and until we provide it with a love that is higher and purer than its worldly love and attachments, it will never be prepared to leave them.

If we were to say to a young woman about to get married: Look here, there is just one month left, so stop loving your mother and father, your sisters and brothers, your friends and companions, so that we can get you married—no matter how hard the poor girl might try, it just would not be possible. But once she is married and starts to love her husband, she forgets mother, father, sisters, brothers, friends and companions: love for one man has freed her from all other love and attachments in the world.

This is why Soami Ji compassionately explains that once you yourself experience the sweetness that is there within the Shabd, your mind will automatically relinquish the pleasures of the senses and its negative inclinations. Guru Sahib says:

> The Word of the Guru is sweet beyond measure....
> *Gur kaa sabad mahaa ras meethaa.*
>
> Adi Granth, M3, p. 753

The Word the saints attach us to is referred to as 'sweet beyond measure' because its sweetness is so great that it cannot be described in words. Hazur Maharaj Ji[*] used to speak of it as 'the molasses of a mute'—if you give molasses to a man who cannot speak and then ask him how it tastes, he cannot but remain speechless.

---

[*] The terms 'Hazur' and 'Hazur Maharaj Ji' are used by the speaker to refer to his Master, Maharaj Sawan Singh (1858–1948). *See also* Translators' Note and Glossary.

... That sweetness cannot be known unless you taste it.
Bin chaakhe saad na jaapai.

Adi Granth, M3, p. 753

Guru Sahib says that without eating it, there is no question of speaking of the joy it brings.

Whether we call it the elixir, the sweetness beyond measure, the nectar of God—whatever we call it—everything that we are to attain will come through our meditation on it, through our practice of listening to the Word. It is that which saints refer to as the true Word or Name.

All the various words we have used to name the Lord out of our love for Him—such as Allah, Wahiguru, Hari Om, Radha Soami, God Almighty, Supreme Being—are all symbols, words that can be written, read and spoken. We can trace the history of the use of each word and its period, its time of usage. Some may be a hundred years old, others five hundred years old, some six or seven thousand years old, and beyond that we have no historical records.

The Word, the Name, that the saints glorify is the power that created the world, the very foundation upon which stand all the regions and universes of the creation. These spoken words and names are a means for us, whereas that—the power itself—is our end and objective.

We must not provoke enmity between the different races, religions and nations by getting attached to these words. They are a means by which we withdraw our attention and focus it at the eye centre, where we are to attach ourselves to the true Word or Name.

It is for this reason that the Masters explain to us the method or practice of withdrawing the scattered attention and focusing it at the eye centre within, so that we can attach ourselves to that power, the Word, the Name.

❧

You will escape from birth and death;
the state of immortality will be yours.

Chhutegaa janm aur marnaa, amar pad jaay too paaee.

What is it that drags us back again and again to the shackles of the body? It is our love for the world and our attachment to it, our karmas, our desires and our longings. Soami Ji says that by listening to the Word, our love for the world and our attachments leave us, we are freed of worldly desires and longings, and the sequence of our karmas comes to an end.

What is this sequence? All our karmas—the interlinking chain of actions and reactions—are connected to the mind. Our soul is at the command of our mind and has to go wherever the mind wants. The mind has allowed itself to become a slave to the sense pleasures, but once we concentrate the mind at the eye centre and give it the bliss of the Word, once we attach it to the Word, it returns to Brahm, its natural home. The soul is then freed from its grasp, and the knot tying the soul and mind is undone. Because all karmic impressions remain with the mind, the soul no longer comes as a prisoner to the body.

We can explain it in whatever way we like—by saying that our karmas are finished, that they have perished, or that their sequence has come to an end. Soami Ji says:

The Word erases the imprint of karmas;
the practice of the Word merges us into the Word.
Shabd karm kee rekh kataave, shabd shabd se jaay milaave.

Soami Ji, *Sar Bachan* 9:5, p. 91

Again he says:

> Without the Word, the whole world is blind;
> who can break the noose of attachment?
> *Shabd binaa saaraa jag andhaa,*
> *kaate kaun moh kaa phandaa.*
>
> Soami Ji, *Sar Bachan* 9:5, p. 91

We will only be able to extricate ourselves from the noose of worldly attachments by meditation on the Name, by listening to the Word.

> Through the glory of the Word
> conquer Kal, the lord of death.
> *Shabd prataap kaal ko jeet.*
>
> Soami Ji, *Sar Bachan* 9:5, p. 91

We are trapped in the domain of Death or Kal, prisoners of suffering in the regions below Trikuti—in the cycle of death and rebirth—and it is only through the practice of the Word that we can escape. Guru Nanak Sahib says:

> By merging into the Shabd, one dies to the self
> and gains everlasting life.
> *Sabad marai so mar rahai fir marai na doojee waar.*
>
> Adi Granth, M1, p. 58

If you engage in the practice of the Word, you will die forever and not have to return again and again to the pain of death and rebirth.

> They who merge with the Word
> become pure beings and Truth-realized.

Pavit paavan se jan saache ek sabad liv laaee.

Adi Granth, M3, p. 910

Those who have detached themselves from all worldly loves and ties and attach themselves to the one Word become pure. Not only do they themselves become pure, they make us pure, too, by connecting our attention to the Word.

That is why saints say that if we practise meditation on the Word, our souls will be purified and the links in our chain of death and rebirth will be broken. Guru Sahib explains this beautifully:

> They who hear the Word within, realize themselves;
> they alone attain the Truth....
> *Jin antar sabad aap pachhaanah*
> *gat mit tin hee paaee.*

Adi Granth, M3, p. 910

People who catch hold of the Word within become self-realized: they transcend the domain of mind and imperma-nence (maya) and attain the supreme state. They are the lovers of the Lord, the saints, who have qualified to unite with the Lord. And what benefit do they receive?

> ... Then the mind enters the state of deep
>   meditation;
> the soul's flame merges with the all-pervading
>   divine light.
> *Eh manooaa sunn samaadh lagaavai*
> *jotee jot milaaee.*

Adi Granth, M3, p. 910

The mind reaches its natural home in Brahm; the soul becomes free from the mind's grasp and its light merges with the supreme light. The light of the soul will dissolve into the supreme light only when it leaves the company of the mind, when all layers of dirt are removed from the soul, when the entire sequence of karmas is finished, and when all worldly desires and longings have left us.

As I have already said, people who have diamonds, have no desire for trinkets. Once a person has found the giver, what gifts can he lack? Someone who has found the emperor, what has he to gain from anything less? So when a person finds the Lord, what more could he want from the world?

That is why saints say: Whatever you are to receive will come only through meditation on the Word, on the Name.

❧

Your dormant fate will awaken;
you will find both the Name and your home.

Bhaag teraa jaage sotaa, naam aur dhaam mil jaaee.

Soami Ji says that when our consciousness attaches itself to the Word within, we awaken after being asleep for countless lifetimes. In what sense are we sleeping? We are asleep to the Lord and wide awake to the world—oblivious to the Lord and hankering after the world.

Once we taste the bliss of the Word within, we fall asleep to the world and awaken to the Lord. We have found that treasure of the Name that makes us emperors when we adorn ourselves with it, and that enables us to escape forever from the prison of the body if we take shelter with it.

∽

What shall I say? Kal has crushed the world
and encircled all creatures with delusion.

Kahoo^n kyaa kaal jag maaraa, jeev sab gher bharmaaee.

Now, looking at our condition, Soami Ji feels sorry for us—
we have become so completely trapped in Kal's net.

Not one person knows the Lord, no one's thoughts turn
to worshipping Him. Because of our worldly inclinations,
physical appetites, and our involvement with social, religious
and political issues, we have no time. We go on thinking
"This world is sweet—who has seen the next! Babar, make
merry now—this life will not come again."[9] In our ignorance,
we think that maybe the Lord has given us this blessing for
us to love our children, or to satisfy our physical appetites and
enjoy the pleasures of the senses. This is why Guru Nanak
Sahib says:

> O father, the world is caught in the great net.
> One can be redeemed only through the Guru's grace
> and through practice of the true Name.
> *Baabaa jag phaathaa mahaa jaal.*
> *Gur parsaadee ubare sachaa naam samaal.*
>
> Adi Granth, M1, p. 1009

The world is grievously caught in Kal's net. While suffering and bewailing the consequences of our actions of previous lives, we keep repeating the same sort of bad and
worthless deeds day and night, forgetting that we will have to

come back here again to undergo their consequences. Soami Ji says that we are so attached to the creation, we love it so much, that we have forgotten the Lord, forgotten our home, and forgotten who we really are. Kal has trapped us in this illusion, and whatever we see in the world we take it to be real.

Our relationship with the world is one of giving and taking; our love is motivated by self-interest. Some people come to us as wives, some as husbands, some as children and some as friends. The moment a particular sequence of karmas comes to an end, all those involved resume their separate ways.

No one has ever accompanied another person into the next world, nor is it possible to do so. Because we take these relations to be real, we busy ourselves night and day trying to possess them; we involve ourselves in thousands of deceptions and dishonesties in order to make them ours.

Still they do not become ours, nor have we ever become theirs. It is through us that our children are born, but they can never belong to us. Our father and mother gave birth to us, but they too do not belong to us, nor we to them. They have to go through their own destiny, their pralabdh karmas, just as we have to go through ours.

When actors come on stage, they all assume their different roles; when they come down from the stage, none of them maintain these relationships any more. This world is a vast stage, and according to our karmas, each one of us is playing our role. But we forget that we will have to step down from the stage. When we do not remember our parents, relatives and friends of previous births, on whose account we are undergoing so much trouble today, who is going to remember these relationships, for which we are suffering so much now? Some have already left us and gone ahead, while we too are getting ready to leave others when we go.

Saints arouse us from our heedless stupor, saying: On whose account are you so restless and suffering so much anguish? For what purpose has the Lord bestowed on you this human form? Why do you take this creation to be real and agitate yourself running around in pursuit of the things of the world? When great kings, rulers and business tycoons had to leave the world in the very process of trying to possess it, and nothing of it went with them, what can possibly go with you?

❧

No one is frightened of death;
Death's henchmen evoke dread in none.

Nahee^n koi maut se dartaa, khauf jam kaa nahee^n laaee.

Soami Ji goes on to explain that we remain so caught up in the endless pleasures of the senses and the world about us that, apart from anything else, we live oblivious to the fact that we will die.

Daily we see our friends taking leave of us. We ourselves accompany them one by one to the cremation ground. We see with our own eyes that not one of the possessions they so proudly claimed to be theirs goes with them. And apart from mourning the fact that we have been separated from each other, we cannot be of any help to anyone else.

Therefore Soami Ji compassionately asks us whether we have ever really imagined the time of our death. Who will help us then? Who will give us support?

How can we even think clearly? All day long we are caught up in that ego of the physical, in the pride of body that we think we are. As human beings, no one even questions why we feel so proud, so arrogant. If we are proud of our youth, then have we not seen what happens when people get old? We only need look at an old man in the street and we will find the poor man cannot even see properly: his head shakes, his knees do not carry his weight, and the light has diminished in his eyes. Are we not going to reach the same age, too?

If we are proud of our beauty, have we never been to a hospital and seen the faces of those who are sick? If we are proud of our money and wealth, can we not find people who were once successful financiers and businessmen, rulers and kings, wandering penniless in the streets and alleys? If we are intoxicated by power, are we not aware of coups? A party is suddenly overthrown and all is finished—those in power are sent to the scaffold or locked up in jail.

As human beings, why are we so full of pride? Soami Ji says:

> O mind, of what are you feeling so proud?
> Your body will mingle with dust
> and you will again have to go into chaurasi.
> *Man re kyo^n gumaan ab karnaa,*
> *tan to teraa khaak milegaa chauraasee jaa parnaa.*
> Soami Ji, *Sar Bachan* 15:15, p. 123

Is it your body you are proud of? It will be consigned to fire or buried beneath the earth. You will then be presented before the lord of death and, on the basis of your actions, desires and longings, you will have to take birth again wherever he sees fit. Who then will you have to call your mother and father? To what miserable surroundings will you have to go? With what friends and associates will you have to play?

One death is hardly over and the next life is already there; we leave one body behind and death is already standing before us. Like habitual criminals, we are always handcuffed.

What can a person who is constantly being sought by the police be proud of?

Just read history and see what happened to the great rulers, dictators and men of vast wealth—men whose very words became law. Where is their importance today? We trample their graves into the ground as we go our way. Their bones are dishonoured by our feet, and it is their dust that blinds our eyes. We forget that others in the same way are to trample our graves, others too will dishonour our bones with their feet, and we too will merge with the dust and blind their eyes.

We say that death, surely, is for others, whereas for us there is nothing but the pleasures and delights of the senses. That is why Kabir says:

> The clay says to the potter,
> Why are you pounding me?
> That day is coming soon when I'll be pounding
>   you!
> *Maatee kahai kumhaar ko, kyaa too roonde mohi^n,*
> *ik din aisaa hoegaa, mai^n roondhoongee tohi^n.*
>
> Kabir, *Kabir Sakhi Sangreh*

The potter makes his vessels by kneading and pounding clay. But the clay warns him: Keep that time in mind when I will knead and pound you in exactly the same way. Then Kabir says:

> The wood asks the blacksmith,
> Why are you burning me?
> That day is coming soon when I'll be burning you!
> *Lakree kahai luhaar ko, too kyaa jaarai mohi^n,*
> *ik din aisaa hoegaa, mai^n jaaraungee tohi^n.*
>
> Kabir, *Kabir Sakhi Sangreh*

The blacksmith makes charcoal by burning wood. The wood warns him: Keep that time before you when I will take you with me and turn you into charcoal in just the same way.

We keep thinking that death is for others and there is nothing but pleasure for us. That is why Soami Ji says that we have become so brazen and arrogant, we have even forgotten we have to die.

$$\backsim$$

The noose of attachment strangles all;
all are struck down and consumed by greed.

Pare sab moh kee phaa^{n}see, lobh ne maar dhar khaaee.

Now Soami Ji goes into more detail. He explains that when we have forgotten the Lord and instead have given our love to our children, properties, communities, religions, countries, wealth and fortunes, we have actually tied a noose around our necks with our own hands. When it starts to strangle us, we shed tears, we call out, we entreat—but who hears our anguished cries for help?

Anything we think of as ours becomes a source of pain and suffering for us. If our spouse has a headache, we stay awake all night; yet no matter what tragedies take place in our neighbour's family, we do not turn a hair.[10] Again, if our own children are ill, we toss and turn all night; yet when large numbers of people are buried alive in an earthquake, we do not turn a hair. This is because we think of some people as ours, and the rest as having nothing to do with us. Those we think of as ours will always cause us suffering. Actually, nothing here belongs to us. Everything belongs to the Lord.

By surrendering to you that which is yours,
what can I possibly lose?
Teraa tujh kao saopate kiaa laagai meraa.

Kabir, Adi Granth, p. 1375

All of this belongs to the Lord. If the Lord wishes to give, so be it; it is His pleasure. If the Lord takes back, so be it; it is God's will. What have we got to grumble about?

But then the dog of greed keeps howling within us. Regardless of what the Lord gives us, we are never content or satisfied. Whenever we happen to come before the Lord, it is with folded hands to beg Him to fulfil our worldly desires and longings. Never do we thank Him: Thank you, Almighty Lord, for giving me such a beautiful house to live in; so many people are in misery, living on the streets. It is thanks to you I have been given such a good life-partner; many of us are involved with partners who are chronically ill. Thank you for giving me enough to eat and drink; half the people of the world go to sleep hungry at night.

We should thank the Lord for whatever He gives us, but instead we are always, day and night, asking for more. Guru Sahib says:

Without any words, He knows everything,
so to whom do we beg and pray?
Vin boliaa sabh kichh jaandaa
kis aagai keechai ardaas.

Adi Granth, M3, p. 1420

To whom do you keep presenting these long lists of demands? Does the Lord not know what you need? He who can fulfil all your needs can also decide what it is you need. Surrender yourself to Him, hand yourself over to Him, and whatever He sees fit, He will give to you.

A beloved son has no need to ask for anything from his father. In fact, the father himself is more concerned for his beloved son: Without him asking anything, I want to give him everything.

Guru Sahib therefore says we should become the beloved sons of the Lord. It is pointless begging all the time—instead, we should be thanking the Lord.

෴

How will you become aware of your condition?
You have not fled to take refuge with the Master.

Chet kaho hoy ab kaise, guroo ke sang nahi[n] dhaaee.

First into lust, and then into anger,
life's creatures are hurled out to burn.

Kaam aur krodh bich bich me[n], jeev se bhaar jho[n]kvaaee.

Now Soami Ji comes to the matter of lust and anger. These two forces are so powerful that we commit numerous sins and wrong actions under their influence. And we have to keep on going down this road of one birth after another to undergo the consequences of those deeds.

Under the influence of lust, the mind is pulled down; under the influence of anger, it is scattered out. Only when we raise our attention to the eye centre, can we start our spiritual journey.

As a result of lust, just see how many children are born. There is no way of supporting them and they have to survive on morsels. We ourselves suffer and cause our children to suffer too. Under the influence of anger, we even go so far as to take someone else's life. When we have to go to prison to serve a sentence, or to the gallows to be hanged, there are cries and entreaties for mercy—but who hears us then? It is anger and our enslavement to it that makes enemies of one brother and another, one race and another, one religion and another, one nation and another. Just see how each one of us dances to its tune. How many nations there are, preparing for terrible wars, making fighter planes, bombs and tanks. Can these be signs of love? They are all signs of anger.

That is why Soami Ji Maharaj lovingly advises that you must withdraw your mind from both lust and anger.

~

Apart from the Master, no one is ours;
who can sever this entangling web?

Guroo bin koi nahee^n apnaa, jaal yaha kaun turvaaee.

*N*ow Soami Ji instructs us: Look carefully throughout the creation. Who really belongs to us?

Only someone who is with us now, and after our death, is truly ours. Those we think of as ours lose interest in us and are ready to abandon us while we are living, so what help can they possibly be to us after death?

Only the supreme Lord, the Almighty, is ours. That is why Guru Sahib says:

> The false are in love with the false
> and have forgotten their Creator;
> whom to love and make one's friend
> when the whole world is in a state of flux?

Koor koorai nehu lagaa wisariaa kartaar.
Kis naal keechai dostee sabh jag chalanhaar.

Adi Granth, M1, p. 468

He says the body is false, it is transient and will perish. It will be consigned to fire or buried in the ground. The attachments and love we develop with the world while living in our body are false in the same way, because they too are transient and will perish. The false remains forever attached to the false, in love with the false, and consequently we live oblivious to the supreme Lord.

He says that even if we search throughout the whole creation, we will find nothing worthy of our love, friendship and devotion except the one supreme Lord. The One who can and does belong to us, we do not think of as ours, and we do not try to attain. Instead, we wander endlessly through the creation, distressed, trying to possess everything that does not belong to us and never can.

Soami Ji explains that only the true Lord and his devotees, his beloved sons, are ours, because they awaken within us love for the Lord, the desire to find Him. It is they who merge us with Him; they tell us the way to find the Lord.

ॐ

Family and relations act from self-interest;
none come near if we have no wealth.

Kutumb parivaar matlab kaa, binaa dhan paas nahi^{n} aaee.

Saints do not spare anyone when giving their teachings. Soami Ji says that all those you call your own—sons, daughters, wife, husband, friends, and so on—are related to you through self-interest; all such love has an ulterior motive. If you have money, all jostle to establish themselves in one way or another as a relative or friend. The moment you have nothing in your pocket, even a son is not prepared to acknowledge his father.

Every day you read accounts of court cases—a father, while dividing his property, gives a thousand rupees or half an acre less to his son, and the son becomes an enemy for life and takes his father to court.

What belongs to us in this world? These are relationships of property, fellowships of inheritance and wealth. A man is about to take his last breath and his beneficiaries are already pressing their claims.

Soami Ji Maharaj warns us to be careful: None of the relations you keep thinking of as yours, in fact, belong to you. You look after your children thinking of your own well-being, and they are glued to you out of self-interest. If you do not give your wife her allowance, just see how long she will stay with you. If you refuse help to a friend in trouble, see what will be left of your friendship. These are relationships of self-interest, of money and material gain—not of love.

That is why Soami Ji says that only the supreme Lord belongs to us, and it is He whom we should make our own.

∽

What words will persuade the mind:
it is our loved ones who gnaw on our flesh.

Kahaa^n lag kahoo^n is man ko, unhee^n se maas nuchvaaee.

Soami Ji says that intellectually all of us understand whatever the saints tell us: that actually, all these worldly relationships will only make us unhappy; no one has ever derived happiness from them; none of them belong to us; only the Lord is ours.

And yet, do we relinquish our attachment to them? Do we stop loving them? Again and again our mind keeps getting drawn to them. By getting involved in this way, we suffer, we cry and complain, and still we do not extricate ourselves from them.

Hazur used to say that when the sheepfold catches fire, people take pity on the sheep and try to save them, but the animals are not prepared to leave each other, so they are burned to cinders.

Saints and Masters come into the world to tell us what is real: Your real self is the Lord; with everything else, your relationship is one of giving and taking, of selfish love. Detach yourself from all this and worship the Lord—develop love for Him instead. And what is the result? As you know, Sarmad was beheaded, Mansur was hanged, Christ was crucified, some Masters were flayed alive, and Paltu was burned alive in his hut. What was their fault? Saints simply explain what is real in the world, awakening within us the desire and yearning to find this reality. They never form sects, religions or nations. They only arouse within us the desire to find the Lord.

We are so bound down by religious codes, we have become such prisoners of our religions—they have made us so blind—that we do not understand what we are doing. What is the use of repenting after an event, of feeling remorse after we have lost control of our senses? That is why Soami Ji says that although all of us understand everything, still we are not ready to give up our worldly attachments, nor let go of our worldly loves.

～

Masters and saints tell in so many ways,
but we never take note of their words.

Guroo aur saadh kahe^n bahu vidhi, kahan unkee na patiyaaee.

Soami Ji says that saints and Masters have left no stone
unturned in their efforts to explain their message to us: they
spend their entire lives explaining simple, straightforward
and basic truths to us. They have spent long periods—often
as much as forty or fifty years—serving us. They have written
many great books and, by collecting together the writings and
discourses of many saints, have explained to us how this
world is transient and perishable; we will never find happiness and peace in it; peace can only be found through devotion to the Lord and by loving Him.

There is nothing lacking in the explanations of the saints.
But we let their words go in one ear and out of the other, saying to ourselves: For whom are the saints saying all these
things? Soami Ji says that it is not because of the saints, but
because of our karmas, our way of thinking, that we do not
understand anything.

～

Without grace, can anyone believe them?
This is what Radha Soami proclaims.

Mehar bin kyaa koee maane, kahee raadhaaswaamee yaha gaaee.

Finally, Soami Ji says that no one can be blamed for this situation, for until the Lord showers his grace and mercy, how

can anyone understand? In this world, everyone is blind, and it is only the Lord who has vision. Those who cannot see will only emerge from the darkness when the One who has sight chooses to call them and lead them into the light.

Therefore only when the Lord showers his grace and mercy will we understand what is real in the world, and only then will our attention turn to worshipping the Lord.

It is for us to take advantage of Soami Ji Maharaj's teachings, to detach ourselves from our love for the faces and forms of the creation, and attach ourselves to the Word, the Name, within.

2

~

O Friend, Observe the Law of This Age

Is jug kaa dharm paroh tum bhaaee

O friend, observe the law of this age;
enlightenment is attained through a perfect Guru.
Here and hereafter, the Lord's Name is your only companion.

Repeat the Lord's Name and contemplate on it with your mind.
With the grace of the Guru, remove all impurities. *(Refrain)*

Through controversies and opposition, the Lord is not realized.
Mind and body are rendered insipid by duality.
Through the Guru's Word, be attached to the true Lord.

This whole creation is stained by egotism.
Ritual baths and pilgrimages do not rid us of ego.
Unless we meet the Guru we are dishonoured by Death.

They alone are true who vanquish the ego.
With the Word of the Guru they defeat the five passions.
They save themselves and those associated with them.

The Magician conjures up his show of illusion and attachment.
The lovers of the world keep clinging blindly to it.
The detached lovers of the Lord remain immersed in Him.

The hypocrite assumes many different appearances;
riddled with inner desires, he parades his ego.
Not knowing the self, he loses the game.

By donning different robes, he cleverly deceives.
Lured by attachment and delusion, he is lost in doubt.
Without service to the Guru, he suffers great misery.

Those dyed in God's Name are forever detached.
While living as householders, they are absorbed in Truth.
Says Nanak, most fortunate are they who serve the Satguru.

Adi Granth, Guru Amardas, p. 230

Is jug kaa dharm paroh tum bhaaee.
Poorai gur sabh sojhee paaee.
Aithai agai harnaam sakhaaee.

Raam parah man karah beechaar.
Gurparsaadee mail utaar. (Rahaau)

Waad wirodh na paa-i-aa jaa-e.
Man tan feekaa doojai bhaa-e.
Gur kai sabad sach liv laa-e.

Haomai mailaa ih sansaaraa.
Nit teerath naavai na jaae ahankaaraa.
Bin gur bhete jam kare khuaaraa.

So jan saachaa je haomai maarai.
Gur kai sabad panch sanghaarai.
Aap tarai sagle kul taarai.

Maa-i-aa moh nat baajee paaee.
Manmukh andh rahe laptaaee.
Gurmukh alipat rahe liv laaee.

Bahute bhekh karai bhekhdhaaree.
Antar tisnaa firai ahankaaree.
Aap na cheenai baajee haaree.

Kaapar pahar kare chaturaaee.
Maa-i-aa moh at bharm bhulaaee.
Bin gur seve bahut dukh paaee.

Naam rate sadaa bairaagee.
Grihee antar saach liv laagee.
Naanak satgur sevah se wadbhaagee.

Shabdarath Sri Guru Granth Sahib Ji (Amritsar: Shromani
Gurdwara Prabandhak Committee), M3, p. 230

O friend, observe the law of this age;
enlightenment is attained through a perfect Guru.
Here and hereafter, the Lord's Name is your only companion.

Is jug kaa dharm paroh tum bhaaee.
Poorai gur sabh sojhee paaee.
Aithai agai harnaam sakhaaee.

ℱor this satsang,* I am taking my text from the writings of
the third Padshahi, Shri Guru Amardas Ji Maharaj, in which
he clearly explains the teachings of the line of Guru Nanak
Sahib.

He says there are four ages that follow one another in a
cycle: Satyug, Tretayug, Dwaparyug and Kaliyug. Each age
has its own various distinct characteristics, with the result that
spiritual practices which worked in Satyug do not achieve
results in Kaliyug.

In Satyug, we lived very long lives, our attention was
hardly dispersed in the world, and we enjoyed excellent
health. With the transition from one age to the next, human
lifespans shortened, our attention spread more and more into
the world, and our health deteriorated.

Now, in Kaliyug, we can see for ourselves how someone who reaches the age of even sixty-five or seventy is considered fortunate. As for our health, we all know how difficult
it is for us to sit cross-legged in satsang for even an hour or
so. And, for our attention, we only have to put our minds

---

* *See* Glossary and Translators' Note for explanations of unusual usage, and technical or Indian-language terms, such as: satsang, Padshahi.

to a minor issue demanding a moment or two of complete concentration, and all the problems of the world appear before our eyes. Guru Nanak Sahib explains, therefore, that the methods that worked for us in Satyug do not work in Kaliyug.

In this age, then, what spiritual technique or method should we practise so we can escape from the endless suffering of the cycle of death and rebirth, so we can worship the Lord and achieve union with Him? It is from the mystics, the lovers of the Lord, that we find out. What do they tell us?

> Here and hereafter,
> the Lord's Name is your only companion.

If you want to live out the brief span of your life in this body in peace and happiness, if you want to return to the Lord, there is only one way: engage in the practice of the Word. Apart from meditation on the Word, there is no other method or technique.

> So many actions have I tried;
> whatever I did resulted in further entanglement.
> Seeds sown out of season do not germinate,
> one forfeits even one's capital.
> Supreme in Kaliyug is the method of the divine
>   Music;
> by the Gurmukh's guidance, with concentrated
>   meditation
> utter the Lord's Name.
> *Anik karam kee-e bahutere.*
> *Jo keejai so bandhan paire.*
> *Kurutaa beej beeje nahee jammai*
> *sabh laahaa mool gavaa-idaa.*

Kaljug mah keertan pardhaanaa.
Gurmukh japeeai laae dhiaanaa.

Adi Granth, M5, p. 1075

Guru Sahib says that everything we do with the mind and intellect to escape from the imprisonment of the body—prayers, penances, austerities, ceremonial worship, reading or reciting scriptures, good deeds, charity, pilgrimages—whatever we do, ends up strengthening the bonds that tie us to the creation, rather than releasing us from them. Why? Because "Seeds sown out of season do not germinate".

If you plant seeds in the wrong season, you will never carry home a harvest. Any farmer will know that wheat is sown in October and November.* If someone sows wheat in the hot months of May or June, then regardless of how much he ploughs, manures, waters and tends the crop, there will be no harvest to take home. That is why Guru Sahib says: "Supreme in Kaliyug is the method of the divine Music; by the Gurmukh's guidance, with concentrated meditation utter the Lord's Name."

If there is one thing saints have openly proclaimed and exalted in Kaliyug, it is the 'divine Music' *(keertan)*, the music that devotees of the Lord listen to with deep concentration within themselves. What he is referring to is the Shabd, the Word or Name. Soami Ji says:

> In Kaliyug ritualistic practices are not required;
> without the Name there is no salvation.
> *Kaljug karm dharm nahi[n] koee,*
> *naam binaa uddhaar na hoee.*

Soami Ji, *Sar Bachan* 38:3, p. 337

---

* This applies in North India.

Try whatever method you want, try any technique you can think of—give what you want in charity, go on endless pilgrimages, bathe in all the holy waters, read all the scriptures, pierce your ears, wear your hair matted, smear ash on your body, go on bowing at the tombs of past saints, renounce your family, hide away in some forest or mountain retreat—without the practice of the Word, you will not escape from the prison of the body under any circumstances whatsoever. That is why the fifth Padshahi says:

> Friends, keep the company of saints
> and cherish the true Name;
> equip yourself with sustenance for this life and
>   the next.
> *Sant janhu mil bhaaeeho sachaa naam samaal.*
> *Tosaa bandhahu jeea kaa aithai othai naal.*
>
> Adi Granth, M5, p. 49

Go to the saints, the holy men, the Masters, and devote yourself to the practice of the true Name. This, he says, is your 'sustenance',* your capital. It stays with you here in this world and it will go with you to the next. No thief can steal it, no fire can burn it, and no one can take it from you. Soami Ji says:

> Remember the Master's Name as you proceed
>   through life—
> it is the only wealth worth securing.
> *Naam guru kaa samhaale chal,*
> *yahee hai daam ga^{n}th bandhanaa.*
>
> Soami Ji, Sar Bachan 19:18, p. 152

---

*See Glossary (sustenance) for discussion of cultural context.

Soami Ji explains that the only thing in the world we can secure and take with us is our earnings from the practice of the
Word, our meditation on the Name.

> Except Nam, you have no friend or companion.
> You will attain salvation only through the practice
>   of Nam.
> *Bin naavai ko sang na saathee*
> *mukte naam dhiaavaniaa.*
>
> Adi Granth, M1, p. 109

Guru Sahib says keep this fact firmly in your mind:
Apart from the practice of the Name, nothing will remain
with you. If you are to attain liberation, it will only be through
meditation on the Name. The third Padshahi, for this reason,
explains:

> O friends, when you find a perfect Gurmukh,
> he will teach you the true way to practise Nam.
> *Santah gurmukh pooraa paaee. Naamo pooj karaaee.*
>
> Adi Granth, M3, p. 910

Only if we meet a devotee and lover of the Lord who explains
to us how to meditate on the Name, will we be able to worship the Lord. He also says:

> Without the Name, there can be no other worship
>   of God;
> in vain, the world strays in doubt.
> *Bin naavai hor pooj na hovee bharam bhulee lokaaee.*
>
> Adi Granth, M3, p. 910

Understand very clearly that there is no devotion or worship of the Lord, other than meditation on the Name. Caught up in their misconceptions, people waste their time running this way and that. In the writings of the first Padshahi, it says:

> By forsaking Nam and treading another path,
> you will be filled with regret at the time of death.
> *Naam wisaar chalah an maarag*
> *ant kaal pachhutaahee.*
>
> Adi Granth, M1, p. 1153

If you abandon this method of meditating on the Name, you will be forced to repent in the end, at the time of death, no matter what path you follow. Why?

> Without the Name,
> no one gains admittance at the royal gate;
> such people are dishonoured by the messengers
> of Death.
> *Vin naavai dar dhoee naahee*
> *taa jam kare khuaaree.*
>
> Adi Granth, M3, p. 754

Without the practice of listening to the Name, no one can reach the Lord's home. We will instead be harassed at the hands of Death's henchmen.

> There is no worship comparable to that of God's
> Name;
> this I have realized after careful personal experience.
> *Harnaamai tul na pujaee sabh dithee thok vajaae.*
>
> Adi Granth, M1, p. 62

Guru Sahib says: I am not just speaking from hearsay, I am not just quoting something I have read. I have tested everything myself, and from my own personal experience I can tell you that there is nothing to be compared with meditation on the Name. That is why he says:

> All other measures fall short of the Truth;
> the practice of the true Word surpasses all.
> *Sach-ho orai sabh ko, upar sach aachaar.*
>
> Adi Granth, M1, p. 62

Whatever benefits we get from prayers, penances and self-imposed austerities, or from charity and good deeds, are far inferior to the benefit we derive from devotion to the Name. The highest and purest reward of all comes from meditation on the Word, from listening to the Name.

> O Nanak, never forget the holy Name;
> liberation is gained through practice of the Word.
> *Naanak naam na veesarai chhootai sabad kamaae.*
>
> Adi Granth, M1, p. 62

Even in your dreams, my friends, try never to forget the Name. Only by practice of the Name will you ever escape from the prison of the body. Soami Ji tells us the same thing:

> The Master speaks out in clear terms:
> My friend, attach yourself to the unending music
>   of the Word.
> There is no way, other than the Word,
> to break out from this mortal vessel of clay.
> *Guru kahe khol kar bhaaee*
> *lag shabd anaahad jaaee,*

> *bin shabd upaao na doojaa*
> *kaayaa kaa chhute na koozaa.*
>
> Soami Ji, *Sar Bachan* 20:10, p. 161

He says engrave this thought deep in your mind: Without the Word, you will never achieve liberation from the body. Then he adds:

> Engage in the practice of listening to the Shabd.
> Now put all other efforts aside.
> *Surt shabd kamaaee karnaa,*
> *sab jatan door ab dharnaa.*
>
> Soami Ji, *Sar Bachan* 20:10, p. 161

We must apply ourselves only to that practice by which the soul realizes the Word *(surat shabd abhyaas)*. There is no need for any other practice. There is no point in even thinking of any other method. Kabir Sahib also refers to this:

> Whenever the Name is fixed in the heart all sin is
>   destroyed,
> just as the smallest spark of fire consumes dry grass.
> *Jab hee naam hirday dharyo bhayo paap ko naas,*
> *maanau chingee aag kee paree puraane ghaas.*
>
> Kabir, *Kabir Sakhi Sangreh*

It makes no difference how much hay you collect together and pile into a stack, it takes only the smallest spark of fire to reduce the whole thing to ashes. It is the same for us humans, weak and dissolute as we are. No matter what sins we may have committed, what bad deeds we may have done, our meditation on the Word will destroy the entire chain of our karmas.

Guru Nanak Sahib says that if there is one way proclaimed by the saints in Kaliyug, it is that of the Word:

> The Dark Age has now arrived.
> Sow thou the seed of the one Lord's Name.
> *Ab kaloo aa-i-o re. Ik naam bovah.*
>
> Adi Granth, M5, p. 1185

Now that we are in Kaliyug, saints openly preach the way of the Word. But the Word that is glorified by the house of Guru Nanak Sahib is no ordinary spoken word; it is the power that created the whole world and from which we have all been born. It is the foundation of all the regions and divisions of the universe. Guru Nanak Sahib says:

> The whole creation emanated from the Name.
> Without the Satguru, the Name cannot be attained.
> *Naamai hee te sabh kichh hoaa*
> *bin satgur naam na jaapai.*
>
> Adi Granth, M3, p. 753

The Name created everything in the world. Now, just reflect! How can the power that has brought the creation into existence possibly be written down, spoken or read? Who can trace its history, who can establish its period, or place it in time? The words we use as names for the Lord out of our love for Him—Allah, Wahiguru, Radha Soami, the Almighty, God, and so on—can all be written, read and spoken. Their history can be traced and the period and time of their usage can be established. But that is the Name that brought the world into existence.

And where is it? It is within us, inside this physical form. That is why Guru Sahib says:

He who searches outside his body
will not find God's Name;
instead he will suffer the fate of bonded labour.
Sareerah bhaalan ko baahar jaae.
Naam na lahai bahut vegaar dukh paae.

Adi Granth, M3, p. 124

People who search for the Name as something outside themselves and their body are like bonded labourers, wasting their precious time. Who are these bonded labourers? They are people who toil their lives away sweating blood and tears, yet end up empty-handed. If something is lost inside one's house and one goes searching for it in the fields or streets outside, how will one ever find it? So where in the body is the Name?

In this body is a multitude of precious treasures,
but one is able to realize them within
only when one meets a true Gurmukh.
Is kaa-i-aa andar vast asankhaa.
Gurmukh saach milai taa vekhaa.

Adi Granth, M3, p. 110

Guru Sahib explains that this physical body is not just a clay effigy some five or six feet long, nor is it just flesh, blood and bones. The Lord has stored a multitude of things within it, He has kept a vast treasury inside it. Most extraordinary of all, He himself lives there. He has also put a path there for us to reach Him. But when will we realize this? "Only when one meets a true Gurmukh"—when we find a real mystic and lover of the Lord. And what do they tell us?

Closing the nine doors,
one finds liberation at the tenth;

there ever resonates the limitless melody of the Word.
Nao darvaaje dasvai muktaa
anahad sabad vajaavaniaa.

Adi Granth, M1, p. 110

They explain that the desires of the senses, the negative tendencies of the mind and the craving for the pleasures of food and drink, all exist below the eyes. The door to our real home is behind the eyes, at a place we call 'the tenth' *(dasvai).*

If we want to enter a house, we must first find the door. Once the door opens—from inside—we can go in. What distinguishes the door to this home of ours? Guru Sahib tells us it is where "ever resonates the limitless melody of the Word". The eternal music of the Word *(anahad shabd)* is resounding within everyone at this entrance to our home. By 'resonates' they are saying that the Word contains sound, it contains melody. That is why they also describe it as the purest music *(nirmal naad)* when they refer to it in the house of Guru Nanak Sahib.

The Word also contains radiance, light, of which Guru Sahib says:

The light of God's Name is latent in everyone
and can be revealed through the Guru's wisdom.
Raamnaam hai jot sabaaee
tat gurmat kaadh la-eejai.

Adi Granth, M4, p. 1323

The light of the Lord's Name is continuously shining in each one of us behind the eyes. Its light is right within us at the eye centre, but we cannot see it until we travel the path shown to us by the saints—which means living according to their teachings. What do they teach?

Nine are the doors, but all nine are insipid;
the divine ambrosia flows from the tenth.
Nao darvaaj nave dar feeke ras amrit dasve chu-eejai.

Adi Granth, M4, p. 1323 ·

   The teaching of the saints is that the pleasures of the
senses and all the negative tendencies of the mind lie below
the eye centre. The nectar that is saturated with sweetness,
that purifies our minds when we drink it, is to be found behind the eyes. Thus, until we make our attention one-pointed
at the eye centre where the nectar is flowing, we can never
drink it, we can never become immortal, we can never escape
from the endless suffering of death and rebirth.

   That is why saints praise the true Word, the everlasting
Name. It is there in everyone—thieves, swindlers, holy men
and saints. The question of race, religion or country does not
arise. Whether Hindu, Sikh or Christian, those who are
blessed and fortunate enough to concentrate their attention
at the eye centre will hear the sound of the Word reverberating within and will see its light or brilliance. By this sound we
can determine the direction of our home. By its light we can
make our journey within. Thus, stage by stage, we return to
our home. This is how the saints have tried to describe the
true Word.

༄

*Repeat the Lord's Name and contemplate on it
with your mind.
With the grace of the Guru, remove all impurities.*
Raam parah man karah beechaar. Gurparsaadee mail utaar.

Guru Sahib explains that our minds have become extremely dirty by getting enmeshed in the web of illusion. Even though our souls are part of the supreme soul, drops of the ocean of Satnam, we have been separated from the Lord and come into this world, where we have taken the mind as our companion.

The mind loves its negative tendencies, physical pleasures, cravings and appetites, and since we act under the domination of the mind, the soul also has to face the consequences. It is because of our worldly desires—trapped as we are in the sphere of the senses—and because of our sins and impure deeds, that we have accumulated such quantities of filth on our minds.

That is why Guru Sahib clarifies for us that it is our mind that has become such a formidable obstacle between us and the Lord. Until the dirt is removed from the mind, the soul will never be worthy of reuniting with the Lord, even though it is a part of Him. And when is the dirt removed? When the mind returns to Brahm, its native place.

We all try countless techniques and methods to purify the mind, each according to our own limited understanding. We repeat sacred names, practise austerities, perform penances, recite prayers and read scriptures. We do good deeds, give in charity, and leave our homes to hide in some secluded place in the mountains or forests. We practise all these methods and techniques solely to purify the mind. We try to withdraw our attention forcibly from the world by means of self-imposed disciplines. We make some progress, but we find that there is nothing to hold our attention, and our minds react, rebounding back into the world.

Guru Nanak Sahib maintains that however hard we try, it is not possible to purify and cleanse the mind by force or discipline. How then can we cleanse the mind? "By Guru's grace" (gurparsaadee). The mind becomes pure by following the teachings given to us by the Master. What does 'Guru's grace' refer to? It refers to the method or technique the Master explains to us of worshipping the Lord. Call it initiation, the gift of the Name *(naam-daan)*, or call it the grace or blessing of the Guru *(gur parshaad)*—it is one and the same thing.

The Master gives only one kind of parshad or blessing: the Name. Grace *(parshaad)* is given freely and happily. A gift *(daan)* is also given freely and happily. The Master's highest grace is the technique for meditating on the Name. When he bestows initiation, it is the greatest gift he can give us. So the Master's blessing and the gift of the Name are the same thing. If our mind is ever to become pure, it will only be by meditating on the Name. Guru Sahib says:

> The living Satguru is the pool of nectar;
> one with great good fortune bathes therein.
> There the dross of countless lives is cleansed
> by repeating God's pure Name.
> *Satguru purkh amritsar wadbhaagee naavah aae.*
> *Un janam janam kee mail utarai nirmal naam driraae.*
>
> Adi Granth, M4, p. 40

Coming to the satsang of a living perfect Master and being in his company is bathing in the pool of nectar. Where is that pool of nectar in which a crow immerses itself to emerge as a swan? In the outside world, there is no such pool where a crow can be transformed into a swan. That pool of nectar lies within us, where we, the lovers of the mind, go to be transformed into swans, into lovers of the Lord. That pool is the satsang of the Masters, it is keeping the company of mystics.

Who bathes in this pool of nectar? Guru Sahib says it is those "with great good fortune"—those who are blessed, the lucky ones, who are not bothered by public opinion, gossip or criticism. And what benefit do they derive? Their "dross of countless lives is cleansed." This dross is the dirt that has adhered to the mind over countless lifetimes, the entire vast store of unpaid karmic debts—our *sinchit* karmas accumulated from previous lives.

Our meditation, the practice of listening to the Name, is done precisely to settle these *sinchit* karmas, whereas our destiny karmas *(praalabdh)* have to be gone through in this life. Laughing or crying, one way or another we have to go through them. In future, we will avoid committing the kind of sinful deeds that bring us back to the prison of the body, but the karmic debts we have already accumulated over so many lifetimes can only be eliminated in one way—by meditation on the Word. That is why Guru Sahib talks about "repeating God's pure Name". Our souls become pure through meditation on the Name, because by this meditation the mind leaves all dirt far behind. Guru Sahib says:

> Friends, the mind becomes pure
> when it merges in the Word.
> This worship alone takes us home.
> *Sabad marai man nirmal santah,*
> *eh poojaa thaae paaee.*
>
> Adi Granth, M3, p. 910

Once we keep our attention in the Word all day long— wherever we are, whatever we are doing—and we are completely absorbed in it, then our mind becomes pure. Guru Sahib says: This is true worship of the Lord. This is the devotion that will take you to your ancestral home.

It is this gift of the Master's grace—meditation on the Word—that releases the knot tying the soul to the mind, cleanses the soul and purifies the mind. The saints say that all

the layers of dirt that we have heaped on the mind, lifetime
after lifetime, will be removed when we meet a Master and
meditate on the Name. The dirt will then be left far behind.
The soul will become pure. The mind will return to its original home, and the soul will reach its home too.

∾

Through controversies and opposition,
the Lord is not realized.
Mind and body are rendered insipid by duality.

Waad wirodh na paa-i-aa jaa-e. Man tan feekaa doojai bhaa-e.

Guru Sahib says that our mind can never be purified by debate, argument, or the study of scriptures. Neither the mind
nor the body can be cleansed in that way. As long as the mind,
through the instrument of the body, remains entangled in
sensual desires and appetites, involved with the family and in
social, religious and political activities, the body is inevitably
rendered unclean. Both mind and body are made unclean.
Guru Sahib explains that if you want to purify them, you cannot do it any way other than meditating on the Name.

> If one reads year after year,
> if one reads month upon month,
> if one reads for a lifetime, breath upon breath,
> Nanak, only one thing is of value;
> all else is but prattling in pride.
> *Pareeah jete baras baras pareeah jete maas.*
> *Pareeah jetee aarjaa pareeah jete saas.*
> *Naanak lekhai ik gal hor haomai jhakhnaa jhaak.*
>
>   Adi Granth, M1, p. 467

He says: You may read for a lifetime, day and night, with every breath, but only one thing will be credited to your account—whether your soul has attached itself to the Word within. If your soul is not attuned to the Word, all your reading and reciting will be useless.

> The learned man reads and teaches others,
> oblivious of the fires that burn his own home.
> *Par pandit avaraa samjhaae.*
> *Ghar jalte kee khabar na paae.*
> Adi Granth, M3, p. 1045

Preachers and theologians keep on reading and expounding to the world. Unaware that their own houses are burning in the fires of lust, anger, greed, attachment and ego, they make no attempt to put them out. Guru Sahib says:

> Without serving the Satguru,
> one is not blessed with the Name;
> one may read till exhausted,
> yet will not find peace.
> *Bin satgur seve naam na paaeeai.*
> *Par thaake saant na aaee he.*
> Adi Granth, M3, p. 1046

You may read till you are exhausted, till you have worn yourself into the ground, but you will have no peace of mind till you go to a Master and learn from him how to listen to the Word.

What exactly are the scriptures? As we know, sages and seers, saints and mystics, devotees and lovers of God, prophets and messengers of the Lord, all put great effort into achieving union with the Lord. They wrote the scriptures to record the visions they had on the path, the difficulties they experienced, and how they overcame them. All spiritual writings and religious books are records of their spiritual experiences.

By reading the scriptures, we can learn about the inner visions of others, but we ourselves do not see anything within. If we read and learn from their experiences, and then act on the advice they give, we will remove the obstacles from our own inner path. Those spiritual experiences will then become ours, and our difficulties will be overcome.

If you want to see the Kashmir Valley, you will first read a book about the area. By reading the guidebook, you will not experience the beauty of Kashmir, but the book will awaken a desire in you to go there. Reading it will give you all sorts of information about getting there, about the difficult terrain and passes and how to deal with them. But unless you use the information to cross the passes and reach Srinagar yourself, how will you ever see the beauty of the Valley?

We lose ourselves in trivial details, and we think that the reading and chanting of scriptures constitutes spiritual liberation. And then sometimes we do not even have the time to read or listen, so we have the priest come to our house: while we are out and about enjoying ourselves, he does the reading, and we actually think that this absolves us of our sins.

We will only benefit from the written word if we ourselves absorb the message of the saints. Then we become aware of our weaknesses, we are inspired with a desire to overcome them, and we look for a method to achieve this. Through services and ceremonies we have ritualized the reading of scriptures so much that we think salvation will come automatically, as long as we go on reading. The saints are not opposed to reading; they are opposed to the attitude with which we read.

If you pick up a medical book and go on reading it the whole day, the disease you are suffering from will not be cured. But if you start taking the remedies prescribed in the book, by this course of action the disease can be cured. No one has ever made a train journey by simply reading a railway timetable. If you act on the information contained in the timetable, buy a ticket and sit in the train, the journey takes place by itself.

This is why the saints emphasize that liberation does not lie in reading scriptures. Reading leads to the habit of debate and argument; soon we begin considering ourselves learned scholars and everyone else to be inferior. Bulleh Shah says:

> Stop gathering knowledge, my friend!
> All you need know is the one letter 'A'.[*]
> Look how much knowledge Satan acquired—
> and how his hearth and home burnt to ashes.
> *Ilamo[n] bas karee[n] o yaar,*
> *ikko alaf tere darkaar,*
> *bahutaa ilam azaazeel ne pariaa,*
> *jhuggaa use daa hee sariaa.*
>
> Bulleh Shah, *Qanun-e-Ishq* 212

Consider Ravan: he was such a great scholar, but where did his intellect get him! Saints therefore stress that salvation lies not in reading, but in putting into practice what we read.

---

[*] *Alif* ('A') designates the first symbol of the Arabic alphabet, which is used for the Arabic, Persian and Urdu languages. The character is a single stroke, the starting point of all other written characters. It thus stands as a metaphor for Allah (God) and the Word, that single power from which all diversity is born.

❧

Through the Guru's Word, be attached to the true Lord.

Gur kai sabad sach liv laa-e.

Our body is purified when we meditate on the Word in the way the Masters teach us, because then the mind does not come down to the level of the senses. Following their teachings, we use simran and dhyan to withdraw our attention from the nine doors of the body and make it one-pointed at the eye centre. Our mind becomes pure when it attaches itself to the Word within and returns to its source in Trikuti.

Guru Sahib says that if you follow the teachings of the Masters, you can make both body and mind pure. True love will awaken within you for the true Lord. Worldly attachments and false love for the false world will leave you, and true love for the true Lord will be born. Guru Sahib says:

> Through the Guru's Word
> one is immersed in Truth.
> *Gursabdee sachee liv laae.*
>   Adi Granth, M3, p. 115

Meditating on the Name as taught by the Masters removes all falseness from within us and awakens within us that attachment and love which is true.

Our mind loves pleasure. Until it is given a higher and better pleasure than those of the world, it will not give up its attachment to the things of the world. What is it, then, that can engender such love and bliss in the mind that it will at once give up its worldly loves and attachments? Guru Sahib says:

The mind becomes content when it finds the Name;
cursed is the life without the Name.
Naam milai man tripteeai bin naamai dhrig jeewaas.

Adi Granth, M4, p. 40

The mind, driven by its own desires and weaknesses, is restless and anxious like a deer. As soon as it tastes the abundant sweetness of the Name within, the ambrosia of Nam, it will be satisfied, content and at peace. Guru Sahib says:

The Lord God's Name is an immortalizing sweet
ambrosia.
Har har naam amrit ras meethaa.

Adi Granth, M4, p. 1323

The Name is the sweetest elixir—the pleasure it gives is sweet beyond measure. We describe it as such because the pleasure we get from our love for our children, from our involvement with social, religious and national politics, from satisfying our physical desires, even from hurting others, all seem insipid by comparison. Someone who has found diamonds and precious stones will not put up with being driven from door to door in search of worthless trinkets. Little girls play with dolls only till they grow up and get married.

It is attachment to the Shabd that gradually detaches us forever from the world. Guru Sahib says:

The Word of the Guru is sweet beyond measure;
that sweetness cannot be known unless you taste it.
Gur kaa sabad mahaa ras meethaa
bin chaakhe saad na jaapai.

Adi Granth, M3, p. 753

The Word we are connected to by the Master is "sweet beyond measure" because no sweetness in the world compares with it. It can be known only by tasting it—by experiencing it—not by talking about it. This, Guru Sahib says, is how true love and devotion for the true Lord is born within us.

❧

This whole creation is stained by egoism.
Ritual baths and pilgrimages do not rid us of ego.
Unless we meet the Guru we are dishonoured by Death.

Haomai mailaa ih sansaaraa.
Nit teerath naavai na jaae ahankaaraa.
Bin gur bhete jam kare khuaaraa.

Guru Sahib explains that all of us, all living beings, are enmeshed in the web of illusion (maya), sleeping the sweet sleep of attachment. No one knows about the Lord—we do not even think about Him. We are all sleeping in sweet oblivion. Guru Sahib says:

> In illusion and attachment, the entire world is asleep.
> Tell me, how will this deception be removed?
> *Maa-i-aa moh sabho jag soiaa*
> *ih bharm kahah kio jaaee.*

> Adi Granth, M5, p. 205

We are all so caught up in this illusion, that whatever we see, we take to be real. In fact, it is all transient and will perish. Because we take it to be real, we get attached to it and we try to possess it. This is not possible, so we suffer, we cry and we complain. This is why Guru Sahib says:

O Nanak, terrible is the disease of the ego;
wherever I look, I see this one agony.
Naanak haomai rog bure.
Jah dekhaan tah ekaa bedan.

Adi Granth, M1, p. 1155

He says that ego is a most terrible disease. Wherever he looks, he sees that we are all sick with this one disease—egotism, me and mine, selfishness and self-centredness. It is all *my* children, *my* inheritance, *my* house, *my* circle of friends, *my* religion, *my* country. These all belong to the Lord, but we think of ourselves as separate from Him and that is why we try to make them ours. They cannot be owned and they never will be. In trying to possess them, we get attached to them and start loving them, and it is this love and attachment that keep dragging us all back again and again to the prison of a physical form. Guru Nanak Sahib says:

Mixing the poison of ego, the Lord created the world.
Haomai bikh paae jagat upaa-i-aa.

Adi Granth, M1, p. 1009

Everything that we see before us in this worldly creation has been created by the Lord through the ego. If there were no ego in us, we would not stay in the creation; we would immediately go and merge with the maker of the creation.

Guru Sahib tells us how we are all caught up in this disease of ego. But even when we become aware that it is our love for an illusory world which has entangled us, what do we do? We go off on pilgrimages, we get involved in prayers, penances, good deeds and charitable works, or we renounce our homes and families to hide away in some remote place. Guru Nanak Sahib makes it clear that we can never detach

our affections from the world in this way. He says that we will
never escape from the world until we surrender ourselves to
the Master and abandon ourselves to him. This means following the teachings and meditating on the Word. We read
in the writings of the house of Guru Nanak Sahib:

> He has made this world an abode of pain and
>   pleasure;
> only they who take refuge with the Satguru are
>   liberated.
> *Harakh sog kaa nagar ihu keeaa.*
> *Se ubre jo satgur sarneeaa.*
>
>   Adi Granth, M5, p. 1075

This world is made from good and bad deeds. We are now
facing the consequences of good and bad deeds we did earlier. Day and night we go on doing more deeds for which we
will again have to come back to face the consequences. There
is only one way to escape: "Only they who take refuge with
the Satguru are liberated"—the ones who gain the protection
of the Master. Guru Sahib also says:

> Beholding his presence, all sins are destroyed,
> thereby bringing union with the Lord.
> *Darsan bhetat paap sabh naasah*
> *har sio de-e milaaee.*
>
>   Adi Granth, M5, p. 915

When we abandon ourselves completely to the presence
(darshan) of the Master, when we surrender ourselves to him,
when we become wholeheartedly and utterly absorbed in him
and assume his identity—then the entire chain of our karmas
is destroyed and he reunites us with the Lord.

The accounts are settled
of those who meet a Satguru, says Nanak.
Naanak jin kao satguru miliaa
tin kaa lekhaa nibriaa.
Adi Granth, M3, p. 435

When do we meet the Satguru? When we entrust ourselves to him, when we become his, when we are not attached
to anyone else in the world, when we are his alone—then the
whole chain of our karmas is destroyed. That is why Soami Ji
says:

Take refuge, my beloved, with a true Master;
your karmic dues will be paid.
Satguru saran gaho mere pyaare,
karm jagaat chukaae.
Soami Ji, *Sar Bachan* 8:13, p. 82

Until we settle whatever karmic debts we have, we cannot unite with the Lord. There is only one way to settle them,
and that is by "taking refuge with a true Master". We have to
go to a devotee of the Lord and follow the path he teaches.
This is why Guru Nanak Sahib lovingly tells us that we will
never be freed from the restrictions of the body until we put
into practice the Masters' teachings. The fifth Padshahi says:

He whose home has been locked,
the key is with the Guru.
Despite many attempts, the key cannot be obtained
without surrender to the Satguru.
Jis kaa grih tin deeaa taalaa kunjee gur saopaaee.
Anik upaav kare nahee paavai bin satgur sarnaaee.
Adi Granth, M5, p. 205

The Lord who made you has kept the wealth of the Name right inside you, for you to use, but He has entrusted the secret of how to attain it to the perfect Masters. However much you try to possess it through your mind and intellect, you will not succeed until you reach the protection of the Master, leave the path of the mind and follow his path instead.

Guru Nanak Sahib tells us, therefore, to surrender ourselves to the Master, abandon ourselves to him, and follow the path he teaches.

∼

They alone are true who vanquish the ego.
With the Word of the Guru they defeat the five passions.

> So jan saachaa je haomai maarai.
> Gur kai sabad panch sanghaarai.

People who rid themselves of the disease of ego become 'true', which means that they escape from the pain of death and rebirth and from the five robbers, the five passions. Guru Sahib means that there is only one way to get rid of the disease of ego: practise meditation of the Name. Guru Nanak Sahib also says:

> Ego is a chronic disease,
> but its remedy, too, is within;
> when the Lord showers his grace,
> he makes one practise the Guru's Word.
> *Haomai deeragh rog hai daaroo bhee is maahe.*
> *Kirpaa kare je aapnee taa gur kaa sabad kamaahe.*

Adi Granth, M2, p. 466

Ego is an age-old disease, but the Lord has kept its cure, also, in each one of us. He has but to shower his grace, mercy and compassion on us, and attach our attention to the Name, and we can get rid of this affliction. Emphatically, Guru Sahib says:

> Who can kill the ego without the Lord's Word?
> *Bin sabdai haomai kin maaree.*
>
> Adi Granth, M3, p. 1046

You can hide yourself away as much as you like, but until you taste the sweetness of the Name, how can you be free of ego and worldly love and attachments? Guru Nanak Sahib says:

> Mixing the poison of ego, the Lord created the
>   world;
> by enshrining the Lord's Name within, one is
>   purged of the poison.
> *Haomai bikh paae jagat upaa-i-aa*
> *sabad wasai bikh jaae.*
>
> Adi Granth, M1, p. 1009

It is precisely because of ego that we remain part of this creation: "By enshrining the Lord's Name within, one is purged of the poison." The very day the Word takes its abode within us, the poison of ego will automatically leave us.

Thus, the only thing that drives away the affliction of ego, of me and mine, of love for this illusory creation and our attachment to it, is the practice of the Word.

∾

They save themselves and those associated with them.

Aap tarai sagle kul taarai.

Those who succeed in removing the barrier of ego from within themselves by listening to the Word, manage to cross the ocean of existence safely. If we keep their company and they connect our attention, in the same way, to the Word, they enable us to cross the ocean too. That is why Guru Sahib says:

> By serving the emancipated, one becomes
>   emancipated.
> Through the Word, one is rid of ego and
>   selfish love.
> *Mukte seve muktaa hovai.*
> *Haomai mamtaa sabde khovai.*
>   Adi Granth, M3, p. 116

Those who rid themselves of ego and all worldly love by meditating on the Word, attain liberation. When we keep their company, they join us, too, with the Word and enable us to be liberated like them. Guru Sahib says:

> They who merge with the Word
> become pure beings and Truth-realized.
> *Pavit paavan se jan saache ek sabad liv laaee.*
>   Adi Granth, M3, p. 910

Those who detach their love from the entire world and give it instead to the one Word will certainly become pure.

When we go to such people, when we associate with them and they connect our attention to the Word, they make us into pure beings, like themselves.

༄

The Magician conjures up his show of illusion and attachment.
The lovers of the world keep clinging blindly to it.
The detached lovers of the Lord remain immersed in Him.

Maa-i-aa moh nat baajee paaee. Manmukh andh rahe laptaaee.
Gurmukh alipat rahe liv laaee.

Guru Sahib warns us that when we see the luxuries of the world—people going about eating, drinking, enjoying themselves and staying in expensive hotels—we should not imagine that this world is a wonderful place or that it is fit to be our home. He says it has no reality at all; here, there is only sorrow and more sorrow, trouble and more trouble. Everything will come to an end, everything will perish.

A magician comes and conjures up his show. Once he has finished and gone away, nothing remains. We have all seen puppet shows—the puppeteer takes the puppets out of a bag, puts them on a table, sits behind a curtain, pulls the strings, and they all begin to dance. The puppets that are mind-lovers, the manmukh puppets, think: I am the one who is dancing; who else could make me dance? The puppets that are lovers of the Lord, the gurmukh puppets, know that the one who makes us dance is sitting behind the curtain: It is you, O Lord, who are making us dance in whatever way you want.

This is the difference between a manmukh and a gurmukh, a lover of the mind and a lover of the Lord. Both have been created by the Lord, and it is in his hands to decide whom He will transform into a gurmukh. But who is exalted? Only the gurmukh.

That is why Guru Nanak Sahib warns that when we see people enjoying the luxuries of the world, we should not be deluded into thinking the world is real. Soami Ji also says:

> Both body and home are unreal;
> why exhaust yourself over an illusion?
> *Deh aur greh sab jhoothaa,*
> *bharm me^n kaahe ko khapnaa.*
>
> Soami Ji, *Sar Bachan* 15:13, p. 121

You are wasting your time caught up in an illusion—there is nothing real in it. Guru Sahib says:

> Apart from the Lord, my friends, everything is
>   impure.
> *Har bin sabh kichh mailaa santah.*
>
> Adi Granth, M3, p. 910

Apart from the Lord, everything is impure, everything is false, because nothing lasts. It is like a dream. Our ordinary dreams last for just minutes or hours, whereas this dream lasts fifty or sixty years. There is no reality in this dream; nor is there any reality in the creation. Saints warn us not to think that this show we are watching is real or to fall in love with it.

When we go to see a film, it lasts about one and a half hours. If we recall that it is just a one- or two-hour show, we do not get involved—we neither suffer nor do we become happy on its account. If we allow ourselves to think of it as real, then everything takes on the appearance of reality and we cry and laugh because we feel it is happening to us. But if we remember that after one or two hours nothing will exist any more, then we experience neither sorrow nor joy. That is why saints lovingly explain to us that this is all just a magician's show. Guru Nanak Sahib points out:

> The true Lord has created his show
> by staging the play of death and rebirth.
> *Sachai aapnaa khel rachaa-i-aa*
> *aavaagaon paasaaraa.*
>
> Adi Granth, M3, p. 754

The Lord has created a play, He has projected a show of death and rebirth.

> The Lord himself is both the doer and the cause.
> *Aape kartaa kare karaae.*
>
> Adi Granth, M3, p. 125

Everything is in the Lord's hands. If He wills, He frees a soul. If He does not so will, He lets the soul remain in his play.

༄

> *The hypocrite assumes many different appearances;*
> *riddled with inner desires, he parades his ego.*
>
> *Bahute bhekh karai bhekhdhaaree.*
> *Antar tisnaa firai ahankaaree.*

Guru Sahib says that it is the Supreme Being who has made the entire creation, but the creation knows nothing of the One who has made it. The creation has forgotten about the

One who made manifest the creation, and imagines that the creation is real. Not knowing what the creation is, we have fallen in love with it.

The gurmukhs, the lovers of the Lord, are absorbed in worship and devotion for the One who made the creation, whereas the lovers of the mind, the manmukhs, are in love with the creation. The gurmukhs are thus able to live in the world without being soiled by its dirt. They keep their attention fixed on the Word; they are always connected to the Name. Guru Nanak Sahib explains:

> Just as the lotus lives detached in water
> and the duck swims on the surface yet remains dry,
> attached to the Word, the soul crosses the ocean of
>   phenomena
> through the practice of the Name, O Nanak.
> *Jaise jal mah kamal niraalam murgaaee naisaane.*
> *Surat sabad bhav saagar tareeai*
> *naanak naam wakhaane.*
>
> Adi Granth, M1, p. 938

We must cross this ocean of existence by connecting our soul to the Word, like the duck, which lives in water yet flies away with dry wings, or the lotus flower, which remains above the water although its roots are in the mud beneath. We must live in this world without letting its filth adhere to us. Guru Sahib, therefore, reminds us that everything we see is transient.

As for yogis and ascetics, who abandon their families, hide themselves away, wear robes of a particular colour, and build rough-and-ready homes for themselves, Guru Sahib says: What is the point of all this? The same desires and cravings are still there, suppressed inside them, so what is the point of running away? Whatever they needed before, they still need it just as much.

Let us consider what we need. We need food for our stomach, clothes to cover our body, and some kind of roof over our head. By retreating from the world, will our stomach stop demanding food? Will we no longer need clothes, or a roof over our head? We will have relinquished the earnings of our own honest labour and the food of our own homes, only to hold out our hands like beggars for others to fill our stomach.

Just because we have renounced normal life, our stomach is not going to leave us in peace—it will bother us there just as much. We can stop wearing ordinary clothes and start wearing ascetics' robes, but we will still need clothes of some kind to cover our body. We may leave the comfort of our homes and look for a hostel, monastery or temple, or we may build a small shelter for ourselves or live in a cave—but we will still need a roof over our head. So have we actually given up anything? On the contrary, we have made ourselves into parasites.

That is why saints do not ask us to give up our homes and families to live in some secluded place. We must live in the world, but we should live in it like brave warriors. Living in the world, we should not to let its dirt stain us.

ᧁ

Not knowing the self, he loses the game.

Aap na cheenai baajee haaree.

Guru Sahib gives a beautiful metaphor. He says that unless we realize who we are, we lose the game we were about to win.

What game is he referring to? After great difficulty we have been blessed with a human form by the Lord. Who knows whether He will ever give us this blessing again—or if He does, whether we will be born somewhere where our thoughts do not turn to Him even inadvertently. But now, in this life, the Lord has given us everything. So, he says, we must realize our true self now, while we have this opportunity of a human form.

> Pure are they who have realized the self.
> *So jan nirmal jin aap pachhaataa.*
>
> Adi Granth, M3, p. 1045

Guru Sahib says that those people who have become capable of knowing the self are absolutely pure. When can we know the self? When we transcend the sphere of mind and the illusion of matter, when the knot that ties the soul to the mind is undone, and all the dirty coverings over the soul are removed.

> Only he who tastes of the Word
> can understand the self.
> *Sabdai saad jaanah taa aap pachhaanah.*
>
> Adi Granth, M3, p. 115

Anyone who enjoys the bliss of the Name becomes capable of realizing the self. Guru Nanak Sahib says:

> They who hear the Word within, realize themselves;
> they alone attain the Truth....
> *Jin antar sabad aap pachhaanah*
> *gat mit tin hee paaee.*
>
> Adi Granth, M3, p. 910

The lovers of the Lord attain the supreme realization by listening to the Word within and first realizing themselves. It is they who attain the highest state and have qualified to unite with the Lord.

> ... Then the mind enters the state of deep
>   meditation;
> the soul's flame merges with the all-pervading
>   divine light.
> *Eh manooaa sunn samaadh lagaavai*
> *jotee jot milaaee.*
>
> Adi Granth, M3, p. 910

Their mind returns to its source in Brahm, while their soul goes on to dissolve its light into the supreme light.

Guru Sahib points out that the Lord has given us the gift of the human form for self-realization and for God-realization, and we are just throwing it away for a song. We waste it in eating and drinking; we spoil it by getting involved in social, religious and political affairs.

∽

By donning different robes, he cleverly deceives.
Lured by attachment and delusion, he is lost in doubt.
Without service to the Guru, he suffers great misery.

> *Kaapar pahar kare chaturaaee.*
> *Maa-i-aa moh at bharm bhulaaee.*
> *Bin gur seve bahut dukh paaee.*

Guru Sahib says that we will achieve nothing in this world, beyond pain and suffering, until we follow the teachings given

to us by the Masters and meditate on the Word. Whatever
rituals we perform, whatever techniques we try, whatever we
attempt in the way of external worship, we will always remain
empty-handed. Only through the practice of the Word will
we receive whatever we are to gain.

"The elephant's footprint covers all."[11] All the benefits of
prayer, penances, austerities, ritual worship, reading or reciting the scriptures, or good deeds and giving in charity, are
included within what we receive through meditating on the
Word.

What greater prayer can there be than to have the Name
of the Lord on our lips day and night through constant sim-
rán? What greater austerity than to be living in the sweet will
of the Lord, abiding by his command day and night? What
greater worship than having the form of a saint with us
twenty-four hours of the day, wherever we go? What greater
recitation than listening at all times day and night to the unending music of the Word within? What greater renunciation
can there be than the indifference to the world that arises
when the mind tastes the nectar of the Name?

This is why Guru Nanak Sahib again and again brings
us back to the same point, saying: My friends, whatever you
are to receive will come only through the practice of Nam,
through meditating on the Word.

∾

Those dyed in God's Name are forever detached.
While living as householders, they are absorbed in Truth.
Says Nanak, most fortunate are they who serve the Satguru.

Naam rate sadaa bairaagee. Grihee antar saach liv laagee.
Naanak satgur sevah se wadbhaagee.

*A*fter discussing everything, Guru Sahib says that there is no need to leave our homes and retreat from the world. We must live a family life and live in the world. We will become detached by attending to our spiritual practice in the context of our worldly responsibilities. He says:

> Imbued with the Name, the supreme swans remain
> detached;
> they live in their own home, their devotion unbroken.
> *Naam rate paramhans bairaagee*
> *nijghar taaree laaee he.*
>
> Adi Granth, M3, p. 1046

Those who are steeped in the dye of the Name all the time, wherever they are and whatever they are doing, become 'supreme swans' even while living a family life. Call such beings supreme swans, gurmukhs, knowers of God, or by any other name—they are the ones who have detached their love from the world and awakened love for the Lord.

That is why Guru Sahib says we must go to such a gurmukh, a knower of God, follow the teachings we are given and meditate on the Word, so that we may derive everlasting benefit from being with him.

3

◈

In the Court of the Lord

Saahib ke darbaar me^n

and

In the Inverted Well in the Sky

Ultaa koowaa^n gagan me^n

In the court of the Lord, devotion and love alone count;
devotion and love alone count, for devotion pleases the Lord.
He declined a royal feast and took gruel with the son of a slave.
They prayed and practised austerities, performed rituals of every kind,
but he chose Shabri's berries, and the ascetics died of shame.
Yudhishtra held a great ceremony, and all assembled there;
pride that day died for all—without Supach, the bell would not ring.
Paltu says, because of high birth, let no one feel proud;
in the court of the Lord, devotion and love alone count.

Paltu Sahib, *Paltu Sahib ki Bani,* Part I, Kundli 218

In the inverted well in the sky, a lamp is shining.
A lamp is shining there without wick or oil;
through six seasons and twelve months, it burns day and night.
Only they who have found a true Master are able to see the light;
without a perfect Master, no one can behold it.
From within the lamp's light emanates a sound;
it is heard by one in deep meditation—no one else can hear it.
O Paltu, those who hear it, their destiny is fulfilled;
in the inverted well in the sky, a lamp is shining.

Paltu Sahib, *Paltu Sahib ki Bani,* Part I, Kundli 169

Saahib ke darbaar me^n keval bhakti piyaar.
Keval bhakti piyaar saahib bhaktee me^n raazee.
Tajaa sakal pakvaan liyaa daasee sut bhaajee.
Jap-tap nem achaar karai bahuteraa koee.
Khaaye shivree ke ber mue sab rishi muni roee.
Kiyaa yudhishtir yagya batoraa sakal samaajaa.
Mardaa sab kaa maan supach bin gha^nt na baajaa.
Paltoo oo^nchee jaati kau jani kou karai ha^nkaar.
Saahib ke darbaar me^n keval bhakti piyaar.

Paltu Sahib, *Paltu Sahib ki Bani* (Allahabad: Belvedere),
Part I, Kundli 218

Ultaa koowaa^n gagan me^n tis me^n jarai chiraag.
Tis me^n jarai chiraag binaa rogan bin baatee.
Chhah ritu baarah maas rahat jartai din raatee.
Satguru milaa jo hoy taahi kee nazar me^n aavai.
Bin satguru kou hoy nahee^n vaa ko darsaavai.
Niksai ek aavaaz chiraag kee jyotihi^n maahee^n.
Gyaan samaadhee sunai aur kou suntaa naahee^n.
Paltoo jo koee sunai taa ke poore bhaag.
Ultaa koowaa^n gagan me^n tis me^n jarai chiraag.

Paltu Sahib, *Paltu Sahib ki Bani* (Allahabad: Belvedere),
Part I, Kundli 169

In the court of the Lord, devotion and love alone count.

Saahib ke darbaar me^n keval bhakti piyaar.

Yesterday I took my text from the writings of Shri Hazur
Soami Ji Maharaj, and the day before from the writings of
Shri Guru Nanak Sahib Dev Ji Maharaj. Today I am taking
my text from the writings of Paltu Sahib Ji Maharaj. I keep
taking the writings of different saints just to show that the
message and teachings of every saint are the same, and that
all saints describe the same one method of worshipping the
Lord.

Paltu Sahib was a fearless and well-known saint from
Uttar Pradesh. He made his home in the city of Ayodhya,
where he openly preached the way of the saints. The priests
and religious leaders burned him alive, for Paltu never spared
them when he was explaining the teachings.

Paltu Sahib says, "In the court of the Lord, devotion and
love alone count." If you want to reach the abode of the Lord,
if you want to meet Him and achieve union with Him, you
need only devotion and love. No one is going to ask about
your caste, creed or class.

This is why many saints describe the relationship between
the soul and the Lord as the relationship of a wife and husband. Soami Ji Maharaj explains:

> Listen to me, dear soul,
> your Husband lives in the regions above.
> *Surat sun baat ree, teraa dhanee base aakaash.*
>
> Soami Ji, *Sar Bachan* 19:6, p. 145

Listen, dear soul, your husband is the Lord, the Supreme Being. You are trapped in the web of illusion whereas He lives
in Sach Khand, the realm of truth.* Until you return to your
own home, you will never know fulfilment *(suhaag)*, you will
always feel incomplete, and you will never escape from the
pain and suffering of death and rebirth. Similarly, Guru
Nanak Sahib says:

> Immortally wedded is the soul bride
> who attains union with her true Lord.
> *Pir sache te sadaa suhaagan.*
>
> Adi Granth, M3, p. 754

Our soul is the wife and the Lord is her husband. Until the
soul comes into the shelter of her Lord's embrace, she cannot experience the joy of fulfilment, nor can she escape from
the pain and suffering of death and birth.

The Rama Krishna Mission compares this relationship with
that of a mother and child; Christ speaks of it in terms of a
father and son. What is the common factor in these relationships that brings them together? It is love, devotion, worship,
and again love. Paltu Sahib says, "In the court of the Lord,
devotion and love alone count." If you want to reach the
Lord's home, only your love and devotion will be considered.

In the writings of Guru Nanak Sahib's successors, it is
said:

> Only those who have loved, have found the Lord.
> *Jin prem kiyo tin hee prabh paayo.*
>
> Dassam Granth, Akal Ustat, M10, p. 14:9:29

---

* *See* Glossary and Translators' Note for explanations of unusual usage, and technical or Indian-language terms, such as: Sach Khand, vital elements.

Only someone whose heart is filled with yearning for union with the Lord, with love and longing for Him and restlessness to find Him, will be privileged to return and merge with Him. Christ says:

> God is love.
> 1 John 4:8

The real form of the Lord is love and love alone. Dadu Sahib says:

> Love is the Lord's essence, love is his nature;
> love is his form, love is his colour.
> *Ishq alah kee zaat hai, ishq alah kaa ang,*
> *ishq alah aujood hai, ishq alah kaa rang.*
> Dadu, *Dadu Dayal*[12]

If you ask the name of God, it is love. If you ask his religion, race or class, they are all love. In the Gospel of Saint Matthew, it is said:

> Blessed are they that mourn:
> for they shall be comforted.
> Matthew 5:4

Most fortunate are they whose hearts are filled with love for the Lord. Theirs is a great destiny. Indeed, we should celebrate their birth as human beings, for one day they will find peace in the lap of the Lord.

That is why the saints say that the relationship between the soul and the Lord is one of devotion and love alone. Guru Nanak Sahib explains this beautifully:

The virtuous bride finds union with her Lord,
for she adorns herself with love and fear.
Kaaman gunwantee har paae.
Bhai bhaae seegaar banaae.

Adi Granth, M3, p. 123

A wife can always keep her husband happy if she possesses two qualities. She must have love for her husband. She must also respect him, show deference to him, be afraid lest she do or say anything that might displease him. She speaks with such sweetness and acts so purely that the husband is always pleased. Guru Nanak Sahib says that a soul that adorns itself with these two qualities, that longs for union with the Lord, will be given the privilege of going back to Him and merging with Him.

Our soul is a particle of the supreme soul, we are drops of the ocean of the true Name. Guru Nanak Sahib says:

God abides in the soul, the soul in God.
Aatam mah raam, raam mah aatam.

Adi Granth, M1, p. 1153

The supreme soul is present in our soul, and our soul is present in the supreme soul. Kabir Sahib says the same thing:

Says Kabir, the soul is a particle of the Lord.
Kahu kabeer ihu raam kee ans.

Kabir, Adi Granth, p. 871

Mystics say that all of us feel and understand that there is only one Supreme Being. No one says that God is different for Hindus, Sikhs, Christians or Muslims. Since ancient times sages and seers have always referred to God as the One, the only One *(ek-ekaa)*. Guru Nanak Sahib says:

There is only one Bestower for all beings.
May I never forget Him!
Sabhnaa jeeaa kaa iku daataa so mai wisar na jaaee.

                    Adi Granth, M1, Japji, p. 2

Everything we see in the world has been created by the one
Lord. He is the generous provider for everybody, the emperor
of all, and He takes care of us all. Muslim saints call Him God
of all the worlds *(rab-ul-aalameen)*, meaning that He is God
of the entire world, not just God of the Muslims *(rab-ul-
musalmeen)*. Guru Nanak Sahib also says:

He has no colour, caste and mark.
By his Command, He creates the whole world.
Varan jaat chihan nahee koee.
Sabh hukame srisat upaa-idaa.

                    Adi Granth, M5, p. 1075

That Supreme Being who created the entire world through
his Command is neither dark nor fair, neither Hindu, Sikh
nor Muslim, nor does He belong to any caste, sect or religion.
Human beings may be divided into the 'four castes', but Guru
Nanak Sahib says the Supreme Being cannot be confined to
any of them.

When the Supreme Being cannot be described as belonging to any particular group, then how can our soul, which is
a particle of that supreme soul, be limited to any particular
race or religion? When the sun belongs to no race or religion,
how can an ordinary ray of light be thought of in such terms?
When the ocean belongs to no particular class, then to what
class can its drops be said to belong?

The Supreme Being created human beings. It is we who
keep on dividing ourselves into these endless classes and

subclasses, sects and religions, races and nations. Then we get caught up in the differences between them. Read the writings of any saint and you will find that they all try to lift our thinking far above such disputes. In the writings of the house of Guru Nanak Sahib, we read:

> Where you render account of your deeds,
> there neither body nor caste go with you.
> *Jithai lekhaa mangeeai tithai deh jaat na jaa-e.*
>
> Adi Granth, M3, p. 1346

When you have to account for your actions, no one will ask what caste or class you belonged to, for your body cannot go to that stage. As you know, all these castes, subcastes, sects and religions are connected with the body, which in the end is left to be consigned either to fire or to earth. One's race and religion come to an end, embraced by fire; one's class and social status merge into the earth. All that will count then is our love and devotion, our actions, and our heartfelt longing to meet the Lord. Kabir Sahib says:

> No one will ask your caste or creed;
> whoever contemplates on Him becomes His.
> *Jaat-paat poochhe nahi[n] koi,*
> *hari ko bhajai so hari kaa hoi.*
>
> Kabir

No one will assess you on the basis of your caste or subcaste. No one will ask you whether you were a Hindu, Sikh or Christian, or whether you came from India, America or Africa. Only your devotion, love and actions will be looked at. That is why Kabir Sahib says that no one should imagine that caste, class or creed can help us cross the dread ocean of existence.

Bulleh Shah was an outspoken and renowned Muslim mystic. He says:

> You will be judged by your actions alone;
> your caste and creed will go unnoticed.
> *Amalaa^n utte hon nibere,*
> *khareeaa^n rahingeeaa^n jaataa^n.*
>
> Bulleh Shah, *Kafian Bulleh Shah*

Only people who pay attention to their actions will be able to settle their karmic accounts. No one will bother about people who are proud of their birth and class. Paltu Sahib says at the end of this poem:

> Paltu says, because of high birth, let no one feel
> proud;
> in the court of the Lord, devotion and love
> alone count.
> *Paltoo oo^{n}chee jaati kau jani kou karai ha^{n}kaar.*
> *Saahib ke darbaar me^n keval bhakti piyaar.*

The thought should not even enter our minds that because we have been born in a particular family—for example, as a brahmin—we alone will have the privilege of union with the Lord. Or that because we have been born in some other group, we might never be able to worship the Lord.* Paltu Sahib says that we are to get such thoughts out of our minds forever; we need only love and devotion to reach the abode of the Lord.

Guru Nanak Sahib does away with these social differences to the point of saying:

---

* *See* Glossary (caste) for discussion of this issue.

> All those bereft of Nam are of low birth;
> they exist like vermin in filth.
> *Bin naavai sabh neech jaat hai bistaa kaa keeraa hoe.*
>
> Adi Granth, M3, p. 426

Who can be inferior to people who do not worship the Lord?
After death they will become maggots or worms living in filth.
And who is truly high-ranking?

> With the Name in the heart, one is revered
> amongst all.
> With the Name in the heart, one is the Creator
> incarnate.
> With the Name in the heart, one is exalted
> above all.
> *Jis naam ridai so sabh mah jaataa.*
> *Jis naam ridai so purakh bidhaataa.*
> *Jis naam ridai so sabh te oochaa.*
>
> Adi Granth, M5, p. 1156

The highest and purest people are those whose hearts are
filled with love and adoration for the Supreme Being. It is
they who will merge into the true Lord. As Guru Nanak Sahib
puts it:

> With the Name in one's heart, there is only one
> great big family.
> *Jis naam ridai tis wad parvaaraa.*
>
> Adi Granth, M5, p. 1156

When the Name has made its home in our heart and the
Lord's love has made a place for itself within us, then the whole
creation becomes one big family for us. And when there is

only one family, there can be only one race, one religion and one class. So the mystics lovingly advise us to avoid these racial, religious and social issues. If we want to meet the Lord, we must awaken true love and devotion within ourselves.

Now the thought comes to our mind that we can only love someone or something we have seen and interacted with. We have never seen the Lord, we have no idea what his face looks like, we have never seen his colour or form, so how can we possibly develop love for Him?

We love the faces and things of the world because we see them before us, because we spend time with them and interact with them, so it is only natural that our minds start getting attached to them. We love our parents because they gave birth to us and brought us up. We love our brothers and sisters because we are of the same blood. We love our children because we ourselves gave birth to them. We love our spouse because he or she is our life companion and the father or mother of our children. We love our friends because we have been together since childhood. We love our community and religion because we have been conditioned since childhood to think of ourselves as part of them. We love our property because we have earned it with our sweat and blood, or inherited it as our proper share, or have been fighting for years to establish our claim to it. But how can we develop love for the Lord?

It is the love we feel for the people and things of the world that pulls us back over and over again to the imprisonment of a physical form. We have come to love them so much that they even come to us in our dreams. At the time of death, it is their forms that stand before our eyes as though on a cinema screen. "Where our desires are, there we dwell."[13] In this world, the direction in which our attention goes in our last moments determines the course of our next life.

If it is our love for the world that is going to pull us back to the prison of the body, then how do we develop love for that Lord whom we have never seen? Who can we love, who can we worship, so that love for the Lord can be born in us? To examine this question properly, we may consider the entire creation and then ask ourselves what is worthy of our love and devotion? With what should we spend our time?

What we find is that everyone and everything in the world is made from the five vital elements *(tattva):* earth, water, fire, air and ether. At least one vital element is active in every living thing. In human beings, all five are active. This is why saints call us 'the five-tattva puppet' and say we are the top of the creation.

The lowest class of life consists of vegetables, grasses, plants, trees, flowers and so on, in which the water element is active. If we five-tattva creatures love vegetables, flowers or trees, how can we hope to progress? As the proverb says, we go in the direction of our desires. Whatever we love, we assume its form when we die. That is why nothing in the plant kingdom is worthy of our love or worship.

The next class is that of earthbound creatures—scorpions, snakes, spiders and insects; in these the earth and fire elements are active, but they too are lower than human beings.

The third class consists of feathered creatures, in which three vital elements are active, whereas in us there are five. So if we love or worship pigeons, parrots or sparrows, what will happen? We ourselves will become sparrows, pigeons or parrots. While trying to transcend the human level, we will do the opposite—by loving and worshipping these creatures, we will come back and take birth as birds.

The fourth class is four-legged animals, in which the element of ether is dormant, so that they have no wisdom, no ability to discriminate. For this reason cows, buffaloes and horses are not worthy of our love or worship, either.

The fifth class is human beings. Should a human being worship or love another human being, and if so, why? Especially in these times when all are equal under the law.

When one human being does not worship another, and no one has ever seen gods and goddesses, and we have no idea of the face or form of the Lord, then we come to a point where we have to consider carefully what may be worthy of our association, love and worship.

Hazur Maharaj Ji* used to make a very nice analogy. If we take a large number of radios without batteries or electrical connections and put them in a room, we will not be able to hear the news from any country. But if we connect them to a power source, we will be able to hear the news from anywhere we like.

We have to search for a devotee or lover of the Lord— one who is connected to the Lord by love. We must spend time with him, associate with him and love him, so that love and devotion for the Lord may be awakened in our hearts through his presence, his company and his love.

The real form of the saints is the Word or the Name. Bhai Gurdas says:

> The Master's form is the Word.
> *Gur moorat gur sabad hai.*
> Bhai Gurdas, *Varan Bhai Gurdas,* 24:25

Their real form is the Word, to which they link our attention. Christ says that the Word is God[14]—it is the Shabd that is God. Guru Nanak Sahib says:

---

* The terms 'Hazur' and 'Hazur Maharaj Ji' are used by the speaker to refer to his Master, Maharaj Sawan Singh (1858–1948). *See also* Translators' Note and Glossary.

All praise and glory!
Formless is the Voice!
Vaahu vaahu baanee nirankaar hai.

Adi Granth, M3, p. 515

Whether you call it the Word, Name or Voice, it is this that is God. And that is why it is the Shabd that is the real form of the Masters. Our Master is the Word, the Name. As the saints say:

The Word is the Guru,
the soul attuned to the Word is the disciple.
Sabad guroo surat dhun chelaa.

Adi Granth, M1, p. 943

The Word is our Master and our soul is the disciple. This body has to be left here by both disciple and Master. The soul of a disciple will never be abandoned by the Word, once it has been inwardly linked to it through the Master. Drawn by the Word, it will definitely merge in the Lord.

Thus, the Word is the real Master, and our soul is the real disciple. Kabir Sahib says:

The soul merges into the Word,
the body does not merge.
Shabd milaavaa hvai rahaa, deh milaavaa naahi[n].

Kabir, *Kabir Sakhi Sangreh*

The body is not going to go there; it is the Shabd or Word that will pull you and unite you with the Lord. That is why we keep the company of saints and mystics.

Christ describes them as the Word made flesh.[15] We should search for someone in whom the Word has made its

home. The real form of the Lord is Shabd. It is to that very
Shabd that we must connect our attention and our soul,
through a mystic or saint.

Guru Nanak Sahib explains this truth beautifully:

> The whole world, the netherworlds, the islands,
>   the spheres,
> have all been put under Kal; such is the Lord's
>   design....
> *Khand pataal deep sabh loaa,*
> *sabh kaalai vas aap prabh keeaa.*
>
> Adi Granth, M5, p. 1076

Whatever you can see in the world—regions, islands, netherworlds, and so on—has been made by the Lord himself, but
He has entrusted its management to Kal. Kal's domain goes
as far as Brahm or Triloki. Whatever comes within Kal's
sphere is caught in impermanence, in the pain of death and
rebirth, entangled in the web of its actions. But the Lord who
actually made manifest this world is unchanging. As Guru
Sahib says:

> ... The only immutable one is the eternal God;
> those who contemplate on Him become
>   immutable too....
> *Nihchal ek aap abinaasee*
> *so nihchal jo tisah dhiaa-idaa.*
>
> Adi Granth, M5, p. 1076

The Creator is unchanging. He exists, not within the painful
sphere of death and rebirth, but in Sach Khand, the true
realm. Those who love and worship Him also become unchanging, and escape from the pain of death and rebirth.

So we come back to the same point: we can only love and worship someone we have seen. Guru Nanak Sahib says:

> ... The Lord's servant is like unto the Lord;
> do not think him to be different because of his
>   human frame...
> *Har kaa sevak so har jehaa.*
> *Bhed na jaanah maanas dehaa.*
>
> Adi Granth, M5, p. 1076

The devotees and lovers of the Lord take on the form of the Lord by worshipping Him. There is no difference, no distinction, between them and the Lord. What is the relationship between them? Guru Sahib says:

> ... just as a myriad waves rise from the ocean,
> and then subside, merging back into its depths.
> *Jio jal tarang uthah bahubhaatee*
> *phir salalai salal samaa-idaa.*
>
> Adi Granth, M5, p. 1076

The relationship of the Masters to the Lord is like that of waves to the ocean—waves rise from the ocean for just a few minutes and then merge into it again. However high a wave rises, it can never be separated from the ocean but will always remain part of it. If we surrender something to a wave, it is lifted and carried by the wave into the depths of the ocean. The saints and mystics are waves of the ocean of the true Name. They come into the world, bear witness to the Word and preach the Name. Then they take us with them and merge back into the ocean of the Name.

The third Padshahi says:

His is the sole kingdom, his Command is but one;
his law and governance prevail from age to age.
Eko amar ekaa paatisaahee jug jug sir kaar banaaee he.

Adi Granth, M3, p. 1046

The Lord is one. He exists beyond the pain of death and rebirth. He is the bestower of all and the emperor of all. Saints
and mystics are sent by Him as his administrators. They come
at his Command; coming into the world they proclaim and
preach that Command; they explain the Cosmic Law. They
come in every era and, taking us with them, they merge back
into the ocean of the true Name.

Saints tell us that we need to associate with the Masters.
Christ says in the Bible: You are merged in me and I am
merged in my Father, the Lord; through me you will also
merge with the Father. You have seen me and I have seen
the Lord, my Father; so now, through me, you also have the
right to see the Lord.[16] That is why we keep the company of
saints.

But what kind of saint should we search for? We need one
who earns his own honest living and serves his or her disciples. A saint will never be a burden on anyone. Saints work
for their own livelihood and teach their disciples that they too
should support themselves by honest means. Saints and mystics have made their own lives into examples, which they have
placed before us.

Take for instance Guru Nanak Sahib, whose spiritual
writings we keep referring to. He worked his farm with his
own hands in the village of Kartarpur, took care of his own
needs and those of his family, and served the sangat all his
life, free of charge. And, at the end of his life, what guidance
did he give the sangat through his writings?

Never bow down before one
who calls himself a Guru and spiritual preceptor
and goes begging.
He who eats what he earns by his honest labour
and from his hand gives something in charity,
Nanak says, he alone knows the true way.

Gur peer sadaa-e mangan jaa-e.
Taa kai mool na lageeai paa-e.
Ghaal khaa-e kichh hathah deh.
Naanak raah pachhaanah se-e.

Adi Granth, M1, p. 1245

If someone claims to be a Master or spiritual leader and goes about begging from his disciples, never bow down before him. What kind of Master should one look for? One who works for his living, earns for his own needs, and serves his disciples while living amongst us.

The saints refer to this service as the grace or blessing of the Master *(gur parshaad)* and as the gift of the Name *(naamdaan)*, because parshad is given freely and no value can be placed on it. A gift is also given away freely, not sold for a price. Saints give the teachings of the Name freely; they do not divulge the teachings to make money.

Kabir Sahib, throughout his life, earned his living by weaving, although people like the King of Balkh-Bokhara were among his disciples and could easily have provided him with a palace to live in. Kabir Sahib says in his writings:

It is for the disciple to give everything to the Master;
it is for the Master to accept nothing from the disciple.
Shishya ko aisaa chaahiye guru ko sarbas dey,
guru ko aisaa chaahiye shishya kaa kachhu na ley.

Kabir, *Kabir Sakhi Sangreh*

It is the disciple's duty to use everything as if it belongs to the Master, but it is a fundamental principle that no Master takes even a pin from his disciples. Kabir Sahib says:

> I would rather die than beg for myself,
> but for spiritual work I feel no shame.
> *Mar jaau^n maangoo^n nahee^n apne tan ke kaaj,*
> *parmaarath ke kaarane mohi^n na aavai laaj.*
>
> Kabir, *Kabir Sakhi Sangreh*

The saints certainly encourage their disciples to give in charity, but they never stretch out their hands before anyone for their own needs.

If we read the life of Saint Ravidas, we see that he supported himself throughout his life by making shoes, although Raja Pipa, whose writings are included in the Adi Granth, and Mira Bai, the famous princess of Marwar, were among his disciples—and was there anything they could not have given him! In the life story of Mira Bai, we read that her relations taunted her for having a Master who lived below the fort stitching shoes, while she was a princess living in the palace.

One thing is certain: it is very difficult for a disciple to bear taunts and criticism concerning the Master. Mira took a valuable diamond and presented herself at Saint Ravidas's hut and entreated him: "Master, my relatives are harassing me. Please sell this diamond and build yourself a nice comfortable home to live in." He replied, "My child, whatever I have received has come from this tanning tank and from cobbling shoes. If this disturbs you, then you may please sit at home and do your meditation."

Even so, she concealed the diamond in the thatched roof of the hut, in the hope that her Master would sell it later and build a house. When she visited him again a month or two

later, she found him in the same state, working at his shoes.
She asked about the diamond and he said, "You can take it,
child, from wherever you left it." And there it was where she
had put it.

My reason for giving these examples is simply to show
that saints always live by supporting themselves from their
own honest earnings. Read the life of Namdev Ji Maharaj and
you will see that he earned his livelihood printing cloth by
hand. Paltu Sahib, whose writings we are discussing today,
worked as a shopkeeper. Dadu Sahib carded cotton; and I
spoke yesterday in some detail about other saints and mystics. My point is that saints are never a burden on society.
They work hard to support themselves, and they teach their
disciples to do likewise.

When we find a saint who earns his own livelihood and
serves the sangat—who has no interest in starting a sect or
religion, or in making money—then what must we do to benefit from his company? Paltu Sahib explains that we must
have humility and love. Soami Ji says:

> Nurture humility and meekness in your mind!
> *Deen gareebee chit me^n dharnaa.*
>
> Soami Ji, *Sar Bachan* 15:15, p. 123

If you want union with the Lord, you should generate humility, meekness and longing in your heart. We can learn the
meaning of humility from the lives and writings of the saints.
If you read Guru Nanak Sahib's writings, you will see that he
refers to himself as a slave of slaves and as a servant. He writes:

> Says Nanak, my deeds are despicable.
> I have taken your refuge:
> oh, protect my honour!

Kah naanak ham neech karamaa.
Saran pare kee raakhah sarmaa.

Adi Granth, M5, p. 378

He says: O Lord, I am a miserable sinner. I have come under your protection; please save me from shame! Why would he make himself out to be such a sinner, except to show us how much humility and longing we must have if we want to unite with the Lord. Saint Ravidas, although he had merged himself with the Supreme Being, wrote:

> Low is my caste, low my rank, low my birth.
> *Jaatee ochhaa paatee ochhaa ochhaa janam hamaaraa.*
>
> Ravidas, Adi Granth, p. 486

How humbly he speaks of himself! As for Hazur, there is no way I can repeat the words he used to describe himself—my voice trembles just thinking about it.

Saints always pass their lives in love and humility, to inspire in us love for the Lord and longing for union with Him.

Why then do we feel proud? Why are we egotistic? Are we proud of our youth? Have we never seen anyone in old age? Are we too not going to grow old? Are we proud of our looks or our beauty? Have we never seen the faces of the sick in hospital? If we get jaundice or chickenpox, it becomes difficult even to look at ourselves in the mirror. We are proud of our money, but have we not seen the wealthiest of people, kings and rulers, roaming the streets like beggars? We are intoxicated by power, but have we not seen influential and important leaders hunted down like animals, made to stand before firing squads or thrown into jail? These are people who were so powerful that others would bow to the ground before them and their every word would be treated as law.

Living in this physical body, what is it that we are proud of? Soami Ji says:

> O mind, of what are you feeling so proud?
> Your body will mingle with dust
> and you will again go into chaurasi.
> *Man re kyo^n gumaan ab karnaa,*
> *tan to teraa khaak milegaa chauraasee jaa parnaa.*
>
> Soami Ji, *Sar Bachan* 15:15, p. 123

What are you so egotistical about? Your body? It will be consigned to fire or to the earth and you will be presented before the lord of judgement. On the basis of your actions and desires, you will have to take on another life wherever he sees fit. We leave the prison of one body, crying, weeping and wailing, only to find another body already waiting for us. We have no sooner come into that body than death is there in front of us again. Like confirmed criminals, we remain forever handcuffed.

We only have to look at history and think of those great kings and powerful dictators who could do whatever they wanted, and ask ourselves: where is their importance today? We trample on their graves as we pass by, their bones crumble beneath our feet and their dust blinds our eyes. We have forgotten that one day people will trample on our graves in the same way, our bones will crumble beneath their feet—we too will have become the dust of the earth and will blind their eyes.

We think that death is meant for others, whereas for us there are sense pleasures, physical appetites, and the issues of race, religion and country. That is why saints awaken us from our sleep of oblivion. Kabir Sahib says:

The clay says to the potter,
Why are you beating me?
That day is coming soon when I'll be beating you!
Maati kahai kumhaar ko,
kyaa too roonde mohi^n,
ik din aisaa hoegaa, mai^n rundhoongee tohi^n.

                                    Kabir, *Kabir Sakhi Sangreh*

The potter makes pots by beating and kneading the clay, so the earth says: Have you ever thought of the time when I will take you into the earth and beat you in the same way? Kabir Sahib then says:

The wood asks the blacksmith,
Why are you burning me?
That day is coming soon when I'll be burning you!
Lakree kahai luhaar ko,
too kyaa jaarai mohi^n,
ik din aisaa hoegaa, mai^n jaaraungee tohi^n.

                                    Kabir, *Kabir Sakhi Sangreh*

We burn wood and reduce it to cinders, but the wood says: Keep that day before your eyes when I will take you with me and turn you into cinders. So Paltu Sahib says: What are you feeling proud about? Why are you so conceited? If you want to benefit from the company of saints and mystics, you must have humility and love in your heart.

Then Paltu Sahib gives examples from mythology to explain how the lovers of the Lord always benefit from their humility and love.

∾

Devotion and love alone count,
for devotion pleases the Lord.
He declined a royal feast
and took gruel with the son of a slave.

Keval bhakti piyaar saahib bhaktee me^n *raazee.*
Tajaa sakal pakvaan liyaa daasee sut bhaajee.

When Lord Krishna went to the city where Duryodhan lived, Duryodhan, in his arrogance and pride, assumed that Lord Krishna would stay in his palace and eat his sumptuous food. But Lord Krishna went straight to Vidhur's home, stayed in his straw hut and survived on whatever simple food Vidhur could provide. Paltu Sahib explains that we can only benefit from the saints through humility and love. We will get nothing if we are arrogant and proud.

∾

They prayed and practised austerities,
performed rituals of every kind,
but he chose Shabri's berries,
and the ascetics died of shame.

Jap-tap nem achaar karai bahuteraa koee.
Khaaye shivree ke ber mue sab rishi muni roee.

Now Paltu Sahib gives an example from the story of Ramchandra Ji Maharaj. When he was exiled to the forest, many ascetics had the same thought—that it would be in their hut that he would come and live. Some were proud of their ability to pray continuously, others of their ascetic practices, some of their celibacy, and others of their great learning. On seeing them, a poor and humble tribal woman named Shabri, out of her love and devotion started to think that maybe Shri Ramchandra Ji Maharaj would even come to her hut.

Now because Shabri was of humble birth, no one would allow her to pluck fruit from the trees. So she went into the forest and gathered up small wild fruits that had fallen to the ground, thinking she would offer them to Ramchandra Ji Maharaj when he came. Then it occurred to her that if the fruits were sour or bitter, they would not be fit to give him, so she tasted each one, saved the sweet ones and threw away the sour ones. She was so intoxicated by her love that she completely forgot that by tasting each fruit she was making them unfit for anyone else to eat. Legend tells us that Ramchandra Ji Maharaj went straight to the poor and lowly Shabri's hut and ate the partially eaten fruits. Paltu Sahib is simply making the point that her love for him was true, and that only through love can we benefit from the devotees of the Lord.

∾

Yudhishtra held a great ceremony,
and all assembled there;
pride that day died for all—
without Supach, the bell would not ring.

Kiyaa yudhishtir yagya bataraa sakal samaajaa.
Mardaa sab kaa maan supach bin gha^n*t na baajaa.*

Then Paltu Sahib gives another very beautiful example.

The war of the Mahabharat has come to an end and the Pandav brothers have organized an impressive religious ceremony *(yagya)*. They have invited and fed a great number of ascetics and holy men. Lord Krishna has told them that their ceremony will be considered complete only when a bell rings in the heavens. Now, they are not short of wealth so they invite and feed everybody, but still the bell does not ring in the skies.

They then beseech Lord Krishna, "O Lord, you yourself should please eat. It is possible that the bell will then ring and our ceremony will be complete." So he eats as well, but still the bell does not ring. They are extremely disappointed. They have spent so much money, invited and fed so many sages and ascetics, and yet the ceremony is incomplete. They therefore beg Lord Krishna to use his inner vision to see which saint or holy man has been left out.

Lord Krishna tells them, "There is a poor devotee of the Lord who lives not very far from here. He is of lowly birth, lame and a hunchback, and he is lost in the joy of his love for the Lord. Until he comes to your home and eats your food, your ceremony will not be complete."

Being rulers and having the arrogance of royal blood—thinking to themselves, "Flies will always come to sugar"—they spread the word through an agent that free food is being served. They assume that when the saint comes to know, he will himself come and eat. But he does not share their way of thinking. The Pandavs themselves then go to him and beg him to come to their home and eat their food. He knows their hearts are not pure, so he puts a condition: "Until you give me the benefit of one hundred ceremonies, I will not come to your house to eat." They come back disappointed. "We haven't yet succeeded in completing one," they say among themselves, "so where is the question of giving the benefit of one hundred?"

Seeing their disappointment, Queen Draupadi gets up early the next morning, bathes, gets ready, and then prepares a meal for the saint with her own hands. Bare-footed, she goes to his hut, bows before him and says very humbly, "Venerable Master, please come to our house and share our food." The saint puts the same condition before her too, and she replies with folded hands and great humility: "O venerable Master, in the company of saints and devotees of the Lord like you, I have heard that when a person goes with a sincere heart to a true saint, every step she takes towards the saint brings the benefit of one hundred sacred ceremonies." The saint, knowing that her heart is pure, does not pause for even the twinkling of an eye but gets up and goes with her.

Again, Paltu Sahib's sole purpose in referring to these stories is to emphasize that we can only benefit from a saint's company if we are humble and loving.

❧

Paltu says, because of high birth, let no one feel proud; in the court of the Lord, devotion and love alone count.

Paltoo oo^{n}chee jaati kau jani kou karai ha^{n}kaar. Saahib ke darbaar me^n keval bhakti piyaar.

Giving examples like these from mythology, Paltu Sahib tells us that none should think that being born into a particular family, as a high-class brahmin, for instance, gives them any special right to union with the Lord; or that by being born into some other class or family, it would be inconceivable for them to worship Him.

Paltu Sahib tells us to eliminate such thoughts from our minds forever: to reach the home of the Lord, we need only devotion and love. As I mentioned earlier, no one there is going to ask our caste, religion, race, nationality or lineage; it is only our deeds and our love that will matter. As one mystic says:

> The lowly and humble all crossed safely,
> in love with the saints' lotus feet;
> those proud of their high birth
> drowned by the thousand.
> *Neech-neech sab tari gae sant charan lavleen,*
> *jaatahi^n ke abhimaan me^n doobe bahut kuleen.*
>
> Tulsi Sahib, *Sant Bani Sangreh*[17]

If we think of ourselves as the lowest of the low and worship the Lord with love and humility in our hearts, we will cross the ocean of existence; whereas people who thrive on the pride of worldly status, of family and religion, drown right here in the ocean of death and rebirth.

That is why Paltu Sahib says that if you wish to worship the Lord you must forget about class, race and religion, forget about nation, honour and fame, and instead develop within yourself true love and true longing to find Him.

The question now arises in our minds as to how the mystics create within us that true love and longing to find the Lord, and how they sever our attachment to the world. Paltu Sahib explains in the following poem *(kundli)*.

∾

In the inverted well in the sky, a lamp is shining.

Ultaa koowaa^n gagan me^n tis me^n jarai chiraag.

Here, right at the beginning, we find the first lesson of the saints, which is explained by every mystic. The Lord for whom we are searching is nowhere outside—He exists in our body, inside us, within this physical form. All who have ever found Him, have found Him within themselves; anyone who is going to find Him, will also find Him within. As Guru Sahib says:

> In the body dwells the bountiful Lord,
> the life of the world, who sustains all.
> *Kaa-i-aa andar jag jeevan daataa wasai*
> *sabhnaa kare pratipaalaa.*
>
> Adi Granth, M3, p. 754

That Supreme Being who gave life to the entire creation, who is the provider for all and emperor of all, who protects and nurtures all, will be found nowhere outside, for He is living in your body, He is present within you. Kabir Sahib says:

> As oil is in sesame seeds and fire in flintstone,
> so is your Beloved within you: wake up, if you can.
> *Jyo^n til maahee^n tel hai chakmak maahee^n aagi,*
> *teraa preetam tujh me^n jaagi sake to jaagi.*
>
> Kabir, *Kabir Sakhi Sangreh*

My friends, the beloved Lord for whom you are searching is present inside you, just as oil is in the sesame seed and fire in the flint. Paltu Sahib says:

> Why are you crying out 'Lord, Lord'—
> the Lord is right there with you!
> *Saahib saahib kyaa kare saahib tere paas.*
>   Paltu, *Paltu Sahib ki Bani*, Kundli

What is this Lord you are searching for, day and night, in bricks and stone, forests, mountains and sacred pools? All the time He is with you, going around with you, because He lives inside you, in your body.

Christ also tells his disciples that the kingdom of God lies within them—and this is why they must repent.[18] He says: Settle and clear the account of your previous deeds. Repent for them, because the Lord is not far away, He is within your body.

If a laboratory exists where we can study the way to the Supreme Being, where we can conduct research into our quest for the Lord, it is the human form itself. The sages and seers of India refer to it as the human form divine *(nar-naraayani deh)*. This form that God himself has created, in which He himself resides, and where the soul has the privilege of becoming God, is none other than the human form. In the Bible, it is called the temple of the living God,[19] the temple in which the Supreme Being resides. Guru Nanak Sahib writes explicitly:

> This body is the Lord's temple;
> it is there that the jewel of knowledge is revealed.
> *Har mandar eh sareer hai giaan ratan pargat ho-e.*
>   Adi Granth, M3, p. 1346

What place would we refer to as the Lord's temple? Any place where God, the Supreme Being, resides. Guru Nanak Sahib says that the true temple, the purest temple of God, is our body, because knowledge of union with the Supreme Being will only be attained in this physical form.

But we worldly people are masters of a strange kind of wisdom. We go on searching for the Lord, day and night, in the places we have made for Him from bricks and stone, instead of in the place the Lord himself has made as his residence. Saints built temples, mosques, gurdwaras and churches so that people might come there and inspire us with longing to find the Lord within, and guide us in the right practice of worshipping Him. They were not built for us to go there each morning for a few minutes, bow down and then come back feeling pleased at how many of our sins have been absolved.

We keep our places of worship sparkling clean so that by seeing them we are inspired with the desire to keep our hearts clean. When we keep those places so clean—places where we sing the Lord's praise and sit and hear stories about Him— then how much greater the need to keep clean our hearts, where the Lord lives and can be attained. Sometimes we put flesh into our bodies, sometimes liquor. We commit sins— some people even go so far as to kill one another. We show so much respect for the sacred places we ourselves have built, but none at all for the temples of God that the Lord himself has made.

Some things we read in history make us feel ashamed. If by chance a crack develops in a wall in a place of worship that we have made, we go out and destroy thousands of those temples of God that the Lord has embellished and that He himself has made. Humans hate humans but love bricks and stones. We then call ourselves martyrs and upholders of the faith. If we could find the Lord by cutting one another's throats, what could be easier? But our thinking is wrong. One who loves the Lord also loves his creation and all his creatures.

If one race looks upon another with hatred, if the people of one religion try to kill those of another, then I say: such a religion or race has not yet developed longing for the Lord or love for Him. Guru Sahib says:

> All belong to you, O Lord; you belong to all.
> Whom shall we call bad, when there is none other
>   than you?
> *Jeea jant sabh tis de sabhnaa kaa soee.*
> *Mandaa kis no aakheeai je doojaa hoee.*
>
> Adi Granth, M3, p. 425

O Supreme Being, you have made all the creatures in the world and you yourself live in each one of them. I could only speak ill of a being made by someone else.

Just see how the saints uplift our thinking and how they guide us to pray before the Lord: "By thy Will, let all be blessed!"[20] We should pray to the Lord to shower his blessings on the whole world. Kabir Sahib also says:

> In the beginning God created light.
> From the light came all created beings.
> When from one light the whole world was made,
> who can be good, who bad?
> *Aval alah noor upaaiaa kudarat ke sabh bande,*
> *ek noor te sabh jag upajiaa, kaun bhale ko mande.*
>
> Kabir, Adi Granth, p. 1349

The Lord's light and brilliance is within each one of us. No one is good, no one is bad; we are all simply rendering the account of our karmas. The saints are explicit in their writings: O Lord, in all these decorated vessels, these human beings that you have created, I see nothing but your light and brilliance. This is why I look upon them all as peerless, and myself as the lowest of the low.

Such humility is made manifest in the mystics in order to teach us. Paltu Sahib reminds us that the Lord is right within us and nowhere outside. So how are we to turn within and seek the Lord inside ourselves? Paltu Sahib talks about 'the inverted well in the sky'.

Our spiritual journey begins at the soles of the feet and ends at the crown of the head. There are two stages in this journey: the first is up to the eyes, the second is above the eyes. In each person's body, the seat of the soul and the mind, as I explained yesterday, is behind the eyes. Some call it the eye of Shiva *(shiv netra)*, others call it the divine eye *(divya chakshu)*, the door to our home *(ghar dar)*, the gateway to liberation *(mukti daa darvaazaa)*, the single eye, the third eye, or the black point *(nuqtaa-e-savaidaa)*.

From this point our attention goes down and spreads out into the whole world through the nine doors or openings of the body. We have to retrace this journey, bring our scattered attention back and concentrate it at the eye centre by following the instructions we have been given by the Master.

Paltu Sahib refers to the part of the head above the eyes as an inverted well, the dome of our head being the bottom of the well. He explains: "In the inverted well in the sky, a lamp is shining." When we withdraw our attention from the nine doors of the body through simran and dhyan and focus it at the eye centre, the first thing we see inside is a light shining within us. All mystics mention this light. Paltu Sahib goes on to describe it.

❧

A lamp is shining there without wick or oil;
through six seasons and twelve months, it burns
day and night.

Tis me[n] jarai chiraag binaa rogan bin baatee.
Chhah ritu baarah maas rahat jartai din raatee.

𝒫altu Sahib explains that this is a flame that has never needed
any wick or oil. Our year is divided into six seasons, twelve
months, and days and nights, so the meaning of this couplet
is that the light is shining in each one of us all the time. Race,
religion or nationality is of no concern: whoever is blessed
with the good fortune of concentrating the attention at the
eye centre, whether Hindu, Sikh, Christian or Muslim, will
see that flame of light within. This is what Buddha calls the
eternal flame *(akhand jyot),* the lamp that never goes out.

The lamps or candles we light in our places of worship all
need oil or wax and a cotton wick or something similar.
When the oil finishes, we have to put in more; when the wick
is finished, we have to put in a new one. But the mystics refer
to a lamp that needs neither oil nor wick. Kabir Sahib says:

> The lamp of Agam
> burns without wick, without oil.
> *Deepak jarai agamm kaa bin baatee bin tel.*
>> Kabir, *Kabir Sakhi Sangreh*

The light of Agam, the inaccessible region, shines in each one
of us, without any wick or oil. Guru Nanak Sahib says:

The flame of God's Name is latent in everyone
and can be revealed through the Guru's wisdom.
Raamnaam hai jot sabaaee tat gurmat kaadh laeejai.

Adi Granth, M4, p. 1323

The light of God's Name shines "in everyone"—our human differences count for nothing. Every single person whom the Lord has made has a light shining at the eye centre. As Christ says:

If therefore thine eye be single,
thy whole body shall be full of light.

Matthew 6:22

If you become single-eyed or one-pointed, your whole body will be filled with brilliance and light. If you withdraw your attention from the nine doors and focus it behind the eyes, you will open your inner eye and begin to see nothing but light within yourself.

In the text I took yesterday from Soami Ji Maharaj's writings, he says:

Come, live at the eye centre;
experience oneness here through concentration.
Here duality is transcended;
fix your attention in the inner light.
Baso tum aay nainan me^n,
simat kar ek yaha^n honaa.
Duee yaha^n door ho jaave,
drishti jot me^n dharnaa.

Soami Ji, Sar Bachan 19:18, p. 152

When you withdraw your attention from the nine doors and collect it here at the eye centre, you will leave duality and enter oneness. It is when you leave the realm of duality, Soami Ji says, that you first begin to see this light which has to be experienced within you, and which has been mentioned by all the mystics.

Paltu Sahib tells us that a light is shining in every one of us here at the eye centre—but when will we be able to see it? He goes on to tell us.

❧

Only they who have found a true Master
are able to see the light;
without a perfect Master, no one can behold it.

Satguru milaa jo hoy taahi kee nazar me^n aavai.
Bin satguru kou hoy nahee^n vaa ko darsaavai.

The saints and mystics explain how we are to collect together our scattered attention, focus it behind the eyes and see the light within ourselves. The saints themselves do not have to light any lamp inside us, since there is a natural divine radiance already there in each person. We know nothing about it because our attention is turned outwards. They tell us the method or technique, the path we need to follow, so that we are enabled to experience that light.

Paltu Sahib says that we can go on searching within ourselves, but we will never find the light with our intelligence and intellect. We will never succeed until we practise the teachings of the Master, regardless of how many books and scriptures we read.

Think how many libraries there are, filled with books on law; how many there are, filled with medical books written by doctors; how many books have been written on engineering. Yet no one has ever become an engineer, doctor or lawyer simply by reading. It takes some fifteen to twenty years of studying in schools and colleges to get a degree, and that is followed by a practical training. Only then do we become proficient in a field of learning.

The question of spirituality is extremely complex. Without the Masters, it would be difficult for us to take even one step inwards. Guru Nanak Sahib says:

> God is attained through the Satguru.
> *Satgur te har paaeeai bhaaee.*
> Adi Granth, M3, p. 425

My friends, if you want to worship the Lord, you can do so only through the saints and mystics.

Each one of us has the ability to learn, but that power lies dormant within us. When we go to school and college and obey our teachers, stay up at night and work hard, little by little that latent power awakens within us. We become B.A.'s, M.A.'s, Ph.D.'s and scholars. People who are frightened of their school and college teachers and run away, have the same power of learning, but it remains dormant. They come with it dormant, they go with it dormant.

Similarly, saints do not put any light within us; it is shining there naturally, provided by the Lord. They are there to explain how to turn inwards by concentrating our attention so that we can experience it.

∽

**From within the lamp's light emanates a sound;
it is heard by one in deep meditation—
no one else can hear it.**

*Niksai ek aavaaz chiraag kee jyotihi[n] maahee[n].
Gyaan samaadhee sunai aur kou suntaa naahee[n].*

Now Paltu Sahib takes us to the next step. Once we see the light within ourselves, our understanding automatically increases. From within the light, there is the most sweet and delightful of sounds continuously welling up which reverberates within each one of us day and night.

Every mystic has made mention of this sound within us. Guru Nanak Sahib calls it the pure Sound *(nirmal naad)*, the unending Word *(anahad shabad)*, and the resounding Melodies *(dhunkaar dhunaa[n])*. Soami Ji calls it the essential Word *(mool-kalaam)*. The Muslim mystics describe it as the Word of God *(kalaam-e-ilaahee)*, the imperial Sound *(nidaa-e-sultaanee)*, and the Call from the skies *(baang-e-aasmaanee)*. The ancient Indian sages call it the Voice from the skies *(aakaash vaanee)*, the Melody of God *(raam dhun)*, the pure Sound *(nirmal naad)*, and the divine Melody *(divya dhuni)*.

This is not an outer sound. It is welling up inside each one of us day and night, irrespective of our race, religion or country. Paltu Sahib explains: "It is heard by one in deep meditation—no one else can hear it." Those who go to a Master, practise what he teaches them and focus their attention at the eye centre, will see the light within themselves and will begin

to hear the sweet sound that emanates from within that light.
Guru Nanak Sahib says:

> Within me is the light of the Word
> from which music arises continuously;
> it is through this that I am attached in love to the
>   true Lord.
> *Antar jot nirantar baanee saache saahib sio liv laaee.*
>   Adi Granth, M1, p. 634

In each one of you a light is shining, and from within it
the most melodious music is pouring forth. If you experience
this inner light *(darshan)* and are able to catch hold of the
sound of the music, your worldly attachments and love will
leave you and instead you will become attached to the Lord.

It is most significant that in all our temples, mosques,
gurdwaras and churches—wherever we worship and pray to
the Lord, each according to our particular understanding—
we light lamps and candles, strike bells and make sounds like
the conch. Do we ever wonder why we use lights, make different sounds and ring bells in all these places?

If we visit a Jain, Buddhist or Hindu temple, the first thing
we see is a bell hanging on the verandah outside. We ring the
bell and then go inside, where we find a lamp burning. If we
go to a church, we find that bells are rung before the service
begins and that candles are lit inside. If we go to a gurdwara,
we find that they too light lamps, ring bells and blow the
conch. If we go to a mosque, we find that the mullah gives
the call to prayer, and they too light lamps at night.

Sages and seers, saints and holy men, prophets and masters, have all explained that the real gurdwara, temple or
mosque is our body: turn inwards and search there, and then

you will experience the inner light and hear the sound of the bell and conch within yourself.

The lights we see outside are not the real thing. Saints use them to explain that this is the kind of sound and the kind of light we will hear and see inside. When we send children to school, we first put them in a Montessori school or in kindergarten. They are not taught lessons, but are given a little something to eat and toys to play with so that they feel happy to be there; then they develop an interest in learning and want to study. The result is that they willingly stay away from their parents and get interested in their studies. As they get older, they leave their toys behind and are taught lessons. They do not stay in the kindergarten their whole life.

Similarly, these outer man-made places of worship—temples, mosques, gurdwaras and churches—are there to develop love and devotion in us, to engender in us love for the Lord. We are not supposed to play with these toys all our life but to progress beyond them and develop that love which is true love. Guru Nanak Sahib says:

> True devotees seek within;
> all others wander in delusion.
> *Gurmukh hovai su kaa-i-aa khojai*
> *hor sabh bharam bhulaaee.*
> Adi Granth, M3, p. 754

The lovers and devotees of the Lord have gone beyond these things. Turning inwards, they search for the Lord inside their body—they turn within themselves and love Him within. Saints explain that outward forms of worship are better than doing nothing at all, but we should not spend our whole life involved with these games. Young girls go on playing with dolls until they grow up, but once they are married, what do they care about dolls? Once true love and devotion are born in our heart, we go far beyond these places of brick and stone.

Paltu Sahib says that when you journey on the path according to the instructions given to you by the Master, you will get to see the inner light and hear the inner sound at the eye centre. This is the light by which you are to see your way within on your spiritual journey, while with the sound, you establish the direction of your home.

For example, you might go for an evening walk and end up by the river, far from the Dera. Night falls and it is very dark, so what do you do? You listen carefully to see if you can hear any sound coming from the Dera. The moment you hear the sound of the siren or a bell, you immediately know the direction of the Dera—whether it is ahead of you or behind you, to your right or left. Since the night is dark and there are bushes and water, you need a torch or lantern to light your way. Once you know the direction of the Dera, even though you may have forgotten the route, you can use the light to guide you on your way back.

If we ask what helped us find our way home, it was the sound and the light. In the same way, we are lost far from the home of the Lord, and to guide us He has kept that sound and light in each one of us, which is why every mystic tells us of the inner sound and light.

ॐ

O Paltu, those who hear it, their destiny is fulfilled;
in the inverted well in the sky, a lamp is shining.

Paltoo jo koee sunai taa ke poore bhaag.
Ultaa koowaa^n gagan me^n tis me^n jarai chiraag.

Now in the end Paltu Sahib says that if, in this life, we are able to see the light and hear the bell and conch within, then the purpose of being born as a human being has been fulfilled. We have begun the spiritual journey and, stage by stage, we will return to our final destination. Such people are blessed with a great destiny; we should rejoice for their presence on earth because it is to love and worship Him that the Lord gives this human form.

Now it is for us to derive benefit from the experience of the saints and mystics by joining our attention within to the true Word, the true Name.

4

~

Cleanse the Chamber of Your Heart

Dil kaa hujraa saaf kar

Cleanse the chamber of your heart
for the coming of your Beloved.
From your attention discard all that is other
so He may be seated there.

With your inner eye look around you:
what a pageant is being played;
what allurements are there to tempt your heart!
One heart, a thousand desires, and still the cravings increase:
where then is the space, tell me, to establish him there?

How sad it is that to man-made temples and mosques
the inhabitants of the natural mosque go, just to suffer pain.
Listen intently in the real Ka'aba's arch:
from the highest, a Call is coming, inviting you to return.

Why wander everywhere in search of your Friend?
The road to your Beloved is through the royal vein.
With patience and love, meet a perfect Master, O Taqi;
he will give you the wisdom to find the royal vein.

Practise for some time and the inner ear will open
to take you to Allah-hu-Akbar, the One without another.
This is Tulsi's call: heed it, O practitioner, and act on it!
The Kun of the Qur'an, it is written, will take you to Allah-hu-Akbar.

Tulsi Sahib, *Santon ki Bani,* Gazal, p. 275

Dil kaa hujraa saaf kar jaanaa^n ke aane ke liye.
Dhyaan gairo^n kaa uthaa uske bithaane ke liye.

Chashme dil se dekh yahaa^n jo jo tamaashe ho rahe.
Dilsitaa^n kyaa kyaa hai^n tere dil sataane ke liye.
Ek dil laakho^n tamannaa us pai aur zyaadaa havas.
Phir thikaanaa hai kahaa^n uske tikaane ke liye.

Naqli mandir masjido^n me^n jaay sad afsos hai.
Kudartee masjid kaa saakin dukh uthaane ke liye.
Kudartee kaabe kee too mahraab me^n sun gaur se.
Aa rahee dhur se sadaa tere bulaane ke liye.

Kyo^n bhataktaa phir rahaa too eh talaashe yaar me^n.
Raastaa shaah rag me^n hai dilbar pai jaane ke liye.
Murshid-e-kaamil se mil sidaq aur saboori se taqee.
Jo tujhe degaa phaham shaah rag ke paane ke liye.

Gosh-e-baatin ho kushaadaa jo kare kuchh din amal.
Laa ilaah allaahoo akbar pai jaane ke liye.
Yaha sadaa tulsee kee hai aamil amal kar dhyaan de.
Kun kuraa^n me^n hai likhaa allahu akbar ke liye.

Tulsi Sahib, *Santon ki Bani* (Beas: Radha Soami Satsang Beas, 1995, 19th edition), Gazal, p. 275

~

Cleanse the chamber of your heart
for the coming of your Beloved.
From your attention discard all that is other
so He may be seated there.

Dil kaa hujraa saaf kar jaanaaⁿ ke aane ke liye.
Dhyaan gairoⁿ kaa uthaa uske bithaane ke liye.

𝄞n this three-day satsang programme,[*] I have already taken one text from the house of Shri Guru Nanak Dev Ji Maharaj and one from the writings of Shri Hazur Soami Ji Maharaj. The text for this satsang is by Tulsi Sahib Ji Maharaj. My sole intention in taking the writings of different saints is to show that they all have the same message and teachings.

It is my constant submission that in every country, religion and age, all spiritual Masters describe the same way of worshipping the Supreme Being. None of them come to the world to create discord between the various nations, religions and social groups. None come to place weapons in the hands of their disciples. They come simply to awaken within us love for the Lord and the desire to find Him. They show us the way to Him, so that by worshipping Him we can become free, we can escape forever from the prison of the body and the cycle of death and rebirth.

It is we human beings who, after the departure of a saint, go far from the real teachings. We get involved in external practices and caught up in rituals and ceremonies. We give

---

[*] *See* Glossary and Translators' Note for explanations of unusual usage, and technical or Indian-language terms, such as: satsang, house of Shri Guru Nanak.

their teachings a national, cultural or religious identity and then start disagreeing and fighting with one another.

Why do we do this? Some of us do it to earn our living, some as a matter of honour and prestige. When their teachings are intended for the whole world, for everyone, and we limit them to such small spheres, just ask yourself: what greater injustice could we do to these lovers of the Lord? If we look deeply into the writings of any great spiritual teacher, with an unbiased mind and an open heart, we will realize this one thing—that they all express the same teaching.

Tulsi Sahib Ji Maharaj was a renowned saint of Uttar Pradesh, generally known by the name of 'the holy man from the south'. He was actually from the ruling family of Pune and Satara in Maharashtra. His father was also a great devotee of the Lord, who thought that since his son was coming of age, he would hand the affairs of the state over to him, renounce the world and devote himself to the Lord. When Tulsi Sahib heard about this, he slipped away under cover of darkness.

There is a substantial portion of his life about which we know nothing, but ultimately he established himself in the town of Hathras. He changed his name so that no one should know who he was, and there he discoursed openly on the way of the saints. Soami Ji Maharaj and his whole family were among his disciples.

Several of Tulsi Sahib's verses were written in order to explain the teachings to Sheikh Taqi, a Muslim faqir who was returning from Mecca after completing a pilgrimage to the Ka'aba. It was his good fortune that he set up camp opposite the place where Tulsi Sahib lived, so that Tulsi Sahib had ample time to explain his teachings to him. Tulsi Sahib had some knowledge of Persian, as did Sheikh Taqi, so Tulsi Sahib used many Persian terms and explained the teachings in the Urdu language.

In the first verse he says: O Sheikh Taqi, the fact is that each one of us would like the Lord to make his abode in our heart—but have we ever considered whether this heart, where we would like the Lord to live, is fit for Him? Even a dog, when it wants to sit down, first prepares the ground with its tail as it turns around. And when we want to sit on the ground, we first sweep it, then wash it, then spread a rug or a carpet, and put out upholstered chairs and cushions. Only then do we consider the place to be fit for us.

This heart where we want the Supreme Being to reside has been soiled by our love for our family, by our involvement with racial, religious and social issues, and by our physical appetites. How then can it be fit for Him?

Our hearts are restless. They yearn day and night for the forms and material possessions of the world, yet we want to meet the Lord. How can these two things be compatible?

A distant relative or friend goes far away and we cry all night and cannot sleep, but have we ever spent a sleepless night out of love for the Lord or because we are separated from Him? Have we even by chance shed tears out of love for the Lord? Our heart longs for the world, and yet we want to meet the Lord. How can this be? This is why Tulsi Sahib says:

> From your attention discard all that is other
> so He may be seated there.

Until you rid yourself of your love and attachment for everything other than Him, your heart will never be fit for the Supreme Being.

The link between our soul and the supreme soul is one of devotion and love. This is why saints generally describe it in terms of the relationship between a wife and husband. Christ speaks of it in terms of a father and son, and the Rama Krishna Mission as that of a mother and child. What is the common factor in these relationships? They are linked simply by love. Similarly, the relationship between the soul and God, the supreme soul, has nothing to do with our country, religion or social background; it is simply one of devotion and love. The saints say:

> Only those who have loved, have found the Lord.
> *Jin prem kiyo tin hee prabh paayo.*
>
> Dassam Granth, Akal Ustat, M10, p. 14:9:29

When a person's heart is filled with love for the Lord and is restless with intense longing for union with Him, then that person will be privileged to reunite with Him. Paltu Sahib says:

> In the court of the Lord,
> devotion and love alone count.
> *Saahib ke darbaar me^n keval bhakti piyaar.*
>
> Paltu, *Paltu Sahib ki Bani*, Kundli 218

If you want to reach the abode of the Lord, you need only love and devotion. In the same vein, Dadu Sahib says:

> Love is the Lord's essence, love is his nature;
> love is his form, love is his colour.
> *Ishq alah kee zaati hai, ishq alah kaa ang,*
> *ishq alah aujood hai, ishq alah kaa rang.*
>
> Dadu, *Dadu Dayal*

If you ask the name of the Lord, it is love, love, and love.

If you ask whether the Lord belongs to a particular place or country, that also is only love. In the Bible it is written:

> God is love.
>> 1 John 4:8

Love, and love alone, is the real form of the Lord.

The real connection between the soul and God is love. It has nothing to do with country, religion or birth. How could we ever say that the Supreme Being belongs to a particular race, religion or country? We all know that there is only one Lord. No one would say that there is one for the Hindus and another for the Sikhs or Christians. That Lord is the same, whether you live in India, America or Africa. That is why the sages of India refer to Him as the One *(ek-ekaa)*. There is only the One.

> There is only one Bestower for all beings.
> *Sabhnaa jeeaa kaa iku daataa.*
>> Adi Granth, M1, Japji, p. 2

Everything that you see before you in the entire world has been created by the one Almighty God. Muslim faqirs speak of this One as God of all the worlds *(rab-ul-aalameen)*, not as God of the Muslims *(rab-ul-musalmeen)*. God is one for the whole world, not just for the Muslims. When God, the supreme soul, cannot be identified with any race, religion or country, then how can an individual soul be thought of in this way?

> Says Kabir, the soul is a particle of the Lord.
> *Kahu kabeer ihu raam kee ans.*
>> Kabir, Adi Granth, p. 871

Our soul *(aatmaa)* is a particle of God, the supreme soul *(parmaatmaa)*. Guru Nanak Sahib says the same thing:

> God abides in the soul, the soul in God.
> *Aatam mah raam, raam mah aatam.*
>
> Adi Granth, M1, p. 1153

God is within our individual soul, and each soul is within God. Guru Nanak Sahib explains this beautifully:

> He has no colour, caste and mark.
> By his Command, He creates the whole world.
> *Varan jaat chihan nahee koee.*
> *Sabh hukame srisat upaa-idaa.*
>
> Adi Granth, M5, p. 1075

The Supreme Being, by whose Command the entire creation has come into being, is neither dark nor fair, Hindu nor Sikh, nor does He belong to any particular country.

Hindu tradition divides the human race into four groups or castes, but the saints state that the Supreme Being cannot be confined to any group. When the Supreme Being or Soul is without race, creed or caste, how can our souls be considered in this way? If the sun is without race or creed, can its myriad small rays be described in these terms? If the ocean has no caste, no social status, then what caste or status can its drops possibly have?

The Supreme Being has created human beings. It is we who have divided ourselves into small groups by race, creed, nation, caste and social group. It is we who get entangled in these differences. Look into the writings of any saint and you will discover that each one tries to lift us high above the level of such disputes. Guru Nanak Sahib says:

Where you render account of your deeds,
there neither body nor caste go with you.
Jithai lekhaa mangeeai tithai deh jaat na jaa-e.
Adi Granth, M3, p. 1346

My friends, your body will not accompany you to the place where you have to render account for your deeds. No one there is going to ask you about your caste or status in this world—to which religion you belonged, or from which country you have come. Only your actions will be considered there, only your devotion and reverence.

These questions of country, caste and creed are connected with our body, and as you know, we leave our body to be cremated or buried. For some of us our national identity and religion go up in flames, while for others our social identity gets mingled with the soil. This is why Kabir Sahib says:

No one will ask your caste or creed;
whoever contemplates on Him becomes His.
Jaat-paat poochhe nahi[n] koi,
hari ko bhajai so hari kaa hoi.
Kabir

No one will ask for details of your position in this life. Any person who worships the Supreme Being takes on the appearance of the Supreme Being. Irrespective of your religion, it is your devotion and love alone that will take you back to the Lord.

Let no one think that it is necessary to become a Sikh, Muslim or Christian. Kabir Sahib says we should remove such thoughts from our mind forever. Bulleh Shah says:

You will be judged by your actions alone;
your caste and creed will go unnoticed.

Amalaa^n utte hon nibere,
khareeaa^n rahingeeaa^n jaataa^n.
Bulleh Shah, *Kafian Bulleh Shah*

By paying attention to your actions, to what you do, you will be able to settle your account. Those who are proud of their birth will be ignored.

Paltu Sahib was a well-known saint who lived in the city of Ayodhya in Uttar Pradesh. He explains through his writings:

> Paltu says, because of high birth,
> let no one feel proud;
> in the court of the Lord,
> devotion and love alone count.
> *Paltoo oo^{n}chee jaati kau jani kou karai ha^{n}kaar.*
> *Saahib ke darbaar me^n keval bhakti piyaar.*
>
> Paltu, *Paltu Sahib ki Bani*, Kundli 218

No one should have the idea that because they have been born into a high-ranking priestly family, they alone have the privilege of union with the Supreme Being; nor that by being born into a humble home they will never meet Him. Paltu Sahib tells us to get rid of such thoughts forever. To reach His abode, only love and devotion are needed. On this question of social standing, the saints have even gone so far as to say:

> All those bereft of Nam are of low birth;
> they exist like vermin in filth.
> *Bin naavai sabh neech jaat hai*
> *bistaa kaa keeraa hoe.*
>
> Adi Granth, M3, p. 426

Who can be inferior to those who do not worship the Lord, to those who have no love for Him? After death, they will become maggots in dirt. And who is of high status?

> With the Name in the heart,
> one is revered amongst all.
> With the Name in the heart,
> one is the Creator incarnate.
> With the Name in the heart,
> one is exalted above all.
> *Jis naam ridai so sabh mah jaataa.*
> *Jis naam ridai so purakh bidhaataa.*
> *Jis naam ridai so sabh te oochaa.*
>
> Adi Granth, M5, p. 1156

Someone whose heart is filled with love for the Name of the Supreme Being, who at all times remains immersed in love for the Lord, is the highest and purest of all and will return to merge with that true Lord. This is why Tulsi Sahib lovingly explains that the link between the soul and the supreme soul is one of love and devotion alone. If you want to find the Lord, then you must awaken love within yourself.

But how can love be awakened within us? He explains:

> From your attention discard all that is other
> so He may be seated there.

What does he mean by 'other'? Everything around us, whatever we experience in this material world, is 'other': children, relatives, friends, houses, money, assets and property. Everything that we think of as ours, apart from the Lord, Tulsi Sahib describes as 'other' *(gair)*. Guru Nanak Sahib refers to it all as illusion *(bharam)*; some talk of it as duality *(doojaa)*.

We may well wonder why the saints speak of all these as 'other'. Our parents gave birth to us and raised us; with our brothers and sisters we have a relationship of flesh and blood; our friends have been with us from the beginning. Similarly, it is through our own sweat and blood that we have property, or through inheritance that we own so much, or through accumulating assets from the start. So why, then, do saints refer to all these as 'other'?

We must understand that any relationship between us and these things is through our body. As long as we are in this body, we think of them all as ours. When we leave the body, however, we will exist apart from these things. This then leads us to question whether even our body belongs to us.

Our body is a rented house belonging to someone else, given to some of us for fifty or sixty years, to others for eighty or ninety years. Once we have gone through the exact number of breaths allotted to us, each one of us will have to leave it. Some leave it to fire, others to the earth. When we are not able to keep even our own body, is there anything in the world that we can really think of as our own? Guru Nanak Sahib says:

> Mother, father, are transient relationships,
> an affliction of the body;
> afflicted is the entire family.
> *Maat pitaa maa-i-aa deh se rogee*
> *rogee kutamb sanjogee.*
>
> Adi Granth, M1, p. 1153

If we are indebted to anyone, it is surely to our parents above all. Not only did they give birth to us, but think what troubles and difficulties they underwent when taking care of us, and what criticism they faced from relatives and others. But, says

Guru Nanak Sahib, even they will have to leave us and will be of no help or support to us in the end. Our relatives cannot help us then. Even the body will be left behind when we go.

These are all relationships of giving and taking, of self-interested love. Some come as parents, some as brothers and sisters, some as relatives and friends. They are there as long as any karmic debt remains. Once it is settled, they all go their separate ways. Just think: some have already left us and gone, while we ourselves are preparing to leave others and go.

In a theatre all the actors have to play their parts. One takes the role of king, one of queen, and one of villain. Once they leave the stage, there is no king, no queen, no villain. Saints explain that, in the same way, this world is a vast stage. We are each playing out specific roles according to our particular karma.

The problem is that in the process of playing these parts, we take them to be real, as though they really belong to us. They can never belong to us, but in trying to possess them, we get attached to them and come to love them. We get so attached through our love for them that we even dream about them at night. At death it is their images that come before our mind's eye, as though we were watching a film. "Where our desires are, there we dwell."[21] In this world, the direction in which our attention goes in our last moments determines the course of our next life.

What is it that brings us back over and over again to the enslavement of the body? It is our worldly love and attachments. And whom do we love? We love our relatives, friends, properties, wealth, country, religion and society. This is why saints say that we are trapped by our love and attachment for all that is 'other'. We have forgotten the Supreme Being, which alone is real and which alone is our real self. This is why they tell us to rid ourselves of these loves and attachments.

Saints do not say that we need to retreat to some remote place to renounce the world. We have to live in the world courageously, like warriors. While living in the world we must not allow the dirt of the world to stick to us. Guru Nanak Sahib says:

> Just as the lotus lives detached in water
> and the duck swims on the surface yet remains dry,
> attached to the Word, the soul crosses the ocean of
>   phenomena
> through the practice of the Name, O Nanak.
> *Jaise jal mah kamal niraalam murgaaee naisaane.*
> *Surat sabad bhav saagar tareeai*
> *naanak naam vakhaane.*
>
> Adi Granth, M1, p. 938

Just as a duck living on the water flies away with dry wings, and a lotus has its roots in the water yet the flower remains above the water, so by attaching ourselves to Nam, to the Name, we can navigate the ocean of this world. If a bee alights on the edge of a jar of honey, it can enjoy the honey and fly off unharmed. If it sinks into the honey, it will not be able to eat it; its wings will get stuck, and after a struggle, it will die.

No saint ever says that to free ourselves from our attachments we have to hide ourselves away. We must live among them, remembering what is real. We must live among them, thinking of them as our duty or responsibility. We must never forget why the Lord has blessed us with this human life: that our relationships with people are just relationships of giving and taking, part of our destiny or karmic chain; but our reality is the Supreme Being alone.

By going off to a forest or mountain, we do not develop any great desire or love for the Lord. People are wrong to think that it is easier to concentrate on the Lord in such places. The fact is that whatever we need in life, the basic necessities are the same wherever we go.

What do we actually need? We need food for the stomach—without it, life would not just be difficult, it would be impossible. We need clothing of some kind to cover our body, and a roof over our head to protect us from the hot and cold weather. These are the three basics that go with us, whether we go to a forest, a mountain, or anywhere else.

We leave our own honest work, the food made in our home, and we stretch out our hands before others to satisfy our hunger. Our stomach is not going to suspend its demands; it will still require food there. We may exchange our everyday clothes for the ascetic's ochre, yellow or blue, but we will still need clothing, just the same. We may leave the peace and comfort of our own home, and look for a cave, build a hut, or search out some shelter, temple or gurdwara; but even there we will need some form of shelter. So what have we renounced? We merely become parasites—a burden on society.

Saints do not tell us to renounce the world. Rather, they say: Extricate your mind from all these things. Apply your mind to worshipping the Lord so that you may acquire that which is yours. You spend your entire life trying to possess those things that can never be yours—and that is why you are always restless and without purpose. Soami Ji says:

> Among your companions, none is your friend.
> Why keep on sleeping among these swindlers?
> *Mitra teraa koee nahee^n sangiyan me^n,*
> *paraa kyo^n sove in thagiyan me^n.*
>   Soami Ji, *Sar Bachan* 15:5, p. 116

Among all the faces and forms we keep with us throughout our lives, there is not one who is our real ally. Not one is our friend, not one is our real relation, because all will leave us in the end. When Death's henchmen stand before us, we will realize this for ourselves.

There are three kinds of people in the world who seek to deprive us of our wealth: the thief, the robber *(dacoit)*, and the swindler *(thug)*. It is a thief's practice to steal a person's goods when he or she has gone out of the house or is asleep, and therefore knows nothing. A robber does not care—in spite of our cries and screams, he takes what he wants by thrusting a knife or gun in our face. Whereas a swindler presents himself so lovingly that he becomes one of us, and with our own hands we happily give him whatever we have. Once he leaves us we realize what we have done, and then we cry that we have been robbed and cheated.

All those we think of as our own are swindlers. We spend our lives entangled in our love and attachment for them. They do not permit us to be aware of the purpose for which the Lord has graced us with this human form; of the relationship between our soul and the Lord, the supreme soul; or of who we really are. We remain trapped all our lives by the debits and credits of our account.

This is why Tulsi Sahib says that if you want to find the Lord, then you must disentangle yourself from such love and attachment.

So now we ask: How did we ever come to love them? How can we get rid of these attachments? We have kept their company from our earliest days. As I have mentioned before, we have never seen the Lord—we do not know his face, his colour or his form. We can love those with whom we have spent time, whose company we have kept, whom we have seen with our own eyes. But this Lord whom we have never seen—how will we ever develop love for Him? Whose love is it that can awaken within us love for the Lord?

In order to consider this question thoroughly, we survey the entire creation and ask ourselves: Is there anything or anyone whose company can engender within us love for the Lord?

And what do we see? We see that in the world everything is made from five vital elements *(tattva):* earth, water, fire, air and ether. All five tattvas are present in each one of us and that is why saints refer to the human being as the five-tattva form and say that it is the top of the creation.

The lowest class, in which the element of water is active, comprises the entire vegetable kingdom, such as plants, grasses and trees. If, after reaching the five-element form, we worship and love these sorts of things, you can imagine what kind of progress we will make. We too will become plants, trees and vegetables, because "Where our desires are, there we dwell".[22] We have to take on the form of whatever we worship and love. This is why nothing in the plant kingdom is worthy of our worship and love.

The next class comprises scorpions, snakes, insects and the like—earthbound creatures, in which fire and earth are active. They too are inferior to humans, because humans have all five vital elements active.

The third class comprises all feathered creatures: sparrows, for example, and doves and pigeons. They have three vital elements, while we have five. If we worship them, what will be the result? We too will become pigeons, doves and sparrows. We were trying to rise above the human birth, but by worshipping birds we do the opposite—we come back in their form.

The fourth class is that of the four-legged animals, which lack the element of ether and therefore have no power of discrimination, but the other four vital elements are all active. For this reason, buffaloes, cows and horses can never be worthy of our worship and love.

The fifth class is the human race itself. Now why would one human being worship another, particularly in these times when everyone is equal under the law.

So when one human does not worship another, when we have never seen the face, colour or form of the Lord, when we have never seen the gods and goddesses, we find ourselves in some difficulty and have to think carefully: whose company can possibly engender devotion for the Lord within us?

Hazur Maharaj Ji[*] used to give a very nice example. You may put any number of radios in a room, but until they are connected to a battery or to any other source of power, you will never hear the news from any country. Once you connect them, however, you can hear the news from wherever you wish.

We have to keep the company of the lovers of the Lord, who are absorbed in his love and whose attention is connected to Him. Through them, through love and devotion, our attention will also be connected to the Lord—as I often say, our mind is easily influenced by the company we keep. Their real form is the Word, the Name, and our real Master is the Word, the Name. Guru Nanak Sahib says:

> The Word is the Guru,
> the soul attuned to the Word is the disciple.

---

[*] The terms 'Hazur' and 'Hazur Maharaj Ji' are used by the speaker to refer to his Master, Maharaj Sawan Singh (1858–1948). *See also* Translators' Note and Glossary.

Sabad guroo surat dhun chelaa.
Adi Granth, M1, p. 943

It is the Shabd that is the Master, and the soul is the disciple. This physical body has to be left here by both the disciple and the Master. When, through the Master, the soul of a disciple attaches itself to the Word, then the Word never leaves that soul—the soul goes straight back and merges into God, the supreme soul.

We keep the company of lovers of the Lord for this very reason—so that through them we can merge into the Word, we can immerse ourselves in the Name. The true form of God is also the Word. Christ says that the Word is God.[23] The real form of the Word is God; there is no difference between the Word and the Lord. The creative power and the Creator are one and the same. So this is why we keep the Masters' company. Guru Nanak Sahib explains beautifully:

> The whole world, the netherworlds, the islands,
>   the spheres,
> have all been put under Kal; such is the Lord's
>   design....
> *Khand pataal deep sabh loaa,*
> *sabh kaalai vas aap prabh keeaa.*
>
> Adi Granth, M5, p. 1076

The entire creation—the regions, islands, netherworlds, and everything that exists—has been created by the Supreme Being and it is He who has entrusted its administration to Kal. Kal's authority reaches up to the level of Brahm, throughout the realm of the three worlds. Whatever comes within his sphere is caught in the pain of death and rebirth. But, Guru Nanak Sahib says,

... The only immutable one is the eternal God;
those who contemplate on Him become immutable
    too....
Nihchal ek aap abinaasee
so nihchal jo tisah dhiaa-idaa.

Adi Granth, M5, p. 1076

The supreme Lord alone is eternal. His home is Sach Khand, the true realm, and He is never subject to death and rebirth. Anyone who worships that Lord, anyone who loves Him, will become, like the Lord, everlasting, and will be released from the pain of death and rebirth.

So now we ask ourselves how we can worship the Lord, since we have never seen Him. Guru Nanak Sahib says:

... The Lord's servant is like unto the Lord;
do not think him to be different because of his
        human frame...
Har kaa sevak so har jehaa.
Bhed na jaanah maanas dehaa.

Adi Granth, M5, p. 1076

The lovers of the Lord assume his form by worshipping Him. There is no difference between them and the Lord. In what way are they connected to the Lord?

... just as a myriad waves rise from the ocean,
and then subside, merging back into its depths.
Jio jal tarang uthah bahu bhaatee
phir salalai salal samaa-idaa.

Adi Granth, M5, p. 1076

A wave arises from the ocean for a few minutes and then merges back into the ocean. Just as waves are connected to the ocean, so are the lovers of the Lord connected to the Supreme Being. A wave, no matter how big it is, can never be separated from the ocean. Similarly, the lovers of the Lord can never be separated from the Lord. If we surrender anything to a wave, it always carries it along with itself into the ocean, and that is why we keep their company. Christ says:

> I and my Father are one.
> John 10:30

He and the Father are one and the same thing. And he also says: You are merged in me and I am merged in the Supreme Being, so you are also merged in the Supreme Being.[24] Guru Nanak Sahib also says:

> Know thou, Guru and God are one.
> *Guru parmesar eko jaan.*
> Adi Granth, M5, p. 864

So the saints and Masters are the waves of the ocean of Satnam, the true Name. They come to the world to bear witness to the Name. They come to spread the message of the Name, and taking us with them, they immerse us forever in the Name. This is why it is through the Masters that we are to awaken within ourselves love and devotion for the Lord and the longing to find Him.

How do they awaken this love for the Lord in us? This, Tulsi Sahib tells us in the next lines.

✄

With your inner eye look around you:
what a pageant is being played;
what allurements are there to tempt your heart!

Chashme dil se dekh yahaa^n jo jo tamaashe ho rahe.
Dilsitaa^n kyaa kyaa hai^n tere dil sataane ke liye.

Now he explains to us that when we see the pomp and show of life—people staying in fancy hotels, travelling by plane, living in palatial homes, driving luxurious cars, wearing beautiful jewellery—we should not assume they are happy. What do we know of the reverse side of the picture?

A picture has two sides. If we look at the front, we see a beautiful painting, and a frame that also looks very nice. But if we look at the back there is nothing but nails and cardboard, which does not appeal to us at all. That is how we see people—from the outside. But just ask anyone, just see what is inside—how pain is throbbing within them, ready to burst out like pus from a wound.

I already explained yesterday how no one can achieve peace and happiness in this phenomenal world. The things through which we seek happiness are impermanent, so whatever happiness or peace of mind we get from them is also temporary and short-lived. With the passage of time, what little happiness there is, gradually gets transformed into pain. Until we attain the imperishable, that which is not subject to decay, until we make it ours, it is impossible to attain real happiness and peace.

As I have already explained, the relationship of the soul and supreme soul is like that of a wife and husband. If a wife has to stay far away from her husband, you may give her a palace to live in, dress her in fine jewels, regale her with good food, and treat her always with respect—but she will not be happy. What she wants is union with her husband; she wants to be with him. When she is with her husband, she likes these things; without him, they taste bitter. As long as our soul is not absorbed in love and devotion for the Lord, we will never be happy—even if the Lord were to give us the sovereignty of the whole world.

This restlessness is on account of the intrinsic pull or attraction of the soul towards its source. The more we let it go in that direction, the more happy and content it will be; the more we keep it at a distance, dispersing it into the creation through the sense pleasures and the negative tendencies, the more we will go on suffering night and day. That is why Soami Ji says:

> Mind, renounce this world of pain and pleasure!
> Rise above it and attach yourself to the true Name.
> *Tajo man yaha dukh sukh kaa dhaam,*
> *lago tum charh kar ab satnaam.*
>
> Soami Ji, *Sar Bachan* 15:9, p. 119

The world is made from pain and pleasure. We have to undergo some degree of pain; we also have to experience pleasure. Both good and bad deeds combine to make a human life. Until both sides of the account are fully settled and we find our home with Satnam, the true Name, the question of real peace and happiness does not arise.

> O Nanak, the whole creation is miserable.
> *Naanak dukheeaa sabh sansaar.*
>
> Adi Granth, M1, p. 954

Only those sustained by the Name are happy.
So sukheeaa jo naam adhaar.

Every living thing, each in its own place in the creation, knows only the terrible extent of its own pain and suffering. Each is ignorant of the other—mistaken and deluded. Real happiness lies only with the one who has taken refuge with the Lord, whose love and devotion are with Him.

This is why Tulsi Sahib is giving us this warning. When seeing the colourful pageantry of the world, we are not to deceive ourselves that we will get happiness from these things. He says: The more you keep looking for happiness in these things, the more unhappiness you will get. If you want to attain happiness, it can only be had through love and devotion for the Lord.

❧

One heart, a thousand desires, and still the
cravings increase:
where then is the space, tell me, to establish him there?

Ek dil laakhoⁿ tamannaa us pai aur zyaadaa havas.
Phir thikaanaa hai kahaaⁿ uske tikaane ke liye.

Tulsi Sahib explains: We have one mind, but day and night thousands of wishes and desires keep arising in it. Those desires and wishes are never fully satisfied, but still the mind keeps on producing more. We should understand that whenever desires remain unfulfilled, they become a cause of suffering for us.

In this world, everyone is being roasted continuously by the fire of desire. That is why he says that if this is our condition, if we are burning on account of our desires, then how will we ever be happy, how will we ever achieve peace and contentment?

The fact is that being people of the world, we do not worship the Lord. We do not have a spare moment from our worldly pleasures and activities. And if we do, then we take along our worldly desires. We cannot even give fifteen minutes of our time to worship the supreme Lord, but then for almost an hour, or sometimes more, we submit lists of our worldly demands to Him. And we forget, as Guru Nanak Sahib says,

> He will go on giving till we tire of receiving;
> throughout the ages, we have been ever consuming.
> *Dedaa de laide thak paahe.*
> *Jugaa jugantar khaahee khaahe.*
>
> Adi Granth, Japji, M1, p. 2

Through the ages we have come before the Lord with our worldly wants and desires. He, the ever-giving, has kept on fulfilling them to this day. And what has been the outcome? Each one of us is still trapped in this prison of chaurasi. Until we ask the Lord for the Lord himself, we will never be released from these ties of the body.

There is a proverb: "Like mountains, our desires—and death is at our heels."[25] Even while death is waiting at the door, our wants and desires go on growing higher than the Himalayas. We have no idea how many years we have left or when we will have to leave everyone behind. Every day we read in the newspapers about sudden death: a morsel of food in someone's hand, and it does not even get to his mouth; a person about to get up from his chair, and his foot does not get as far as the ground. If we were to fulfil all our desires, how long would we have to live!

We should realize that when the Lord is capable of giving, He is also capable of knowing. The Lord, before whom we keep on presenting our worldly wants and desires, also knows what it is that we need. When He can give to us, then He also knows what is good for us. That is why Guru Nanak Sahib says:

> Without any words, He knows everything,
> so to whom do we beg and pray?
> *Vin boliaa sabh kichh jaandaa*
> *kis aagai keechai ardaas.*
>
> Adi Granth, M3, p. 1420

Why do we keep on making these long lists of demands to the Lord? Do we think He is deaf, or that He does not understand what is in our hearts, or that He does not know what we need in this world?

A much-loved son has no need to make demands of his father; it is the father who is always concerned for his beloved son. But when a son keeps on asking his father for things throughout the day, when he continuously ignores the authority of his father and does not love him—then the father too tries to keep him at a distance.

We must become beloved children of our Father, not go before Him with our worldly demands. Tulsi Sahib is saying that we must worship the Lord so as to be united with Him, not to fulfil our desires. That is why saints say that we should worship the Lord while living in his will. Remaining within his order, at his pleasure, we have to devote ourselves to the Lord. 'In his will' means taking before Him none of our own desires. Whatever our destiny is, we should meet it gladly. Whatever He gives to us, we should go through it thanking the Lord and taking it to be his will. Baba Namdev says:

Should you make me king, whose would be the
    glory?
Should you make me a beggar, what would I lose?
Jau raaj deh ta kavan badaaee.
Jau bheekh mangaavah ta kiaa ghat jaaee.
Namdev, Adi Granth, p. 525

O Lord, if you were to make me ruler of the world, I would have no other work but to worship you. If you were to have me driven from door to door through the world, still I would have nothing else to do but worship you. Just as a crow out at sea can take rest only on a boat, where, other than with the supreme soul, can the soul make its home? Ultimately it has to come within the will of the Lord.

As long as we do not conduct our lives according to his will, we will go on suffering. To live in his will, we should worship Him not by taking before Him our own desires and wants, but by surrendering ourselves to Him and meditating on the Word wherever He chooses to keep us. We need to be customers *(gaahak)* of the Lord when we worship Him—not customers of the world.

Just imagine a small child playing in the care of its nanny. When the child cries, the nanny tries everything to make it happy, sometimes giving it sweets or toys, sometimes telling little stories or rhymes. As long as the child remains happy, the parents can go about their own activities without a care. However, if the child is crying for its parents and nothing else will satisfy it, how can they resist? They will run and pick the child up and hug it to their breast.

As long as we go on playing with the toys of the creation, the Supreme Being goes on ignoring us. Once we remove our attention from everything else and turn towards the Lord, He unites us with Him, showering his grace and mercy upon us.

That is why Tulsi Sahib says that we must live in the Lord's will and worship Him—we must worship Him in order to be united with Him. We must not do so to fulfil our desires for pleasure, to satisfy worldly wants, or because of fear that if we do not worship Him then our children or spouse may turn out to be no good, there may be friction in the family or somebody may get ill. This is no way to worship the Lord. It is like when people worship a snake, the plague or small-pox. They do it not because they love these things, but to avoid them. We must not worship the Lord with this attitude of mind.

The basis of religion is love, not fear. We must bring Him our love. That is why Tulsi Sahib says we must always worship the Lord for himself. That Lord who takes care of the life in each leaf, who satisfies even their need for food—is He likely to give us birth and then forget about us, when we are at the top of the creation? He has had our destiny written from the start. That is why Tulsi Sahib says: Turn towards the Lord, make Him your priority when you worship Him.

ॐ

How sad it is that to man-made temples and mosques the inhabitants of the natural mosque go, just to suffer pain.

Naqli mandir masjido^n me^n jaay sad afsos hai.
Kudartee masjid kaa saakin dukh uthaane ke liye.

So now he notes with great sadness what we go and do when that love awakens within us, when we feel that longing for union with the Lord. Some of us run to the temple, some to the gurdwara, some to the church, and some to the mosque; not one of us, poor fools that we are, turns inward to the place where He is actually living, the place that He has made for himself. Not one of us searches for Him there.

The Supreme Being is not to be found anywhere outside. He is to be found in our body, inside our physical form. If a laboratory exists where we can study the way to find the Lord, that laboratory is the human body itself. Guru Nanak Sahib says:

> True devotees seek within;
> all others wander in delusion.
> *Gurmukh hovai su kaa-i-aa khojai*
> *hor sabh bharam bhulaaee.*
>
>   Adi Granth, M3, p. 754

Real lovers and devotees of the Lord always turn within to search for Him, whereas everyone else wanders about in ignorance, caught up in their illusions and imaginings. That is why he emphasizes that the Lord lives within our body. In reference to this, Kabir Sahib says:

> As oil is in sesame seeds and fire in flintstone,
> so is your Beloved within you: wake up, if you can.
> *Jyo^n til maahee^n tel hai chakmak maahee^n aagi,*
> *teraa preetam tujh me^n jaagi sake to jaagi.*
>
>   Kabir, *Kabir Sakhi Sangreh*

Just as there is fire in flint, and oil in sesame seeds, so the Supreme Being permeates each one of us. Paltu Sahib says:

> Why are you crying out 'Lord, Lord'—
> the Lord is right there with you!
> *Saahib saahib kyaa kare saahib tere paas.*
>
>   Paltu, *Paltu Sahib ki Bani*, I:39, Kundli

What Lord are you searching for in the forests and mountains? He is with you all the time and goes with you wherever you go. Guru Nanak Sahib says:

> Always with us, think Him not distant,
> the One who created the creation.
> *Sadaa hajoor door nah dekhah rachnaa jin rachaaee.*
>
> Adi Granth, M3, p. 909

The Almighty, who created the whole world, is always with you—present in your body, in your physical being.

Christ also tells his disciples that the kingdom of God lies within them—and this is why they must repent.[26] He says: Repent for your earlier actions, for which you are responsible, and settle their account. God does not live anywhere in the outside world, but right inside you.

If there is a real gurdwara, temple or mosque, it is the human form alone. This is why the rishis and sages chose to call it the human form divine *(nar-naraayani deh)*. The form which God himself has made, in which He lives, and in which the soul can have the privilege of meeting Him—this is none other than the human being. In the Bible it is described as the temple of the living God.[27] Guru Nanak Sahib says explicitly:

> This body is the Lord's temple;
> it is there that the jewel of knowledge is revealed.
> *Har mandar eh sareer hai giaan ratan pargat ho-e.*
>
> Adi Granth, M3, p. 1346

Your body is the real abode of the Lord and if you are ever to find Him, you will find Him there. But we creatures of the world are masters of a strange kind of wisdom. We put together bricks and stones and then start trying to find the

Lord within them, instead of in that place which the Lord made for himself to live in and where He actually resides.

We construct our temples, mosques, churches and gurdwaras so that we can come together to sing his praises; so that when a devotee or beloved of the Lord comes, he can engender within us longing for union with the Lord and explain to us how to reach Him. Then, when we go home, we can search for the Lord within ourselves, we can love and worship the Lord according to the saints' instructions.

We do not construct these buildings with the idea that we will find the Lord just by going to them. We keep them looking so beautiful because it is there that He is honoured and praised, it is there that we are inspired to find Him.

If we take so much care of those places where our love for Him is nurtured, then just think how important it is for us to clean our self, the place where the Lord lives and where we are to attain Him. Yet sometimes we put flesh or liquor in it; sometimes we do the most terrible deeds in spite of living in this precious house; or we hate people or start looking down on them with scorn.

We show respect for what we ourselves have built, but no respect for what the Lord has made.

It makes one feel ashamed that when someone accidentally damages a wall, for example, in a man-made place of worship, we go out and destroy thousands of those beautiful temples of God that the Lord himself has made and embellished. Humans hate humans but love bricks and stones. Then we call ourselves martyrs, upholders of the faith. If we could find God by cutting one another's throats, what could be easier? But our thinking is wrong. One who loves the Lord also loves his creation and all his creatures.

When there is only one Supreme Being, and that One has created all of us alike and lives within each one of us, then if anyone hates another, I say he is hating God. If one race looks upon another with hatred, then that race or religion has not yet developed love and longing for the Lord. Guru Nanak Sahib says:

> All belong to you, O Lord; you belong to all.
> Whom shall we call bad, when there is none other
>   than you?
>
> *Jeea jant sabh tis de sabhnaa kaa soee.*
> *Mandaa kis no aakheeai je doojaa hoee.*
>
> Adi Granth, M3, p. 425

O Supreme Being, you have made all the creatures in the world, and you yourself live in each one of them. I could only speak ill of a being if it were made by someone else, in which some other Supreme Being were to reside.

Just see how high the saints raise our awareness. This is why Tulsi Sahib explains here with such compassion: How sad that we never turn inwards towards the place where the Lord is living, which has been made by Him as his own residence, nor do we keep it clean. But the places we have made for the Lord—we keep dusting and washing them every day, we are always concerned about how clean they are kept, and it is there that we go on searching for Him. How then will we ever attain the Lord?

ॐ

> *Listen intently in the real Ka'aba's arch:*
> *from the highest, a Call is coming, inviting you to return.*
>
> *Kudartee kaabe kee too mahraab me^n sun gaur se.*
> *Aa rahee dhur se sadaa tere bulaane ke liye.*

Because Sheikh Taqi was on his way back from a pilgrimage to Mecca, Tulsi Sahib explains: The Ka'aba you have to visit, the pilgrimage which brings liberation, does not exist anywhere in the outer world. The Lord has already endowed each and every one of us with it. That Ka'aba is our body.

Our pilgrimage will start from the soles of our feet and when we reach the crown of the head, we will have completed it. There is a mosque at the Ka'aba where the priest stands and gives the call to prayer, and people believe that by hearing the call, they will attain liberation. Tulsi Sahib says that, in the same way, our body is the Ka'aba—we must remove the attention from the nine doors of the body and bring it behind the eyes. Here at our forehead is the archway (mehraab) of our own Ka'aba's mosque—archway and forehead have a similar shape. The outer archway is where the priest gives his call, but here in nature's archway is where the supreme Lord gives his unending Call.

Within each person, this most beautiful and sweet Call from the heavens (baang-e-aasmaanee) surges forth from the Lord, from the court of the Lord. This Word of God (kalaam-e-ilaahee) reverberates in everyone. Call it the Word (shabd), the Name (naam), the Melody of God (raam dhun), the Name of God (raam naam)—call it what you like—but as I keep saying, until we attach ourselves to it, we will never be able to detach ourselves from the world and develop love for the Lord and become attached to Him.

As we read in the writings of Guru Nanak Sahib:

> Closing the nine doors,
> one finds liberation at the tenth;
> there ever resonates the limitless melody
> of the Word.

Nao darvaaje dasvai muktaa
anahad sabad vajaavaniaa.
          Adi Granth, M1, p. 110

The pleasures of the senses, our negative tendencies and taste for eating and drinking, all exist below the level of the eyes. The Lord has placed the gateway to liberation *(mukti daa darvaazaa)* between and behind the eyes in each person—a place called the black point *(nuqtaa-e-savaidaa)* by saints in the Muslim tradition. We call it the eye of Shiva *(shiv netra)*, the divine eye *(divya chakshu)*, the door to our home *(ghar dar)*, the third eye or the single eye.

It is here that we must concentrate our attention. It is here behind the eyes that the melody of the Word goes on reverberating within everyone. Until we catch hold of its sound, and our mind sees its light and brilliance, we will never be able to detach ourselves from our love for the world.

I often explain how the different religions have their own codes of conduct and ritualistic practices because they have originated with human beings. But the spirituality in them—the reality, truth, essence or spiritual base—is always the same.

The saints simply awaken in us the desire to attain that spirituality. They try to explain it to us, calling it by many different words. Regardless of whether we are Hindu, Sikh, Muslim or Christian, there is no way we can be freed from the limitations of our physical bodies until we dye ourselves in the colour of that spirituality.

Codes of conduct can support spirituality, they can help to protect it, but they cannot be a substitute for it—they can never take its place. If we have a beautiful picture, we need a beautiful frame to set off the beauty of the picture. To protect it from the elements—the heat and cold, the wind, storms and dust—we need a frame and glass. If there were no picture, what good would a frame be?

If we own precious gold jewellery, we need a beautiful box to keep it safe. If there is no jewellery, what would we do with the box? If we have a sword, we need a scabbard for it. If there is no sword, what good is the scabbard on its own? When the spirituality has gone in a religion, what use is the code of conduct on its own?

It is a sad thing to have to say, but we have already gone far from spirituality, enslaved as we are by our religious practices. This is why the various religions keep on maligning each other, cursing each other, criticizing and despising each other.

If the spirituality were still present, there would be no question of criticism and abuse. The spirituality in each and every religion teaches the same thing: it awakens in us love for the Lord, and reverence for Him, fear of the Lord, so that we are spared from doing wrong or sinful deeds.

But so often the Lord is hardly mentioned, nor are we encouraged to think of Him. People are either hatching political plans or thinking up schemes for cutting each other's throats. This is not the fault of the religion, but of those in positions of power within it. That is why there is no point in only having a code of conduct; unless we also keep the spirituality before us, these codes, on the contrary, turn us into fanatics.

That is why Tulsi Sahib says that until you are able to hear the Shabd, the Call from the heavens, the Kalma—that power which I talk about every day as the Word or Name—you will never be able to extricate your love from the world.

ᕎ

Why wander everywhere in search of your Friend?
The road to your Beloved is through the royal vein.

Kyo^n bhataktaa phir rahaa too eh talaashe yaar me^n.
Raastaa shaah rag me^n hai dilbar pai jaane ke liye.

When saints teach, they never show disrespect to anybody
or speak ill of others, but one has to call a spade a spade when
discussing its worth.

Tulsi Sahib explains compassionately that the Lord exists
within each one of us, and the way to find the Lord also exists within each one of us and nowhere outside. He explains
that it is by travelling the royal vein *(shaah rag)* that one com-
pletes the inner spiritual journey to one's home. By the 'royal
vein' he does not mean a blood vessel in the body. This is a
mystic term referring to a place behind the eyes, which rishis
and sages describe as the channel of bliss *(sushmanaa naadee)*.

He says: Why are you wandering around uselessly in the
outside world? You will achieve nothing from these pilgrimages, from reading scriptures, from recitations and prayers,
or from renouncing your family and hiding away in forests
and mountains. Nothing will be gained by going about with
pierced ears, matted hair, and with ash all over your body.
Do you think the Lord disapproves of unpierced ears, so that
to meet Him you must pierce them? Does He dislike clean
hair, so that to meet Him you must keep it matted? Does He
disapprove of cleanliness, so that you must smear your body
with ash?

However clean or pure water may be, it can only wash
away the dirt on our body. Ask yourself, then, how will water

clean the dirt that has accumulated from our deeds in each life, for lifetimes and lifetimes? Guru Nanak Sahib says:

> This body is the pool of nectar, friends,
> bathe in it with love and devotion.
> They who bathe in the pool of the Name are
>   purified;
> through the Word is all dirt cleansed.
> *Eh sareer sarvar hai santah*
> *isnaan kare liv laaee.*
> *Naam isnaan karah se jan nirmal*
> *sabade mail gavaa-ee.*
>
> Adi Granth, M3, p. 909

Friends, you will find no better pool in the world to bathe in than your own body. Turn within and bathe in this body, if you want to find the Lord. Bathe in the Word, bathe in the Name, by collecting your attention inside, behind the eyes, and attaching it to the Word. That is why they say:

> Within the body lies the real pool of nectar.
> *Kaa-i-aa andar amritsar saachaa.*
>
> Adi Granth, M3, p. 1045

The true pool of nectar—where crows go to bathe and emerge transformed into swans, where the maimed are made whole—is nowhere outside. It is in our body. You will never find such a pool in the outside world where a crow is turned into a swan. It is worldly people who are being described as crows, and once they go there, they are turned into lovers of the Lord. We call them crows because crows eat dirt and filth, and the diet of worldly people is sense pleasures, negative habits, and cravings for food and drink.

So, when we worldly people keep the company of the lovers of the Lord and practise meditation of the Word, we too become gurmukhs, we become pure and worthy of meeting the Lord. We keep looking for Him through external things, so saints tell us that we will achieve nothing that way. Whatever we are to achieve will only be through practice of the Word. They explain:

> By merging into the Shabd, one dies to the self
> and gains everlasting life.
> *Sabad marai so mar rahai fir marai na doojee waar.*
>
> Adi Granth, M1, p. 58

People who remain attached to the Word all the time, wherever they are and whatever they are doing, 'die' once and for all. They never have to come again in the painful cycle of death and rebirth.

Christ says that worship of the Spirit is worship of the Father—no other worship pleases the Father.[28] Whether we call it Spirit, Shabd, the Name, the Word or anything else, this worship alone constitutes true worship, and no other worship is acceptable to God. Two days ago I quoted Soami Ji's words:

> The Master speaks out in clear terms:
> Attach yourself to the unending music of the Word.
> Other than the Word there is no way to break from
>   this mortal clay pot.
> *Guru kahe khol kar bhaaee lag shabd anaahad jaaee,*
> *bin shabd upao na doojaa*
> *kaayaa kaa chhute na koozaa.*
>
> Soami Ji, *Sar Bachan* 20:10, p. 161

The only method by which you can escape from the ties of the body is meditation on the Word—there is no other way. Kabir Sahib says:

> Whenever the Name is fixed in the heart
> all sin is destroyed,
> as dry grass is consumed by the smallest spark
> of fire.
>
> *Jab hee naam hirday dharyo bhayo paap ko naas,*
> *maanau chingee aag kee paree puraane ghaas.*
>
> Kabir, *Kabir Sakhi Sangreh*

It only takes one small spark of fire to reduce a great heap of straw to ash, no matter how much we may have piled up. Similarly for us sinful human beings, no matter how many bad deeds we may have done, our meditation on the Word destroys the entire chain of our karmic debts.

In praise of Nam, Kabir Sahib goes to the extent of saying:

> All praise to the leper, repeating the Name
> though his flesh festers and decays.
> What worth a body, perfect as gold,
> where those lips never know the Name?
>
> *Naam japat khaudhee bhalaa, chui chui parai jo chaam,*
> *kanchan dei kis kaam kee, jaa mukh naahee[n] naam.*
>
> Kabir, *Kabir Sakhi Sangreh*

A leper whom no one will go near, sitting lost in love and devotion for the Lord, is a hundred times better than someone with a 'golden body'—someone adorned with the entire beauty of the world—but who lives oblivious to the Lord. Kabir Sahib says:

> Plunder and amass, if you can, O friend,
> plunder the booty of God's Name;
> otherwise you will be sorry
> when you discard this physical frame.
>
> *Looti sakai tau looti le, raam naam hai looti,*
> *paachhe phiri pachhitahuge praan jaayenge chhooti.*
>
> Kabir, *Kabir Granthavali*[29]

If there is anything to be 'plundered' during our life in this human form, it is the Lord's love and devotion alone. Without this, we will inevitably be filled with regret at the time of death, realizing that we have wasted our precious time on a worthless illusion.

Saints say that only meditation on the Word will bring you anything. Do not waste your time wandering through life with no purpose, do not wear yourself out searching here and there. The Lord has kept everything you need within you, and whatever you are to attain, you will attain it from within yourself.

∾

With patience and love, meet a perfect Master, O Taqi;
he will give you the wisdom to find the royal vein.

Murshid-e-kaamil se mil sidaq aur saboori se taqee.
Jo tujhe degaa phaham shaah rag ke paane ke liye.

When does our attention extricate itself from these outward rituals and practices, from these illusions and misgivings? Tulsi Sahib says it is when we meet a perfect Master, a perfect saint, a devotee of the Supreme Being. He will sever us from these illusions. So search for such a saint, believe in him and have faith in him. He will explain how to make the spiritual journey right here, within our body, and how to reach our home by going from one stage to the next.

These stages are not far away. They are within the body. We must keep our objective before our eyes and search for that specific destination. We must complete our spiritual journey so that the aim and purpose of achieving this human life is fulfilled.

∾

Practise for some time and the inner ear will open to take you to Allah-hu-Akbar, the One without another.

Gosh-e-baatin ho kushaadaa jo kare kuchh din amal.
Laa ilaah allaahoo akbar pai jaane ke liye.

𝓗e says that if we put into practice the method explained to us by the saints, if we work to join the soul with the Word *(surat shabd abhyaas)* and meditate on the Name in the way they tell us, then our inner ears and eyes will open. The reverberating melody of the Call from the heavens, God's Word, which Tulsi Sahib mentioned earlier, and the light and brilliance which is referred to by the saints, cannot be heard or seen with these outer ears and eyes. Those are different ears within us with which we hear the sound of the Shabd, and different eyes with which we see its light.

That is why he lovingly says that if we do our meditation in the way the saints explain, and join our attention to the Shabd through simran and dhyan, our inner eyes and ears will open. We will start hearing the sound of the Shabd within us and seeing its light.

The sound is not outside. It vibrates in each one of us here behind the eyes, where the light, too, projects its brilliance. It goes on constantly, throughout the twenty-four hours, day and night. When our mind reaches this level, we see it; but when it goes downwards, we see only darkness. It is not the light that comes and goes, but we who come and go. In reference to this, Christ says:

> Having eyes ye see not, having ears ye hear not.
>
> Mark 8:18

In spite of these eyes and ears, we cannot see the light or hear the Call from the heavens. Guru Nanak Sahib also says:

> Seeing without eyes, hearing without ears,
> walking without feet, working without hands,
> speaking without tongue, thus dying while living,
> O Nanak, comprehending this divine Law
> shalt thou be able to merge in the Lord.
> *Akhee baajhah vekhnaa vin kan-naa sun-naa.*
> *Pairaa baajhah chalanaa vin hathaa karnaa.*
> *Jeebhai baajhah bolnaa io jeevat marnaa.*
> *Naanak hukam pachhaan kai tao khasmai milnaa.*
>
> Adi Granth, M2, p. 139

When you contact the divine Law, the Word, then you will find your Beloved who has never been seen with these outer eyes, heard with these ears, described with this tongue, written of with these hands, or approached by these feet. You can only attain Him by dying while living.

Dying while living means withdrawing the attention from the nine doors of the body and collecting it behind the eyes. The Muslim scriptures also say: learn to die before your death (*Mautu qabal aan tamutu*),[30] if you want to live forever. And

Saint Paul says, "I die daily."[31] Similarly, Guru Nanak Sahib says:

> If one serves the Satguru, dirt is removed;
> dying while living, one unites with God.
> *Satgur seve taa mal jaae.*
> *Jeevat marai har sio chit laae.*
>
> Adi Granth, M3, p. 116

Learn to die while living if you really want to love the Lord.

It is called dying while living because whenever anyone dies, first the feet and then the legs go cold while the soul is still in the body and the person may still be conscious. Once the attention collects behind the eyes, it leaves the body and passes on, and we say the person has died.

In the same way, saints say that through simran and dhyan, we are to collect the attention behind the eyes while living, if we want to hear the sound and see the light of the Word. Our inner eyes and ears then open, and as a result we are able to make our inner spiritual journey.

This stage of which he is now speaking is referred to by rishis and sages as *Sahasradal Kamal* because their language is Sanskrit. Tulsi Sahib, on the other hand, because he is using Arabic terms to speak to Sheikh Taqi, calls it *Allah-hu-Akbar*. Everyone has to pass through the same stages or levels on the inner spiritual journey before they reach their home. Arab and Persian mystics give them Arabic and Persian names; Indian mystics use Sanskrit.

If you are travelling by train from here in Jaipur to Delhi, the stations will be the same, whether you refer to them in English, Hindi, Persian or Arabic—the stations will not change. Similarly, the stages on the spiritual journey are always the same; it is just a question of language that we give them different names.

By catching onto the sound and watching the light, we reach the first stage, and then gradually, stage by stage, we begin the journey towards our home.

 споро

This is Tulsi's call: heed it, O practitioner, and act on it!
The Kun of the Qur'an, it is written, will take you to
Allah-hu-Akbar.

Yaha sadaa tulsee kee hai aamil amal kar dhyaan de.
Kun kuraan men hai likhaa allahu akbar ke liye.

*H*e ends by saying that what he has tried to explain is not something he has heard from others. He is speaking from his own personal experience. No saint speaks from hearsay. Dadu Sahib says:

> With his own eyes, Dadu has seen,
> whereas people tell what they hear.
> *Daadoo dekhaa deedaa sab koee kahat shuneedaa.*
> <div align="right">Dadu, <i>Santon ki Bani</i>[32]</div>

Others speak from hearsay, but I tell you only what I have seen with my own eyes. Guru Nanak Sahib says:

> There is no worship comparable to that of
>   God's Name;
> this I have realized after careful personal
>   experience.
> *Harnaamai tul na pujaee sabh dithee thok vajaae.*
> Adi Granth, M1, p. 62

There is nothing that can be compared with devotion to the Word. I myself have tested everything and I am telling you from my personal experience.

That is why Tulsi Sahib is saying: O Sheikh Taqi, whatever I am saying is from my own experience. If you act upon it, you will understand what Prophet Muhammad means by the term *Kun* when he explains in the Qur'an that the creation was made by the Kun. Call it the Kalma, call it the Kun, in the end it is into that Kun, that Word or Name, that everything has to merge.

So, as I said at the beginning, in these past three days I have referred to many different saints simply to show that they all have one message, that their teaching is the same. We should therefore try to avoid these petty arguments about nation, caste and creed. Rather, we should grasp the real message of the saints and nurture it, in order to join our attention to the true Shabd within us.

5

Among Your Companions, None Is Your Friend:
A Warning

Mitra teraa koee nahee^n sangiyan me^n:
Chitaavanee

Among your companions, none is your friend.
Why keep on sleeping among these swindlers?
Wake up and put your heart in satsang;
the Master will then dye you in the Name beyond colour.
Wealth and possessions will be of no use to you;
you will leave them in a second and depart.
Before you lies the darkest of nights;
attend to your work while the daylight lasts.
You will not get this human form again;
you will wander, lost in the forest of chaurasi.
Please your Master by serving him;
now is the time to adopt this way.
Apart from the Master, none is your friend;
engrave these words in your heart and mind.
Do not get caught in the net of this world;
stay absorbed in devotion day and night.
Mark well the words of the true Master:
live detached, filled with yearning, in the world.
Abandon the ways of deceit and cunning—
why let yourself sink to this low state?
Keep your mind in simran and serve your Master;
rise today to the spiritual sky!
Death will otherwise determine your tomorrows:
you will roast in the fires of hell.
Understand this now and make no delay.
Who knows even what will happen next?
Thus explaining, Radha Soami declares:
one instruction should be enough!

Soami Ji, *Sar Bachan* 15:5, p. 116

Mitra teraa koee nahee^n sangiyan me^n,
paraa kyo^n sove in thagiyan me^n.
Chet kar preet karo satsang me^n,
guroo phir rang de^n naam arang me^n.
Dhan sampat tere kaam na aave,
chhor chalo yaha chhin me^n.
Aage rain andheree bhaaree,
kaaj karo kuchh din me^n.
Yaha dehee phir haath na aave,
phiro chauraasee ban me^n.
Guru sevaa kar guroo rijhaao,
aao tum is dhang me^n.
Guru bin teraa aur na koee,
dhaar bachan yaha man me^n.
Jagat jaal me^n pha^{n}so na bhaaee,
nis din raho bhajan me^n.
Saadh guroo kaa kahanaa maano,
raho udaas jagat me^n.
Chhal bal chhoro aur chaturaaee,
kyo^n tum paro kugati me^n.
Sumiran karo guroo ko sevo,
chal raho aaj gagan me^n.
Kal kee khabar kaal phir legaa,
vahaa^n tum jalo agin me^n.
Abahee samajh der mat kariyo,
naa jaanoo^n kyaa hoy is pan me^n.
Yo^n samjhaay kahe^n raadhaaswaamee,
maano ek bachan me^n.

Soami Ji, *Sar Bachan Radhaswami, Chhand Band*
(Beas: Radha Soami Satsang Beas), p. 116:15:5

Among your companions, none is your friend.
Why keep on sleeping among these swindlers?

Mitra teraa koee nahee^n sangiyan me^n,
paraa kyo^n sove in thagiyan me^n.

𝐹or this satsang,* I am taking my text from the writings of
Soami Ji Maharaj. Soami Ji explains that everything we see
with our eyes—the world, the whole creation—is a vast
prison, the prison of chaurasi. To escape from this prison, the
Supreme Being has provided only one door. And what is this
door? It is the human form.

We are living as prisoners in this jail because of our previous actions: our karmas, our desires, our longings. The
world is a field of karmas, a field where we harvest the consequences of actions we ourselves have sown.[33] Because we are
dominated by our mind, we have to keep coming back into
the prison of chaurasi to experience the results of each and
every action we do, irrespective of whether those actions are
good or bad.

When we do good deeds, we come back to the world to
enjoy their pleasant results. When we do bad ones, we suffer
unpleasant results. We cannot free ourselves from the ties of
the physical body by doing good actions, nor can we escape
the pain and suffering of the cycle of death and rebirth by
doing bad ones.

---

* *See* Glossary and Translators' Note for explanations of unusual usage, and technical or Indian-language terms, such as: satsang, prison of chaurasi.

If we do good deeds, what is the result? We may come to the world as millionaires, royalty or rulers. We may become leaders in our communities, religions or countries. At best, we may go to a paradise or one of the lower heavens—but even there we will be given a form of life with no free will *(bhog jooniaa*^{n}*)* and for a certain time only. And then again we will have to return here to the prison of chaurasi. If we do bad deeds, then hell and the endless cycle of transmigration stand ever ready to welcome us.

King or subject, rich or poor, woman or man, every soul in the world is here to pay for its own actions. And it is because of our actions that we all have to suffer and face problems, as we know from our own experience—irrespective of the particular life form we are given. No physical form exists in which we can find only peace and happiness.

It is not possible for us to imagine what it is like to live in the lower forms of life, nor can words describe it. But we are in a position to talk about the human form, described by Indian sages as the body in which God resides *(nar-naraayani deh)*, and which we refer to as the top of the creation *(ashraf-ul-makhluqaat)*. What peace or happiness can be experienced living in this form? We do not get a moment's rest from the tensions and conflicts of race, religion and nation. How many unfortunate people are killed, how many women widowed, how many children orphaned! What life form can there be that brings happiness and peace in a world where people have to suffer and struggle just to secure their basic needs of food and clothing? Soami Ji says:

> Listen to me, dear soul,
> your Husband lives in the regions above.
> *Surat sun baat ree, teraa dhanee base aakaash.*
>
> Soami Ji, *Sar Bachan* 19:6, p. 145

O soul, your Husband is the Lord, the Supreme Being. He is present in Sach Khand, the everlasting realm, while you are entangled in this web of illusion. You will only experience fulfilment and feel complete when you return home and are free from the suffering of death and rebirth.

It is for this reason that saints awaken within us love for the Lord and the desire for union with Him. Soami Ji explains that a human birth is given to us by the Lord as an opportunity to love Him and worship Him. He writes:

> Now you have this human body,
> do something for yourself.
> Don't toil vainly in this world—
> it is only a passing dream.
> Both body and home are unreal;
> why exhaust yourself over an illusion?
> *Milee nar deh yaha tumko,*
> *banaao kaaj kuchh apnaa,*
> *pacho mat aai is jag me^n,*
> *jaaniyo rain kaa supnaa,*
> *deh aur greh sab jhoothaa,*
> *bharm me^n kahe ko khapnaa.*
> Soami Ji, *Sar Bachan* 15:13, p. 121

This human form has been bestowed on us by the Lord so that we can do our real work. And what is our real work? It is any activity that frees us from the prison of the body and re-unites us with the Lord. Soami Ji says that our body is not real—it will leave us. Indeed, the creation, the world we see around us, is equally unreal—it is transient and perishable. Everything is illusory; there is nothing real about it, for all of it will come to an end. Guru Nanak Sahib says:

The body is like a township, a beauteous township,
where the bargain of God's nectar may be struck.
Kaa-i-aa nagar nagar hai neeko wich saodaa har ras keejai.

Adi Granth, M3, p. 1323

He describes the human body as a very beautiful town
because, while living in it, we are able to strike the ultimate
bargain—God. The one real bargain we can get in the human
form is love and devotion for the Lord and union with Him.
Saints therefore teach us that if we wish to fulfil the purpose
of being given a human life, we should take full advantage of
this opportunity, keep our objective clearly before our eyes,
search for our destination, and thus complete our spiritual
journey.

However, when the Lord does give us the opportunity
of a human birth, we completely forget its real purpose. We
get caught up in love for our children, and in issues of race,
religion and nation. We get trapped by our appetite for the
pleasures of the senses. We feel so restless for wealth and possessions, we are such slaves of our desires and cravings, that
we forget that one day we will die. This is in spite of seeing
our friends and relations dying every day.

We accompany our friends one after another to the cre-
matorium or the cemetery and see for ourselves that they all
leave the world empty-handed. Of all the possessions they
accumulated, they could take nothing with them, and yet we
do not stop to ask ourselves what we will be able to take with
us. Guru Nanak Sahib says:

Everyone is caught up in worldly activities;
no thought is given to finding a solution.
Man remains oblivious to the cycle of
    birth and death,

being foolish and ignorant under the sway
of his mind.

Dhandhai dhaavat jag baadhiaa
naa boojhai weechaar.
Jamman maran wisaariaa
manmukh mugadh gavaar.

Adi Granth, M1, p. 1010

How obsessed and foolish we are, so completely dominated by the mind. We spend all our time restlessly running
around just to satisfy our physical appetites. We are forever
dissatisfied and unhappy because of our attachment to the
forms and images of the creation. Our own house is on fire,
but we are not aware of it and have never tried to put it out.
Instead, we busy ourselves worrying about extinguishing the
fires in other people's houses. We cannot lift our own load,
but we have made ourselves into beasts of burden for others.
Our own houses are being robbed, and yet we are busy guarding other people's. We deceive ourselves and we deceive the
world.

Soami Ji explains that we will not get this opportunity
again and again; it is vital therefore that everyone should
search for the Lord and worship Him.

He tells us that the people we associate with throughout
our lives—our children, spouse, brothers, sisters, friends and
other relatives—are not really helping us. None of them are
really related to us. None of them belong to us. All will leave
us in the end. They have taken on these particular roles out
of self-interest; if there was no self-interest connecting us,
they would not even bother about us. Trapped by such love
and attachment, we are lulled to sleep. And what is this sleep?
That we are oblivious of why the Lord has given us the opportunity of a human life.

Soami Ji shakes us awake from this state of careless oblivion when he says: Just think of the moment of your death—who will come to help you then? Who will give you support? Not your relatives and friends, on whose behalf you so often deceive, dishonour and sacrifice your most precious values. They do not even know where the agents of Death have come from, nor where they are taking you. What help can people possibly give you when they do not even know where you have come from and where you are going?

Your real friend, supporter and relative is someone who cares about your well-being and has your best interests at heart; not these people, who are concerned with their own well-being and their own advantage. They are not concerned in the least about your interests or what is beneficial for you.

There are three kinds of people whose one aim is that we should be deprived forever of our true self, our true wealth: the thief, the robber (dacoit), and the swindler (thug). Thieves try to break in when the owner of the house is not at home or is fast asleep, so that they can gather up the contents and take them away. Robbers do not care whether we are at home or not. They threaten us at knife point or with a gun to our head, ignore our screams, and rob us of our belongings by force. Swindlers befriend us, gain our confidence and win our trust—we willingly and happily give them everything with our own hands. Once they have gone, we wake up, we come to our senses and realize that we have been deceived and robbed.

That is why Soami Ji says that the people you think of as being close to you are cheating you. They keep you so entangled by love and attachment for them throughout your life that you do not wake up until the agents of Death stand before your eyes and give the order: "Come on, let's go!"

Who will help us at that moment? Who is able to help us? Guru Nanak Sahib says:

> Except Nam, you have no friend or companion.
> *Bin naavai ko sang na saathee.*
>
> Adi Granth, M1, p. 109

Apart from what we have earned through our practice of the Name, nothing and no one will give us any support, will go with us or will help us. Regardless of the property and possessions we accumulate, the progeny we produce and the fame and reputation we establish, in the end we have to go alone. No one can help us then.

Soami Ji tries to arouse us from our state of oblivion, warning us not to stay entangled all our life in this web of love and attachment. We must give some thought to the purpose for which the Lord has given us the opportunity of a human birth. Guru Nanak Sahib says:

> He who slips on this rung of the ladder
> suffers in the wheel of birth and death.
> *Is paoree te jo nar chookai so aae jaae dukh paa-idaa.*
>
> Adi Granth, M5, p. 1075

The human form is the top rung of a ladder, the very last step on the stairs. We can reach the roof of the house from here, if we try.* But if our foot slips on this last step, we will fall right to the bottom, despite having got so close to the top. If we are steadfast and achieve union with the Lord through

---

* Traditional Indian houses have a flat roof with a parapet, used as a sunny place to work and rest in winter days, and as a cool sleeping area on hot summer nights.

devotion, we can escape forever from the bonds of the physical body and from the pain and misery of death and rebirth. If we want to go on being trapped by our love for our children and families, by our destructive tendencies, negative habits and sensual appetites, then we will have to keep coming back into the prison of chaurasi to undergo the consequences. Kabir Sahib says:

> Rare is the human birth,
> it occurs not again and again;
> like ripe fruit once fallen
> cannot be rejoined to its branch.
> *Kabeer maanas janam dulambh hai*
> *ho-e na baarai baar.*
> *Jio ban fal paake bhue girah*
> *bahur na laagah daar.*
>
> Kabir, Adi Granth, p. 1366

Just as we cannot attach a ripened fruit to a tree once it has fallen, however hard we may try, similarly, if we allow this opportunity to pass through our hands, we will not get it again and again. Saints warn us, therefore, never to lose sight of the purpose of this God-given opportunity of human life. Soami Ji advises us:

> From this home, go to that home.
> *Is ghar se us ghar jaavo.*
>
> Soami Ji, *Sar Bachan* 20:10, p. 161

As long as the Lord gives you the opportunity of living in 'this home', you should keep searching for your true home, since this one, the human body, is only a temporary residence—Kal's cage, a rented house belonging to someone else.

Some people are given this home for fifty or sixty years, others for seventy or eighty years. When we have exhausted the number of breaths allotted to us by the Lord, each of us must vacate it and move on, leaving it here to be burned or buried in the ground. By 'that home' he means the home of the Supreme Being. Once we reach it, we will never again have to come back into the creation and inhabit any other home.

As long as we are blessed with the human form, Soami Ji says, we must search for this true home, the home where the Lord himself lives. Going there will free us forever from the bonds of a physical form, the pain of death and rebirth, and the prison of chaurasi—the endless wheel of transmigration.

That is why Soami Ji says: Take your attention away from those whose love traps you in the creation. Search for the Lord and devote yourself to Him.

಼

Wake up and put your heart in satsang;
the Master will then dye you in the Name beyond colour.

Chet kar preet karo satsang me^n,
guroo phir rang de^n naam arang me^n.

When can we learn what is real in these worldly relationships, and in the images and forms of the creation? Soami Ji says: When we go into the presence of the lovers of the Lord, when we are blessed with the satsang of the Masters, it is then that we discover how we are connected to everything by relationships of giving and taking, and how our 'love' is based on self-interest. We will come to understand the relationship between the soul and the Lord, the supreme soul, the barrier that separates them, and why the Lord has bestowed on us this covering of a human form. Guru Nanak Sahib says:

> When the Satguru wishes to shatter the chains
>   of attachment,
> he places those souls in the company of saints
> and immerses them in his love.
> *Jin ke bandhan kaate satgur*
> *tin saadh sangat liv laaee.*
>
> Adi Granth, M5, p. 205

Whenever a perfect Master wishes to guide souls towards union with the Lord, the first thing he does is to bring them into his presence, his satsang. By attending the satsang of saints we learn what is real. We come to realize that this creation, which we take to be real and are busy trying to possess, is transient and perishable.

Even the richest and most powerful people—millionaires, royalty, dictators—depart from the world empty-handed, in spite of trying their best to own it. When they have to leave with nothing, how then do we think we can make any of these things ours? It is in the satsang of the Masters that we gain a true perspective on all these things.

The saints explain to us that our soul is part of the supreme soul, that we are drops of the ocean of the true Name. Separated from the Lord, we have taken the mind as our companion and are enmeshed in this web of illusion. Whatever actions we perform under the domination of the mind force us to come back again and again into this prison of chaurasi to undergo the consequences. Until the account of these karmic debts is settled, it is impossible for any of us to escape from the imprisonment of the body and the unending pain of transmigration.

It is our worldly love and attachments that keep dragging us back to the body. Guru Nanak Sahib says:

> In illusion and attachment, the entire world is
> asleep.
> Tell me, how will this deception be removed?
> *Maa-i-aa moh sabho jag soiaa*
> *ih bharm kahah kio jaaee.*
>
> Adi Granth, M5, p. 205

In this creation, all living things are entangled in the web of illusion (maya), sleeping the sweet sleep of attachment. They are so caught up in delusion that whatever they see, they take to be real. Guru Nanak Sahib says:

> The false are in love with the false
> and have forgotten their Creator;
> whom to love and make one's friend
> when the whole world is in a state of flux?
> *Koor koorai nehu lagaa wisariaa kartaar.*
> *Kis naal keechai dostee sabh jag chalanhaar.*
>
> Adi Granth, M1, p. 468

Our physical body is false because we have to leave it here; the worldly love and attachments that we get involved in while living in this body are just as false, because they also are temporary and will dissolve. That which is unreal is caught up all the time in its attachment to that which is also unreal, so we remain oblivious of the Lord. Guru Sahib says: Look carefully at the whole creation. Nothing is worthy of your love, devotion or friendship except the one Lord. We realize this after we go to the satsang of the Masters and spend time in their company.

How do the Masters detach us from our love for the creation? How do they awaken in us love for the Lord, devotion to Him and longing for Him? Soami Ji tells us:

> The Master will then dye you in the Name beyond
>   colour.

They explain to us the technique for listening to the Word, the method of meditating on the Name. Guru Sahib says:

> Through the Guru's Word,
> one is immersed in Truth.
> *Gursabdee sachee liv laae.*
>   Adi Granth, M3, p. 115

When we meditate on the Word according to the instructions of the Master, false love for this false world leaves us, and true love and longing for the true Lord develop within us. But until we go to a perfect Master and meditate on the Name, we cannot free ourselves from our attachment to this creation, nor can we develop love for the Lord. That is why devotees and lovers of the Lord, the saints and perfect Masters, explain this technique for meditating on the Name.

If you examine the writings of any saint, you will find that they all praise the Name, in verse after verse and page after page. The Name they praise is not a written word, but the creative power that gave birth to the entire creation and supports all the countless regions and universes.

This creative power permeates each one of us—every particle is dyed in its hue. Soami Ji speaks of it as the melodious Name *(dhunaatmak naam)*, to distinguish it from the names we use in our love for God, such as Allah, Wahiguru, Hari Om, Radha Soami, the Supreme Being and Almighty God.

These he describes as attributive *(varnaatmak)* words, because they can be written, read and spoken.

Consider how many countries there are in the world, and how many languages and dialects are spoken in each country, and in each language how many names and words are used to remember God. Countless saints have come to the world and have remembered the Lord with countless names. Countless saints are yet to come and they too will remember the Lord with countless other names. We keep on forgetting the names given by saints from earlier times and, out of our love, we keep on giving Him more and more new names. These are all descriptive or attributive names.

A mother uses many terms of endearment for her child when she is moved by love, but this does not make the relationship between the mother and child one of words. It is a relationship of devotion and love. She can express her love using any words she likes. Similarly, the relationship of the soul with the supreme soul is not one of words—it is all devotion, love, and more love. That is what saints refer to as the melodious Name *(dhunaatmak naam)*, the true eternal Word. This true Name is present in our bodies; it is to be found within this physical frame.

Our spiritual journey begins at the soles of the feet and ends at the crown of the head. There are two stages in the journey: the first is up to the eyes, the second is above the eyes. For each one of us, the seat of the soul and mind in the body is behind the eyes, at a place Soami Ji calls the tenth window *(dasvee khirkee)*. The other nine windows or doors of the body open outwards, whereas the tenth window opens inwards.

Through the technique of simran and dhyan explained to us by the Masters, we have to collect our scattered attention, reverse its outward flow, and focus it at the eye centre or tenth window. Then we will automatically realize that the Name, that sweet and most melodious sound emanating from the court of the Lord, is present in everyone—in thieves and swindlers, in saints and enlightened beings. The question of race, religion or nationality does not arise.

Anyone who is blessed with the good fortune of being able to make the attention one-pointed at the eye centre, whether Hindu, Sikh, Christian or of any other faith, will hear the melodious resonance of the Word ringing within, and will see the light, the brilliance of the Word, inside. By following this melody *(dhun),* this voice *(aavaaz),* this pure sound *(nirmal naad),* we establish the direction we must follow to reach our home within. By the radiance of its light we travel the inner journey, so that stage by stage, region by region, we finally arrive back home.

The Word, the Name that is praised by the saints, has both sound and light within itself. Guru Sahib is speaking of this when he says:

> Within me is the light of the Word
> from which music arises continuously;
> it is through this that I am attached in love to the
>   true Lord.
> *Antar jot nirantar baanee saache saahib sio liv laaee.*
> Adi Granth, M1, p. 634

A light is shining within each one of us behind the eyes, and a sweet melodious music emanates from its light. Those who see that light and listen to that sound, escape from the false love and attachments of the world, and in their place true love and attachment for the true Being are born. It is the Word, the true Name, that detaches us from the world and awakens love for God within us. It is present in everyone without exception, regardless of background, character, or belief.

Soami Ji explains that before we came into the presence or the satsang of the Masters, we were dyed in worldly colours: our love for our children and family; our involvement with our race, religion and nation; our enjoyment of meat and drink; our obsession with wealth and property. Once we come to the satsang of a Master and practise meditation on the Word, the colours of the world fade away and we are dyed instead in the colour of love and devotion for the Lord. The first Padshahi says:

> Bliss comes to the soul when it hears God's Word;
> the essence of joy is to be dyed in God's hue.
> *Sabad surat sukh oopajai prabh raatao sukh saar.*
>
> Adi Granth, M1, p. 62

When we attend to the practice of uniting the soul with the Word, we become imbued with the colour of devotion for the Lord, dyed in the hue of his love, and we experience our first taste of true happiness. That is why Soami Ji says we need to go to the Masters, the lovers of the Lord, and meditate on the Word.

❧

*Wealth and possessions will be no use to you;
you will leave them in a second and depart.*

Dhan sampat tere kaam na aave, chhor chalo yaha chhin me[n].

Soami Ji explains how nothing that we think of as ours in the world, such as family and friends, fame and prestige, or wealth and possessions, will be of any help to us in the end. We are separated from them by death without even a

moment's notice. Our relationship with them is a karmic in-
terchange of giving and taking; our love for them is motivated
by self-interest. Some people come as wives, sons or daughters, some as friends, some as husbands. We stay together as
long as any debt is outstanding; the moment an account is
settled, we go our separate ways.

No one has ever accompanied another to the next world,
nor can anyone ever do so. Actors, once on stage, play out
their particular roles. One has the role of king, one of queen,
one of villain, but as soon as they leave the stage they cease to
be king, queen and villain.

Similarly, saints describe this world as a vast stage; according to our actions in previous lives, each one of us is acting
out a role. In the process of playing our part, however, we
forget that these relationships are based on karmic debts and
obligations, that our love is selfish love. Believing our friends
and relatives to be ours, we try to possess them. We cannot
own them, but the very business of trying to possess them
brings us nothing but pain and sorrow. It is our love for them
that keeps dragging us back to the captivity of the body.

If we look at our own lives we see that some family members have already left us and passed on, while we ourselves are
preparing to leave others behind. Anyone who has watched
pieces of wood floating down a river will have noticed how
one current brings them all together, and then another disperses them. It is the same with worldly relationships. Guru
Nanak Sahib says:

> Mother, father, are transient relationships,
> an affliction of the body;
> afflicted is the entire family.
> *Maat pitaa maa-i-aa deh se rogee rogee kutamb sanjogee.*
> Adi Granth, M1, p. 1153

Of all our relatives, we are most indebted to our mother and father. They gave birth to us, took care of us and nurtured us; they accepted criticism, pain and troubles on our behalf. Yet even they, Guru Nanak Sahib explains, cannot help us or support us in any way. They have brought their own karmic destiny with them into this world and we have brought ours. Unquestionably it is through them that we have taken birth, but this does not mean we can possess them, nor can they make us theirs. In the same way, we give birth to our children, but they never belong to us, nor we to them.

Our relationship with each one of them is the result of a debt, an obligation of giving and taking, and our love is selfish. When even our bodies do not belong to us, what can we possibly make our own in the creation? Guru Sahib says:

> Apart from the Lord, my friends, everything is
>   impure.
> *Har bin sabh kichh mailaa santah.*
>
> Adi Granth, M3, p. 910

Apart from the Lord, everything is impure, everything is false. Everything will pass away, everything will perish. Nothing, absolutely nothing, will help us in the end. Take, for instance, these large properties, mansions and estates that we carefully register in our names. Is it likely that our children will allow them to stay registered in our names, when we ourselves have not allowed them to remain registered in someone else's name? Just look through the land register. We acquire these things here and we have to leave them here.

That is why Soami Ji pointedly asks who it is that we love; who and what holds us entangled in love and attachment? The rich and powerful leave their property and possessions in just a fraction of a second, and at death we too will have to leave everything in exactly the same way. As long as the Lord gives us life in a human form, we should make use of the opportunity to fulfil our real purpose.

❧

Before you lies the darkest of nights;
attend to your work while the daylight lasts.

Aage rain andheree bhaaree, kaaj karo kuchh din me^n.

Soami Ji explains that after death we go on alone. We are surrounded by the darkness of ignorance; we cannot see the way; we bear a heavy load of sins on our head; we have no friend to guide us out of the darkness; we stumble around lost. He therefore instructs us:

Attend to your work while the daylight lasts.

What is the daylight? It is our human life. The Lord gave us this opportunity so that we can dispel the darkness of ignorance, search for a companion for the spiritual journey, and lighten the load we are carrying by settling our karmic debts. He gave us this chance so that we can travel on the spiritual path and search for our true destination. He emphasizes that this is our one chance; each of us should take full advantage of it because we will not be given such an opportunity time and again. He keeps warning us, "Attend to your work while the daylight lasts", because no work can be done in the dark.

If we have to make a journey through a forest at night, we will make all the arrangements during the day. We get a torch, make sure we have a strong stick, and look for a guide who is familiar with the paths through the forest; only then will it be possible to travel in the dark. If we wait until nighttime, we will not be able to find the torch, batteries and walking stick, we will not find our guide, and we will not be able to see the path, so we will end up stumbling around lost in the forest.

Soami Ji reminds us that now is the time to drive the darkness away, the time to pursue our objective, the time to return to our true home—and this opportunity does not come again and again.

∽

You will not get this human form again;
you will wander, lost in the forest of chaurasi.

Yaha dehee phir haath na aave, phiro chauraasee ban me^n.

Soami Ji repeatedly comes back to the same point to stop us from thinking that when we die, we will automatically be re-born as humans. Who knows whether we will or not? We may be born in a situation in which our thoughts cannot possibly turn towards devotion for the Lord. We need only look about us to see how many nations, religions and peoples are devoid of true devotion for the Lord.

Soami Ji keeps emphasizing this message: Now is your chance to worship the Lord and search for Him. There is no point in being filled with regret at the time of death.

∽

Please your Master by serving him;
now is the time to adopt this way.

Guru sevaa kar guroo rijhaao, aao tum is dhang me^n.

Soami Ji explains that we should serve the Master in such a way that we please him. By service he does not mean that we should give him our wealth, or put our land in his name, or massage his feet and legs when he is tired.* To serve the Master means to live our lives according to his teachings. It means withdrawing our attention from the nine doors of the body through simran and dhyan, bringing it to the eye centre, and joining it with the Shabd, the Word. Guru Nanak Sahib says:

> Dirt is removed if one serves the Satguru;
> dying while living, one unites with God.
> *Satgur seve taa mal jaae. Jeevat marai har sio chit laae.*
> Adi Granth, M3, p. 116

It is by serving the Master that the dirt of the mind is removed. But what is that service? It is dying while living *(jeende jee marnaa)*. This is love for the Lord. This is service of the Master. Dying while living means withdrawing our consciousness from the nine doors of the body through simran and dhyan and then joining it with the Word. This is real service to the Master. We please the Master and also benefit ourselves through such service. It is we who get the benefit, but we also enjoy the Master's pleasure.

When a sapling that a gardener has planted bears fruit he is very pleased, even though it is the owner who will eat the fruit, not the gardener. The gardener is happy just watching the fruit ripen on the tree. Similarly, when the Master who puts us on the path sees us attending to our meditation, he is happy, even though the benefit comes to us. Soami Ji says:

> Now is the time to adopt this way.

---

* It is customary for younger members of an Indian family to serve their elders by massaging the muscles of their legs and feet when they are tired.

This is the way we must do our meditation, this is the way we must practise the Word.

∾

Apart from the Master, none is your friend;
engrave these words in your heart and mind.

Guru bin teraa aur na koee, dhaar bachan yaha man me^n.

Soami Ji warns us that other than the Lord we have no one in the whole world whom we can call our own. All those who are close to us, who we think of as ours, stay close to us only as long as it suits them. The moment they cannot get what they want, even sons will refuse to acknowledge their fathers, and wives their husbands.

If you put honey on your finger for a small baby, it will go on sucking happily as long as the taste of the honey lasts. The moment the sweetness disappears, the infant will dig its sharp little teeth right into your finger with great zest. This is the nature of worldly relationships. As long as their interests are being served, everyone tries to be as close to us as possible, all jostling with one another to be the closest. When there is nothing left to gain, or they see that their expectations will not be fulfilled, then they start biting us, just like the baby.

Soami Ji cautions us by asking us whose love we are entangled in; whom are we attached to? If anyone can really be said to belong to us, it is the one Supreme Being. We can only possess something that is really ours. We cannot possess those who do not belong to us. Thinking of them as ours, we keep trying to possess them, but we never try to possess the One who really belongs to us.

The devotees of the Lord, those who are beloved of Him, are also ours because it is through them that the Lord becomes ours. Guru Nanak Sahib says:

> The Lord's servant is like unto the Lord;
> do not think him to be different because of his
>   human frame …
> *Har kaa sevak so har jehaa.*
> *Bhed na jaanah maanas dehaa.*
>
> Adi Granth, M5, p. 1076

Through love and devotion, the devotees and lovers of the Lord assume the form of their Beloved. Nothing remains between the two to distinguish the one from the other. What is the nature of their relationship to the Lord?

> … just as a myriad waves rise from the ocean,
> and then subside, merging back into its depths.
> *Jio jal tarang uthah bahubhaatee*
> *phir salalai salal samaa-idaa.*
>
> Adi Granth, M5, p. 1076

Just as waves rise from the surface of the ocean for a few moments and then merge back into the ocean, so are the Masters, the lovers of the Lord, related to the Supreme Being.

If we surrender something to a wave, it is lifted and carried by the wave into the depths of the ocean. Similarly, if we surrender ourselves to the devotees of the Lord, they take us with them to merge in the ocean of the true Name. Soami Ji says:

> Radha Soami has assumed the human form
>   in this world;
> He comes as a Master and awakens souls.

Raadhaaswaamee dharaa nar roop jagat me^n,
guru hoi jeev chitaaye.

Soami Ji, *Sar Bachan* 1:2, p. 6

The perfect Lord has come as a human being and has himself awakened within us the desire to find and love Him. He has explained the technique whereby we can reach Him, and he has then taken us back with him to the Supreme Being and merged us in Him.

It is the Lord and his beloved servants, his devotees, who belong to us, who are truly ours.

&

Do not get caught in the net of this world;
stay absorbed in devotion day and night.

Jagat jaal me^n pha^{n}so na bhaaee, nis din raho bhajan me^n.

Soami Ji explains how helplessly entangled we are in the great net of Kal. No one knows about the Lord, no one even thinks of Him. We complain and cry, and we get so involved in undergoing the consequences of actions we did in previous lives that we are oblivious to the fact that we are continuously doing the same kinds of bad deeds even now. It never occurs to us that we will have to come back again to this same prison of chaurasi to face the consequences. Guru Nanak Sahib says:

> O father, the world is caught in the great net.
> *Baabaa jag phaathaa mahaa jaal.*
>
> Adi Granth, M1, p. 1009

Every being in the creation is grievously caught in Kal's

net. Like a fisherman who uses a net that allows small fish to get away, and then casts a net so fine and extensive that it prevents even the smallest fish from escaping, so Kal has trapped the entire creation in a vast net. This is why either we do not worship the Lord at all, or if we do, then we present Him with our worldly desires and longings. And what is the result? We have to take another birth in order to fulfil those desires.

We worship the Lord either to fulfil our desires, or out of fear—fear that if we do not pray to Him, He may call our children back to Him, send sickness to our home, or reduce our wealth. We are then worshipping God out of self-interest and fear, not because we long to meet Him or are filled with love for Him.

So Soami Ji is alerting us as to how badly we are caught in Kal's net—that it is to fulfil our desires that we keep on being reborn. To this day, no one's desires have ever been satisfied, nor can they ever be. There is a proverb, "Like mountains, our desires—and death is at our heels."[34] Our desires and longings reach higher than the Himalayas, yet death is standing right behind us. Until the very end, we have no idea when we might have to leave our friends and relations and go. No matter what the Lord gives us, no matter how much He gives, our mind is never satisfied and content.

> The worldly man remains ever hungry;
> never satisfied, he craves for more and more.
> *Saakat nar praanee sad bhookhe*
> *nit bhookhan bhookh kareejai.*
>
> Adi Granth, M4, p. 1323

It makes no difference how much wealth, honour and respect we are given, or whether we are provided with good health and an excellent companion, we are always hungry for more, and the dog of greed keeps barking and whining inside us. We never experience contentment or satisfaction. Seeing our condition, Soami Ji takes pity on us and tells us how to escape:

> Stay absorbed in devotion day and night.

He says: Keep your attention connected to the Shabd all the time if you want to escape from Kal's net. Be attentive to the Shabd whatever you are doing, wherever you are.

We can only be taken beyond the influence of mind and the illusion of matter by a power that arises from beyond their orbit. The Shabd, the Word, arises in the everlasting realm of Sach Khand. When we collect our attention at the eye centre and attach ourselves to the Word, it pulls us beyond both mind and matter. Guru Nanak Sahib says:

> Through the grace of the Guru we rise above Trikuti
> and become absorbed in the fourth realm.
> *Gur parsaadee trikutee chhootai chaothai pad liv laaee.*
>
> Adi Granth, M3, p. 909

By following the teachings given to us by the Master, we go beyond Trikuti, leave the domain of Kal, and reach the fourth realm, Sach Khand. That is why Soami Ji says:

> Through the glory of the Word
> conquer Kal, the lord of death.
> *Shabd prataap kaal ko jeet.*
>
> Soami Ji, *Sar Bachan* 9:5, p. 91

Through meditation on the Word, my friends, defeat Kal, settle your karmic accounts. Guru Sahib says:

One can be redeemed only through the Guru's grace
and through practice of the true Name.
Gur parsaadee ubare sachaa naam samaal.

Adi Granth, M1, p. 1009

He says: If you want to cross the ocean of existence and escape from endless pain and suffering in the cycle of death and
rebirth, then follow the path given by the Masters, attend to
your meditation and listen to God's Name.

∽

Mark well the words of the true Master:
live detached, filled with yearning, in the world.

Saadh guroo kaa kahanaa maano, raho udaas jagat me^n.

In this beautiful verse, Soami Ji explains that we should not
renounce our families or worldly commitments and retreat
to some remote place, but should live in the world like warriors, bravely and courageously. He says: Live in the world
but remain detached. How do we remain detached? When we
long to be with someone, when we miss him, when we love
him and are restless and yearning to see him, when our heart
beats restlessly with desire for union—this detaches us, in
spite of ourselves, from the rest of the world. Soami Ji urges
us to develop this intense love and longing to meet the Lord
within ourselves.

He says that it is not by going off to mountains or forests
that our love will grow, since life's basic necessities will follow
us and trouble us there as much as anywhere else. We can
worship the Lord just as well while living in the context of
our home. That is why Guru Sahib says:

Imbued with the Name, the supreme swans remain
    detached;
they live in their own home, their devotion unbroken.
Naam rate paramhans bairaagee
nijghar taaree laaee he.

Adi Granth, M3, p. 1046

He says it is no easier to become a 'supreme swan', an in-
habitant of the highest spiritual regions, by renouncing your
home and family. You can achieve that spiritual purity and
detachment while living in the world, if you are steeped in
the colour of the Name—steeped in love and devotion for the
Lord. Again he is telling us to develop true love and longing
within ourselves. Guru Sahib says:

The virtuous bride finds union with her Lord,
    for she adorns herself with love and fear.
Kaaman gunwantee har paae.
Bhai bhaae seegaar banaae.

Adi Granth, M3, p. 123

A wife with these two particular qualities is always pleasing to her husband. One is love for him; the other is that she
fears him—she is always careful lest she do or say anything
that might displease him. A wife endowed with these two
qualities will always please her husband. Similarly, Guru
Sahib says, if we want to meet and merge with the Lord, we
too must develop these qualities—we must adorn ourselves
with them. We must develop true love for the Lord within
ourselves, and we must also nurture fear and reverence in our
hearts so that we do not commit bad deeds, do not gossip
about others, and thus displease the Lord. Instead, we must speak
and act in such a way that our Lord is always pleased with us.

If we take this path, we will automatically be pleasing to
the Lord.

❧

Abandon the ways of deceit and cunning—
why let yourself sink to this low state?

Chhal bal chhoro aur chaturaaee, kyo^n tum paro kugati me^n.

Soami Ji explains that hypocritical worship—worship done
to create an impression of piety, to appeal to public opinion
and to win praise—is of no use whatsoever. We must worship the Lord with a true heart. We do not do it for others, or
for show, or so that we ourselves may be venerated, but only
to please the Lord.

Soami Ji warns: Do not waste your time in a show of spirituality, like the contemplative white heron standing on one
leg.[35] He says that if you want to worship, do so sincerely—
understand what true love and longing is. Hypocritical worship will be of no benefit whatsoever.

❧

Keep your mind in simran and serve your Master;
rise today to the spiritual sky!

Sumiran karo guroo ko sevo, chal raho aaj gagan me^n.

Keep your mind in simran and serve your Master; rise today to the spiritual sky!" Soami Ji says: Do simran, concentrate your attention by keeping the form of the Master before
your eyes, and join your consciousness to the Shabd. Once

liberated from the body, you can meet the Lord today, if you so wish. It is through simran and dhyan that you will detach yourself from worldly love and attachment, and by holding onto the Sound, you travel stage by stage, region by region, back to your home. Soami Ji explains that this is the kind of devotion you need and this is the path you must follow.

～

**Death will otherwise determine your tomorrows:
you will roast in the fires of hell.**

Kal kee khabar kaal phir legaa, vahaa^n tum jalo agin me^n.

What Soami Ji means here is that we must meditate daily. We must not waste time with pencil and paper making schemes for the future, making fools of ourselves thinking that in another six or seven years the children will grow up, get married, settle in their careers and take over the family responsibilities, so then we will have time to worship the Lord; for the moment we have too many duties and responsibilities, too much worldly work piled up in front of us.

Soami Ji says that however good our intentions may be when we keep making such plans, what do we know of the Lord's plans? We do not even know when we will have to leave this world. At our level we do not know what will happen to us in the next second, let alone the next hour.

We often hear how people suddenly die of heart failure— food in their hand, halfway to their mouth; or getting out of their cars, before their feet can even reach the ground. That is why it is essential that we worship the Lord every day. Whether the mind enjoys it or not, we should sit in meditation, looking on it as our duty. Little by little, the mind will turn by itself towards devotion to the Lord, although in the beginning we have to keep up a constant fight with it.

There is no particular time of day that is best for worshipping the Lord. If we get time in the morning, take advantage of it; if it is in the afternoon, meditate then; in the evening, then meditate in the evening. Whenever we sit in remembrance of the Beloved, our Friend—whether for a quarter of an hour, half an hour, one hour or two hours—it will be credited to our account and we will receive the benefit accordingly.

Soami Ji warns us not to delude ourselves: We must attend to our meditation every day.

༄

Understand this now and make no delay.
Who knows even what will happen next?

Abahee samajh der mat kariyo, naa janoo^n kyaa hoy is pan me^n.

Thus explaining, Radha Soami declares:
one instruction should be enough!

Yo^n samjhaay kahe^n raadhaaswaamee, maano ek bachan me^n.

Through these few verses, Shri Hazur Soami Ji Maharaj has given us a beautiful explanation of why the Lord has blessed us with a human form and how we have forgotten the real purpose of our life. We are so involved with family and friends, and with social, religious and political issues, that we lose sight of our real goal. It is now up to us to benefit from his teachings, and, whatever we are doing, wherever we are, to be attentive all the time to the true Word, the true Name.

Hold Fast Your Mind
in Contemplation of the Guru's Form

Gur kee moorat man mah dhiaan

Hold fast your mind in contemplation of the Guru's form;
understand that his Word is the path to spiritual transformation.
Enshrine within your heart the Guru's lotus feet;
the Guru transcends Brahm—salute him reverently.

Let no one in the world be deluded:
none can attain liberation without a Guru. *(Refrain)*

The Guru has brought the misguided to the path;
detaching them from all else, he has led them to divine worship.
He has obliterated the fear of birth and death.
Infinite is the glory of the perfect Guru!

By the grace of the Guru the inverted lotus turns straight and blooms;
the prevailing darkness is illumined with effulgent light.
The One who made all is realized through the Guru;
by his grace, the wayward mind is chastened.

Guru is the creator, Guru is omnipotent;
Guru is God, and shall ever be.
Says Nanak: O friend, the Lord has made this known:
Without a Guru, there is no salvation.

Adi Granth, Guru Arjan, p. 864

Gur kee moorat man mah dhiaan.
Gur kai sabad mantar man maan.
Gur ke charan ridai lai dhaarao.
Gur paarbraham sadaa namaskaarao.

Mat ko bharam bhulai sansaar.
Gur bin koe na utras paar. (Rahaau)

Bhoole kao gur maarag paa-i-aa.
Avar tiaag har bhagtee laa-i-aa.
Janam maran kee traas mitaaee.
Gur poore kee beant vadaaee.

Gur prasaad ooradh kamal bigaas.
Andhkaar mah bha-i-aa pragaas.
Jin keeaa so gur te jaaniaa.
Gur kirpaa te mugadh man maaniaa.

Guru kartaa guru karnai jog.
Guru parmesar hai bhee hog.
Kah naanak prabh ihai janaaee.
Bin gur mukat na paaeeai bhaaee.

Shabdarath Sri Guru Granth Sahib Ji
(Amritsar: Shromani Gurdwara Prabandhak
Committee), M5, p. 864

Hold fast your mind in contemplation of the Guru's form;
understand that his Word is the path
to spiritual transformation.

Gur kee moorat man mah dhiaan.
Gur kai sabad mantar man maan.

This text is from the writings of the fifth Padshahi,* Shri
Guru Arjan Dev Ji Maharaj. All the Gurus in the line of Guru
Nanak Sahib speak in praise of the Word and the Name, and
they all explain the many aspects of the path of the saints, but
it was Guru Arjan Dev who emphasized devotion to the Satguru,
the perfect Master. His Master was in fact his father, but he
did not look upon him as a father; rather, he loved him as his
Master. In each verse of this brief composition, Guru Sahib re-
veals the way of the saints in a clear and systematic manner.

Guru Sahib says that we are all seeking the Lord, and we
do indeed feel that we are part of the Supreme Being, that our
souls are drops of the ocean of Satnam, the true Name. But
because we have become separate from the Lord and dominated by the mind, we have to keep coming back to this
prison of chaurasi—we have to undergo the consequences of
all our actions, regardless of whether they are good or bad.

This, the saints tell us, is because the world is a field of
karmas, of actions.[36] It is the kind of seeds we sow that determines the crop we have to harvest. It is thus our actions that
cause us to face suffering and problems in whichever form of
life we take birth.

---

* *See* Glossary and Translators' Note for explanations of unusual usage, and technical or Indian-language terms, such as: Padshahi, the Name.

There simply is no form of life in which we can live that can bring peace and happiness alone. When even human beings have to struggle day and night just to feed and clothe themselves, then you may well question whether any form of life exists in which peace and happiness can be found. Guru Sahib explains:

> Immortally wedded is the soul bride
> who attains union with her true Lord.
> *Pir sache te sadaa suhaagan.*
>
> Adi Granth, M3, p. 754

Our soul is the bride, the Lord is the groom. As long as the soul-bride does not find herself in the embrace of her beloved Groom, she will never be fulfilled, never be liberated from the painful cycle of death and rebirth.

This is why each one of us is seeking the Lord and why all saints awaken within us the desire and longing to find Him. Guru Sahib says:

> The whole world is engaged in the worship
>   of the Lord,
> but worldly people do not find their bearings.
> *Poojaa karai sabh lok santah*
> *manmukh thaae na paaee.*
>
> Adi Granth, M3, p. 910

Everyone worships the Lord—each one of us according to the inclination of our mind. The yearning to find the Lord and restlessness for union with Him is within everyone. All are aware that without union they will never be happy or achieve peace of mind. As a result, some go to bathe in holy waters; some get caught up in performing recitations, austerities and external forms of worship; some get caught up in doing charitable deeds; some have the impression that liberation lies in reading the scriptures; some undertake pilgrimages; some grow their hair long, pierce their ears or smear their bodies with ash.

We do all these things simply to try to find the Lord, to unite ourselves with Him. But Guru Nanak Sahib informs us that the Lord we seek cannot be found anywhere outside because He lives within us. Up till now, no one has found Him in the outer world, nor is it possible to find Him there. In the scriptures we read:

> True devotees seek within;
> all others wander in delusion.
> *Gurmukh hovai su kaa-i-aa khojai*
> *hor sabh bharam bhulaaee.*
> Adi Granth, M3, p. 754

The Lord's lovers, his devotees, his beloved ones, always turn inwards to worship Him. They seek to find Him within their own bodies.

> Within the body the Lord himself resides;
> invisible, He remains unseen.
> The foolish egoist understands nothing
> and goes on searching outside.
> *Kaa-i-aa andar aape vasai alakh na lakhiaa jaaee.*
> *Manmukh mugadh boojhai naahee*
> *baahar bhaalan jaaee.*
> Adi Granth, M3, p. 754

The Supreme Being is living right inside us, yet—fools and simpletons that we are, lovers of the creation—we keep

searching for Him outside. We search in bricks and stone, in
holy waters, in remote secluded places, in books and scriptures. Guru Sahib says:

> In the body dwells the bountiful Lord,
> the life of the world, who sustains all.
> *Kaa-i-aa andar jag jeevan daataa vasai,*
> *sabhnaa kare pratipaalaa.*
>
> Adi Granth, M3, p. 754

The Supreme Being, giver of life to the whole universe, benefactor and emperor of all, who takes care of and nurtures all,
lives nowhere outside. He lives within us. He says:

> Always with us, think Him not distant,
> the One who created the creation.
> *Sadaa hajoor door nah dekhah rachnaa jin rachaaee.*
>
> Adi Granth, M3, p. 909

The Lord who has given birth to the entire creation will
never be attained in the outside world. He is with you all the
time, twenty-four hours of the day, going with you everywhere, because He lives within you, inside your body. So
Guru Sahib says:

> This body is the Lord's temple;
> it is there that the jewel of knowledge is revealed.
> *Har mandar eh sareer hai giaan ratan pargat ho-e.*
>
> Adi Granth, M3, p. 1346

What place would we call 'God's temple'? The place
where He lives, the Supreme Being's abode. Guru Sahib says
that if any place can be described as God's true temple—the

place the Lord himself lives in—that place can only be the human form, this mortal frame. Only inside this human body can we attain that knowledge or experience of union with the Lord.

How are we to worship the Supreme Being by turning inwards? He says:

> Hold fast your mind in contemplation of the
> Guru's form.

The natural seat of the soul and mind within everybody is at a place between and behind the eyes. The saints speak of it as the door to our home (ghar dar), the tenth (dasvaa^n), the grain of sesame (til), and the gateway to liberation (mukti daa darvaazaa). It is from here that our attention descends and, through the nine gateways of the body, dissipates itself by going into every corner of the world.

As we sit here, we are sometimes thinking of our families, sometimes of our household activities, sometimes of our businesses. The mind does not stay still; it is constantly preoccupied with some thought or another. This habit we have acquired of unceasing mental activity is referred to by the saints as doing simran. It is a natural habit that is established right within each one of us. Even if we shut ourselves in the darkest of rooms, we are not really there because our attention spreads out into the whole world.

Whenever we do simran of something, its form or image automatically comes before our eyes. If we think of our sons and daughters, their forms appear before us; if we think about our homes, then that is what passes before our eyes. The saints speak of this as doing dhyan. It is natural that whatever we constantly think about—whatever is the focus of our simran—we will also start visualizing or doing its dhyan.

Whenever we keep thinking of something and visualize it constantly, little by little we become attached to it and start loving it. We become so attached to these forms and images that they even appear in our dreams at night. It is they that stand before our eyes at the moment of death, as though projected on a cinema screen. "Where our desires are, there we dwell."[37] In this world, the direction in which our attention goes in our last moments determines the course of our next life.

What keeps bringing us back into the body? Our worldly loves and attachments. How did these come about? Through simran and dhyan. What is the focus of our simran and dhyan? Things that will perish and pass away. Everything we see in the world is transient and will perish.

Saints say that since the practice of simran and dhyan is natural to all of us, we should take advantage of this mental habit. Simran will eliminate simran, dhyan will eliminate dhyan. But, saints say, do the simran and dhyan of that which is permanent and will never perish. What can that be? It can only be the one Supreme Being, the Almighty Lord—He who has been given a thousand names by all of us out of our love for Him. Guru Sahib says:

> Apart from the Lord, my friends, everything is
>   impure.
> *Har bin sabh kichh mailaa santah.*
>   Adi Granth, M3, p. 910

Everything, other than the Lord, is impure because it is transient and perishable. He explains:

> The false are in love with the false
>   and have forgotten their Creator;

whom to love and make one's friend
when the whole world is in a state of flux?
Koor koorai nehu lagaa wisariaa kartaar.
Kis naal keechai dostee sabh jag chalanhaar.

Adi Granth, M1, p. 468

Our body, through which we relate to the creation, is false in that it leaves us. The manifest world, in which we are so entangled through our attachments and love while living in the body, also passes away. The false thus remains eternally trapped by attachment and love for the false, and we live oblivious to the Lord.

Guru Sahib says: Be attentive, look carefully about you. Apart from the one supreme Lord, there is nothing in the world that is worthy of your friendship, your love, or your true affection. Your soul *(aatmaa)* is a particle of that supreme soul *(parmaatmaa),* the Supreme Being, which alone will never perish or pass away. Guru Sahib in the first verse of Japji Sahib says:

True in the beginning, True through the ages,
True He is, and True He shall be.
Aad sach jugaad sach.
Hai bhee sach naanak hosee bhee sach.

Adi Granth, M1, Japji, p. 1

He says that after a very long search, he has now experienced something, he is in touch with something, that was true in the beginning and will ever remain true through all the ages. What is that? The one Supreme Being, the Almighty, who is imperishable and eternal. Everything else will come to an end.

Saints tell us how to do the simran of the Name of that Supreme Being. Following their instructions, we use simran to bring back our scattered attention from the nine doors and concentrate it at the eye centre. When we focus our attention at the eye centre, it does not stay there because it is in the habit of going down towards the pleasures of the senses. Unless we also do dhyan, unless we give it someone's image to contemplate, it will never develop the habit of staying at the eye centre.

Whose form should we contemplate on, since whenever we contemplate on anything, we ourselves will begin to assume its form? We grow to love that face, and it is into that form that we will merge.

Now, we have never seen the Lord. We do not know his face, his colour, or his form. Guru Sahib says:

> He has no colour, caste and mark.
> By his Command, He creates the whole world.
> *Varan jaat chihan nahee koee.*
> *Sabh hukame srisat upaa-idaa.*
>
> Adi Granth, M5, p. 1075

The Almighty Lord, who gave birth to the entire creation through his Command, is neither black nor white, Hindu nor Sikh, nor can He be said to live in India, America or Africa. He cannot be fitted into any category. When no one has seen the Supreme Being and we only know about Him from hearsay, how then can we contemplate on Him?

We can only devote our attention to someone whom we have met, with whom we have had some interaction, whose face we have seen, and for whom we have developed love. When we have not seen the Lord, how can we possibly love Him? How can we possibly contemplate on Him—how can we do his dhyan? Other than the Lord, is there anything, any face, that is deserving of our love?

Since everything that we can see in this creation is made from the five vital elements *(tattva)*, and all five are transient, anything made from them is not worthy of our contemplation. We have to seriously consider what can be worthy of our contemplation. It is not appropriate for one human being to practise contemplation on another; humans do not speak the language of animals; we have never seen the gods and goddesses; and we do not know the face, shape or form of the Lord. Whom can we love, to whom can we direct our attention, who will then channelize that attention and love towards the Lord?

Hazur* used to make a fine analogy. You may place any number of radios in a room, but as long as they are not connected to a battery or other source of power, you will never be able to hear any news. Once they are connected, however, you will be able to receive the news from any country you choose. We have to search out the beloved of the Lord, those connected with the Supreme Being through devotion and love, and it is on their form that we must concentrate our attention. We have to contemplate on the form of those lovers of God who live their lives in Him, who exist as part of Him, in spite of living in the physical form. Their real form is the Shabd or Name, and it is the Shabd, the Name, that is our real Master. Guru Nanak Sahib says:

> The Word is the Guru,
> the soul attuned to the Word is the disciple.
> *Sabad guroo surat dhun chelaa.*
>
> Adi Granth, M1, p. 943

---

* The terms 'Hazur' and 'Hazur Maharaj Ji' are used by the speaker to refer to his Master, Maharaj Sawan Singh (1858–1948). *See also* Translators' Note and Glossary.

The physical body has to be left behind by both disciple and Master. But if our attention is connected to the Word within, by the Master, then that Word will take us back to our home. Thus, we have to contemplate on a lover of the Lord who connects our soul with the Word. Such a Master lives in the body, but his real form is in fact the Word or Name. This is why we do the dhyan of our Master's form.

Our relationship with Masters who left the physical form before we were born is the same as the one we have with the Supreme Being. We have never seen them and we never had the opportunity to keep their company. They have become one with the Supreme Being. If we are going to contemplate on them, why do we not simply contemplate on the Supreme Being? If we could contemplate on them, we might just as well devote our attention to the Supreme Being. They have gone as far from us as is the Supreme Being.

If we are going to practise contemplation, we can only do it on a saint who is living in our time. We must contemplate on the form of the saint who has connected our attention with the Word, the Name. It is through such a saint that we will develop the habit of holding our attention at the eye centre. That is why Guru Nanak Sahib explains the purpose of dhyan so thoroughly. He says:

> The whole world, the netherworlds, the islands,
>   the spheres,
> have all been put under Kal; such is the Lord's
>   design....
> *Khand pataal deep sabh loaa,*
> *sabh kaalai vas aap prabh keeaa.*
>
> Adi Granth, M5, p. 1076

Having created the whole world—the regions, islands, netherworlds, and all that exists—the Supreme Being has entrusted its management to Kal. Kal's realm extends as far as Brahm, and everything that falls within it—within the three worlds—is subject to the painful cycle of death and rebirth. But, Guru Sahib says, where is the Being who created the world and handed over its administration to Kal? He explains:

> ... The only immutable one is the eternal God;
>   those who contemplate on Him become
>   immutable too....
> *Nihchal ek aap abinaasee so nihchal jo tisah dhiaa-idaa.*
> Adi Granth, M5, p. 1076

The Supreme Being is the unchanging Reality itself, never entering the realm of death and rebirth, residing eternally in Sach Khand, the true realm. Kal's sphere reaches only as far as Brahm. People who contemplate on the Supreme Being, who worship Him and love Him, become unchanging like Him and escape forever from the circle of death and rebirth.

So the question again arises: When we have never seen the Supreme Being, how can we worship Him? How can we love Him? How can we contemplate on Him? Guru Sahib says:

> ... The Lord's servant is like unto the Lord;
>   do not think him to be different because of his
>   human frame ...
> *Har kaa sevak so har jehaa.*
> *Bhed na jaanah maanas dehaa.*
> Adi Granth, M5, p. 1076

The Lord's beloved ones become the Lord by devoting themselves to Him. There is no distinction or difference between
them and the Lord. What is the nature of their relationship
with the Supreme Being? In what way are they connected to
Him? Guru Sahib says:

> … just as a myriad waves rise from the ocean,
> and then subside, merging back into its depths.
> *Jio jal tarang uthah bahubhaatee*
> *phir salalai salal samaa-idaa.*
>
> Adi Granth, M5, p. 1076

The relationship between the lovers of the Lord and the
supreme Lord is like that of waves with the ocean. The waves
arise from the ocean for a few minutes and then merge back
into the ocean. Waves may rise high above the ocean but they
will never separate from it. They always remain part of the
ocean.

If someone abandons himself to a wave, then the wave
will enfold him in itself and merge him in the depths of the
ocean. When we surrender ourselves to the lovers of the Lord,
when we follow their teachings and devote ourselves to contemplating on their form, they carry us with them and merge
us in the folds of the ocean of Satnam, the true Name. That is
why we contemplate on the Master, on our Satguru's form.

It is through simran that we focus at the eye centre, pull-
ing the attention back to this place behind the eyes. It is
through dhyan that we are able to hold it there. Imagine there
is a river flowing continuously from somewhere—if you
build a dam across it, certainly you can stop the water flowing for a limited time. But if too much water falls in the catch-
ment area, the pressure will be such that the water will burst
through the dam and flood over the banks. If, after building

the dam, we make proper arrangements for the water to flow in another direction, then the dam remains safe and, as the water flows along the new channel, the banks of the river are able to dry.

Similarly, through simran and dhyan we are building a dam at the eye centre, to prevent the mind going towards the sense pleasures. But it is not possible to keep our attention at the eye centre forever just through simran and dhyan. We have to divert the flow of attention in another direction. For this reason, Guru Sahib says:

> Understand that his Word is the path to spiritual
> transformation.

The saints connect our consciousness to the Word. It is to the Word—that power to which they have connected us—that we must divert our mind. As the mind develops a taste for the Word, it turns increasingly inward and upward, unlike before, when its orientation was outward and downward, spreading continuously into the outer world. This is why we attach our attention to the Word through the saints.

The first stage is to collect the attention at the eye centre through simran and dhyan. The second is to make our spiritual journey, which we do by attaching our mind to the Word. Once we have linked our attention with the Word, we return stage by stage to our home.

We will experience true contemplation when we have crossed the realm of the mind—the sphere of illusion—and have merged in the Word, in the Name. Guru Nanak Sahib indicates this in several places in his writings, when he speaks of merging in the Name, through the Satguru.[38]

We become so absorbed in contemplating our Master's Radiant Form that we actually merge into him. We become so engrossed in beholding the Master, so taken by his dar-shan, that we surrender ourselves to him, we offer ourselves up, we annihilate our identity by merging in his identity. This is inner contemplation.

To do this, we must first fix our attention on his form at the eye centre so that our mind develops the habit of staying there. Only then will we be able to catch hold of the sound of the Word. The Word itself will transport us to the level where we will be able to see the Radiant Form of our Master, where we will merge into that form and become that form.

All true lovers of the Lord connect our attention to that true Word, the Name. Guru Sahib says:

> By merging into the Shabd, one dies to the self
> and gains everlasting life.
> *Sabad marai so mar rahai fir marai na doojee waar.*
>
> Adi Granth, M1, p. 58

You would die forever if, wherever you are, whatever you are doing, every moment of the day, you were to attach your attention to the Word of which they speak. You would then never have to come back into the cycle of death and rebirth. Guru Sahib says:

> They who hear the Word within, realize themselves;
> they alone attain the Truth....
> *Jin antar sabad aap pachhaanah gat mit tin hee paaee.*
>
> Adi Granth, M3, p. 910

Anyone who experiences this Word within, becomes self-realized. This means that such a person transcends the realm of mind and impermanence; the knot which ties the mind and soul together is undone; and all the soiled coverings of

the soul are removed. They "realize themselves; they alone
attain the Truth"—such a person attains the highest state and
has qualified to unite with the Lord.

> ... Then the mind enters the state of deep
>   meditation;
> the soul's flame merges with the all-pervading
>   divine light.
> *Eh manooaa sunn samaadh lagaavai*
> *jotee jot milaaee.*
>
>   Adi Granth, M3, p. 910

The mind had descended from the eye centre and spread
into the creation through the nine doors of the body. Now,
through listening to the Word, it has become absorbed in a
state of transcendent consciousness. The soul goes beyond
Brahm, becomes absolutely pure and separates from the
mind. Then, "the soul's flame merges with the all-pervading
divine light"—the brilliance of our soul dissolves in the brilliance of the supreme light.

Until the mind reaches this state of consciousness, the
light of the soul cannot merge with the supreme light. Guru
Sahib says:

> Friends, the mind becomes pure
> when it merges in the Word.
> This worship alone takes us home.
> *Sabad marai man nirmal santah,*
> *eh poojaa thaae paaee.*
>
>   Adi Granth, M3, p. 910

By purifying the mind through meditation on the Word or
Name, we are worshipping the true Lord. This worship will

take us back to our ancestral home. It is this Word, this Name, that Guru Nanak Sahib praises so highly. The third Padshahi says:

> Closing the nine doors
> and restraining the wandering mind,
> in the tenth one finds one's true abode.
> There the unending music of the Word plays
>   day and night.
> Through the Guru's guidance, the celestial
>   Word is heard.
> *Nao dar thaake dhaavat rahaae.*
> *Dasvai nijghar vaasaa paae.*
> *Othai anahad sabad vajah din raatee*
> *gurmatee sabad sunaavaniaa.*
>
> Adi Granth, M3, p. 124

Withdraw your consciousness from the nine doors of the body and concentrate it at the eye centre in the way the saints explain. You will reach the entrance to your home. What feature will enable you to recognize that door? You have only to remember one thing: day and night, the unending music of the Word is reverberating there. Only by reaching that place is our soul able to hear the limitless Word and travel inwards on the spiritual journey. Guru Nanak Sahib says:

> Closing the nine doors,
> one finds liberation at the tenth;
> there ever resonates the limitless melody
>   of the Word.
> *Nao darvaaje dasvai muktaa*
> *anahad sabad vajaavaniaa.*
>
> Adi Granth, M1, p. 110

Below the eye centre lie sense pleasures, immorality and perversions, and the weaknesses of the flesh. The Lord has kept the gateway to liberation at a point between the eyes. That is the point where we are to concentrate the attention by doing simran and dhyan of the Master's form. The first Padshahi also explains that we will recognize this place by the limitless sound of the Word that resonates there.

Until our souls become conscious of the sound of the Word by coming to this level, there can be no question of our attaining liberation. Guru Sahib says:

> Attached to the Word,
> the soul crosses the ocean of phenomena
> through the practice of the Name, O Nanak.
> *Surat sabad bhav saagar tareeai*
> *naanak naam vakhaane.*
>
> Adi Granth, M1, p. 938

Fix this thought firmly in your mind: the only way you will ever cross the fearful ocean of existence is by the practice of joining the soul with the Word *(surat shabd abhyaas)*, by meditating on the Name. He says:

> One who dies while living, through God's holy
>   Word,
> becomes whole and perfect;
> this is what Satguru, the brave warrior, proclaims.
> *Sabad marai soee jan pooraa.*
> *Satguru aakh sunaae sooraa.*
>
> Adi Granth, M3, p. 1046

Those who 'die' in the Word, who are absorbed and immersed in it, are fulfilled. They become whole. They become pure. Our valiant Master has enabled us to understand that anyone who hears the Word becomes complete, pure and worthy of union with the Lord. That is why the saints link our attention to this Word.

The Word that is praised so highly by Guru Nanak Sahib has within it a voice, a melody, a sound. It has within it light and brilliance. He says:

> When the vibrant melody of the five sounds is
>   heard—
> that music signifies the Word.
> *Panch sabad dhunkaar dhun tah baajai*
> *sabad neesaan.*
>
> Adi Granth, M1, p. 1290

The Word is made known by the audible reverberations that continually emanate from within it. Guru Sahib also says:

> Without the Word, there is utter darkness within;
> one neither finds the precious treasure of Nam
> nor escapes the cycle of birth and death.
> *Bin sabdai antar aaneraa.*
> *Na vast lahai na chookai feraa.*
>
> Adi Granth, M3, p. 124

No one has ever been able to dispel the darkness of ignorance, or find the Lord, or escape from the shackles of the physical form, without the practice of the Word. The fourth Padshahi gives a beautiful analogy:

> Just as fire is latent in wood
> and can be produced with skill,

so is the flame of God's Name latent in everyone
and can be revealed through the Guru's wisdom.
Kaasat mah jio hai baisantar
math sanjam kaadh kadheejai.
Raamnaam hai jot sabaaee tat gurmat kaadh laeejai.

                                                    Adi Granth, M4, p. 1323

We may say that fire is present in wood, but we cannot
see or use this fire until we rub one piece of wood against
another, using the correct technique. The fire is then mani-
fested and can be both seen and used. Similarly, Guru Sahib
says that the light of God's Name shines within everyone at
the eye centre, but it can only "be revealed through the Guru's
wisdom". Although it is present in everyone, it is only when
we follow the path given to us by the saints that we will see
the inner light.

What is the path of the saints?

Nine are the doors, but all nine are insipid;
the divine ambrosia flows from the tenth.
Nao darvaaj nave dar feeke ras amrit dasve chu-eejai.

                                                    Adi Granth, M4, p. 1323

The pleasures of the senses, negative tendencies and physical
appetites all lie below the eye centre; whereas at the eye centre itself, the nectar that is laden with sweetness rains all the
time in abundance. We have to focus our attention at the
point where the nectar of the Name rains down, where the
spiritual light shines in everyone, and where that reverberating sound constantly surges forth in all of us. It is with the
help of that light and melody that we are to travel on our inner spiritual journey. Guru Nanak Sahib says:

Hold fast your mind in contemplation of the
   Guru's form;
understand that his Word is the path to spiritual
   transformation.

Concentrate your attention at the eye centre by doing
simran and dhyan in the way the lovers of the Lord explain
to you. Attach your mind to the Word to which you have
been linked by the saints, attach it to the Name.

～

Enshrine within your heart the Guru's lotus feet;
the Guru transcends Brahm—salute him reverently.

Gur ke charan ridai lai dhaarao.
Gur paarbraham sadaa namaskaarao.

Guru Sahib says we must develop love for the saints, we must
keep their company, we must associate with them. There is
no difference of any sort between them and the supreme
Lord. Theirs is the form of the Supreme Being. They are the
embodiment of the Supreme Being, and that is why we keep
their company.
   The capacity or potential for learning exists in everybody.
Only when we go to school or college and obediently follow
the instructions of our teachers, when we stay awake till late
at night and put in our best efforts, is this latent power awakened. Only then do we become scholars and obtain degrees.
Some people run away from school or college because they
do not like the discipline. They have the same power as
everyone else within them, but it is never awakened. They
come and go without realizing their potential.

When we enrol in school or college, we do not ask whether our teacher is Muslim, Hindu, Sikh or Christian. We do not say that we will only study with a teacher belonging to a particular religion, and not with any other. To acquire knowledge of a subject, you have to go wherever that knowledge is available. The field of spirituality is just the same: it must also be acquired wherever it can be found.

Our minds, as you know, are easily influenced by the company we keep. When we spend time with drinkers, we take on the habit of drinking; with smokers, we get into the habit of smoking; with thieves, we begin to steal. When we keep the company of saints, devotees and lovers of God, we automatically develop the habit of devotion, whether we want to or not. That is why they tell us to associate with saints.

By worshipping the Lord, saints assume his form; there is nothing to distinguish them from Him. When we keep their company, our attention automatically engages in devotion of the Lord. We start loving Him. Guru Sahib entreats the Supreme Being on our behalf, saying:

> O beloved Lord!
> Grant us the company of the true ones,
> that we may contemplate on God.
> *Gobind jeeo sat sangat mel har dhiaaeeai.*
> Adi Granth, M4, p. 1179

O Lord! Give us the company of holy people, the satsang of saints and great souls, so that we may know about you and our attention might turn to worshipping you.

We must understand, however, that when one religion maligns and slanders another religion, saints do not call that a satsang. There is never any pettiness or criticism of others in the satsang of the saints. Nor do they recount tales or stories of bygone kings and princes. They simply pay homage to the Word and praise the Name. Guru Nanak Sahib says:

> Know that as true satsang
> where the doctrine of the one Name is explained.
> *Satsangat kaisee jaaneeai.*
> *Jithai eko naam vakhaaneeai.*

Adi Granth, M1, p. 72

My friends, that alone can be called satsang where the desire and longing to find the Lord is awakened and the method for uniting with Him is described.

It is wrong of us to abuse or speak ill of someone who does not worship the Lord in the way we think he should. Rather, we should explain lovingly to this good person: My friend, here is how we have benefitted by following this path. If it appeals to you and your way of looking at things, you could also benefit in the same way.

Saints clear up our misconceptions and remove our doubts and illusions through their company, through their satsang. They arouse within us the desire and longing to meditate on the Name.

෧

> *Let no one in the world be deluded:*
> *none can attain liberation without a Guru.*
> *Mat ko bharam bhulai sansaar. Gur bin koe na utras paar.*

The fifth Padshahi now warns—in no uncertain terms—that we should not be deluded into thinking that we will be able to achieve union with the Lord by virtue of intellect, birth or religion, or because we are highly knowledgeable or intelligent. He tells us to throw out these delusions and superstitions. For us to take even one step without a Master is difficult; the question of attaining salvation on our own does not arise.

Is there any knowledge in the world that can be had without a teacher? When a child is newly born, it cannot even sit on its own. First the mother is the teacher—she guides the child to sit and stand. She teaches him to talk, walk and run. Then the father becomes the teacher. Taking the child by his little finger, he leads him out beyond the door of the home. How many different teachers he has in his life before he is capable of standing on his feet and earning his own livelihood!

Spirituality is so complex that it is hard to take even one step without a teacher. Just think of the academic world: how many libraries there are, filled with books on engineering and medicine—yet no one has ever qualified as a doctor or engineer just by reading books. We attend school and college year after year for twenty-five years or more. We read and study night after night, burning the midnight oil. We then need practical training. Only after that do we qualify in our particular field.

The subject of spirituality is extremely difficult. That is why Guru Sahib says that we must rid ourselves of the idea that we can find and truly worship the Lord by any means other than through the help of a perfect Master, a lover of God.

The first thing that the saints do when they wish to liberate people from the shackles of the body is to attract them to their satsang. Through satsang, they engender within them the desire to find the Lord. They detach them from external rituals and practices, and free their minds of doubts and wrong thinking. They awaken within them a desire to practise meditation of the Word.

When, after coming into contact with a saint, people meditate on the unutterable Lore *(akath kathaa),* on the Word, the Name, they reach such a high state of consciousness that "between them and the Lord, now no difference remains."[39] By worshipping the Lord, they go back and become the Lord.

That is why they say we need the saints. It is through them, through the lovers of the Lord, that we return and attain union with the Supreme Being.

∾

The Guru has brought the misguided to the path; detaching them from all else, he has led them to divine worship.

Bhoole kao gur maarag paa-i-aa. Avar tiaag har bhagtee laa-i-aa.

*H*ow are we misguided? We flounder around, misguided, because we are caught in the net of impermanence and illusion (maya), trapped by our worldly attachments and love.

We are enmeshed in our love for family, in matters of race, religion and country, in our enjoyment of the physical pleasures, in earning our livelihood and acquiring wealth. We are perpetually trapped by our attachment to these things. We are caught up in our love for them. Because of this, we have to die again and again and be reborn again and again. Saints disengage our attention from all these things for this very reason, and redirect it towards love for the Lord.

Could there be any greater kindness than that which the Lord's lovers bestow upon us? We were separated from what we really are—from our true home—for lifetime after lifetime. They have enabled us to know what our reality is. They have awakened within us the longing to realize that reality; and taking us with them, they have united us with that Truth. What is false, we took to be real, and what does not belong to us, we kept trying to possess.

Our relationships with everyone are connections of debits and credits, sometimes giving and sometimes taking—but always with an ulterior motive. Whenever a particular chain of karmas comes to an end, all leave us and go their own way. After being asleep for countless lifetimes, we awaken in the satsang of a saint. We ask ourselves: What are these attachments by which we are so trapped? What is this love that has ensnared us so? Guru Sahib says:

> Mother, father, are transient relationships,
> an affliction of the body;
> afflicted is the entire family.
> *Maat pitaa maa-i-aa deh se rogee rogee kutamb sanjogee.*
>   Adi Granth, M1, p. 1153

If we have any real obligation, it is to our parents. Not only did they give birth to us, but they took care of us, suffered so much criticism on our behalf and faced so many difficulties and problems. But, Guru Sahib says, even our parents cannot support or be of help to us. We have to account for our karmas in our lifetime. They have to account for their karmas in their lifetime.

Similarly, our children take birth through us, but they do not belong to us, nor we to them. That is why Guru Sahib says that they are all afflicted with impermanence, subject to death, and will all leave us. Even the body deceives us—after sixty or seventy years, it too falls away and the soul stands apart. The body is then cremated or buried. When someone dies, everyone sits about watching—they have no idea from where Death's henchmen have come, nor to where they have spirited us away.

Guru Nanak Sahib says that saintly people, God's lovers, rid us of all these misconceptions and illusions. What illusions are they referring to? Since everything we see is unreal, it is all an illusion. The real is what we cannot see, and the saints awaken within us the desire to experience it. They detach us from our love for the creation and engender within us a longing to find the real.

∽

He has obliterated the fear of birth and death.
Infinite is the glory of the perfect Guru!

Janam maran kee traas mitaaee. Gur poore kee beant vadaaee.

𝐴ll of us are frightened of death. We have no idea of the suffering and difficulties we will have to endure. People say that when we die, Death's henchmen come and drag us away. Where will they give us our next birth? Whom then will we call our mother and father? In whose lap will we have to play? What neighbourhood will we frequent? We tremble in fear because of our sins, because of our karmas, our deeds.

Guru Sahib says that when people take refuge with the Masters, the lovers of the Lord, and practise meditation of the Name, the fear of death leaves them completely. They become the ones who know. The dark veil of ignorance has been removed from their eyes, and they have found a companion for the journey who will travel with them to their destination.

That is why they say that the saints shower grace. They carry us along with them and enable us to merge into Sach

Khand, the realm of truth. What greater happiness can there be than finding one's home and returning to it after living in exile for countless lifetimes? Hazur used to say that spiritual practitioners are more joyous at the time of their death than on their wedding day.

Our daily meditation is indeed a rehearsal for death. Every day we are practising dying. At the time of death, our consciousness withdraws from the nine doors, collects behind the eyes, leaves and stands apart. This is our rehearsal—when we sit in practice every day for two or two and a half hours. Why then would we fear death, when we have made it our daily practice thousands of times?

Saints explain that through our practice of meditation on the Word and Name, the fear of dying and of suffering in the cycle of transmigration leaves us forever. Guru Sahib says:

> Blind and foolish are they who do not serve the
>   Satguru;
> how can they reach the gate of salvation?
> They die to be born, they are born to die;
> they suffer repeated blows at the hands of Death.
> *Satgur na sevahi moorakh andh gavaaraa,*
> *phir o-i kithahu paa-in mokhduaaraa.*
> *Mar mar jammahi phir phir aavahi,*
> *jam dar chotaa khaavaniaa.*
>
> Adi Granth, M3, p. 115

How is it possible for such people to attain liberation when they do not associate with a Master or practise the teachings he gives? They have to take birth again and again and die again and again. Wherever they take birth in the circle of chaurasi, they will have to put up with ill-treatment, with suffering and difficulties.

This human life is bestowed upon us by the Supreme Being so that we can worship Him and love Him. If we do not take advantage of it, we will have to keep returning to the prison of chaurasi.

∽

By the grace of the Guru the inverted lotus turns
straight and blooms;
the prevailing darkness is illumined with effulgent light.

> *Gur prasaad ooradh kamal bigaas.*
> *Andhkaar mah bha-i-aa pragaas.*

What is our condition? After death we are completely alone. Everything is darkened by our ignorance. We are weighed down by the load of sins on our head. We cannot see the way and we cannot find anyone to help us escape. When we come into the presence of a saint and practise meditation of the Word, the darkness of ignorance is removed from our path forever. The load of sins we are carrying gets very light—in fact, it is no longer there.

At the moment, our souls are in the grasp of the mind, and the mind is enslaved by the pleasures of the senses. When we start following the path given to us by the saints, this whole process is reversed. The soul comes to dominate the mind and the mind comes to dominate the senses. The soul becomes pure and the mind becomes pure. We rid ourselves of our physical appetites and are freed from the creation.

When we no longer have any attachments in the world, when we lose all love for the world, and our souls are able to leave the mind, what is there to bring us back? It is our mind, our actions, our karmas, that drag us back again and again to the imprisonment of a physical form. The soul is always yearning to be united with the Lord. It is filled with love, longing and restlessness for Him. A needle will always be attracted by a magnet, but if we put a stone on top of the needle, what can it do? In the same way, the soul is restless for immediate union with the Lord, the supreme soul of which it is a part. When the mind's load of karmas weighs down the soul, it becomes helpless and cannot do anything.

By contacting a lover of the Lord and meditating on the Name, the weight of the mind is removed from the soul, which then becomes pure and worthy of uniting with the Lord. Thus, the whole process has been reversed: first the soul was controlled by the mind and the mind was a slave of the senses; now this has been turned around—the soul has been freed, the mind has been made pure, and we have escaped both from our physical desires and from the pain of death and rebirth.

∾

The One who made all is realized through the Guru;
by his grace, the wayward mind is chastened.

Jin keeaa so gur te jaaniaa. Gur kirpaa te mugadh man maaniaa.

The One who made all" refers to the Supreme Being who created the whole world. It is always from the Masters—the holy men, saints and great souls—that we get to know about the Lord. Our mind then submits—that mind which is wayward, foolish and naive in the extreme. Enslaved as it is by the senses and always sitting over the soul, dragging it back again and again into the prison of the body, the "mind is chastened" and becomes pure.

The mind itself suffers greatly from being trapped by the senses. From its perspective, it was merely trying to find peace and happiness through the physical pleasures. As a result, however, it had to face more and more suffering. By holding onto the sound of the Word, the mind also reaches its own home, and it too breathes a sigh of relief. Guru Nanak Sahib says:

> When the Guru puts the collyrium of wisdom in
>   the eyes,
> truth is attained;
> effulgent inner light dispels the darkness of ignorance.
> *Gur giaan anjan sach netree paa-i-aa.*
> *Antar chaanan agiaan andher gavaa-i-aa.*
>
> Adi Granth, M3, p. 124

Once we have contacted a lover of the Lord and use the collyrium of wisdom in our eyes, once we make contact with the Word by concentrating our attention at the eye centre according to our Master's instructions, the darkness of ignorance disappears and we are filled with the brilliant light of the Lord. What benefit do we derive from this?

> When the soul's light merges with the supreme
>   light
> and the chastened mind stands still,
> we are exalted at the gate of the Lord.
> *Jotee jot milee man maaniaa*
> *har dar sobhaa paavaniaa.*
>
> Adi Granth, M3, p. 124

Our minds are chastened, reformed. At present they are used to going in a downward and outward direction. By listening to the Word and becoming motionless, they return to their home in Brahm. Once the mind reaches Brahm, the light that is our soul is able to dissolve into the supreme light. When we reach the court of the Almighty, we are in a position to enjoy our real splendour and worth. That is why he says here that our wayward minds come under control by the practice of meditation on the Word—they become pure.

If you keep on rubbing a rusty knife steadily against a grindstone, no matter how much rust has accumulated, it will all be gradually removed and a clean blade will emerge. Similarly, go on polishing your mind with the Word, and no matter how bad or dirty it has become, every layer covering it will be removed and it will become absolutely pure. Once the mind becomes pure, the soul is automatically released from its grasp. That is why Guru Sahib says:

> They who merge with the Word
> become pure beings and Truth-realized.
> *Pavit paavan se jan saache ek sabad liv laaee.*
>
> Adi Granth, M3, p. 910

People who detach themselves from all worldly love and connect themselves to the one Word, attain a state of absolute purity. If we associate with them, they attach us to the Word in the same way and make us pure also, forever.

∽

Guru is the creator, Guru is omnipotent;
Guru is God, and shall ever be.
Guru kartaa guru karnai jog. Guru parmesar hai bhee hog.

*H*e now praises the perfect Masters: Between them and the Supreme Being, there is no difference. They are the Creator— it is they who brought the universe into existence. He says:

> Know thou, Guru and God are one.
> *Guru parmesar eko jaan.*
>
> Adi Granth, M5, p. 864

No difference exists at all between the lovers of the Lord and the Lord. Christ says the same:

> I and my Father are one.
>
> John 10:30

And Bulleh Shah says:

> The Lord has transformed himself
> and come as a man.
> *Maulaa aadmee ban aaiaa.*
>
> Bulleh Shah, *Kulyat Bulleh Shah*[40]

The Supreme Being has come to me in the guise of a human being. Soami Ji says:

> Radha Soami has assumed the human form in this
>   world;
> He comes as a Master and awakens souls.
> *Raadhaaswaamee dharaa nar roop jagat me*[n]*,*
> *guru hoi jeev chitaaye.*
>
> Soami Ji, *Sar Bachan* 1:2, p. 6

Radha Soami, the absolute Being, in the guise of a human being, takes the form of a Master and is waking us up through his satsangs. By linking our consciousness to the Word, he is taking us back and merging us in the Lord.

That is why he says—in that the form of the Masters is one with the Supreme Being—the Masters are the Creator; it is within their power to do whatever they choose. He affirms that the Masters are the Supreme Being—they are, will be, and will always be. It is not that a past Master was the Lord, while some future Master will not be the Lord. Guru Sahib says:

> His is the sole kingdom, his Command is but one;
> his law and governance prevail from age to age.
> *Eko amar ekaa paatisaahee jug jug sir kaar banaaee he.*
>
> Adi Granth, M3, p. 1045

The Lord is one. He is the emperor and benefactor of everybody. His Command, his Will, is the one Cosmic Law for everyone. Saints and Masters come through his Command, and they come with his Command. Coming into the world, they stand witness to his Command—they preach his Command. They come in every age and they return to merge into his Command.

Guru Sahib says saints come into the creation "from age to age". Just as with the sea it is not possible for there to be only one wave, after which there are no more, so it is with saints and Masters, who come to the world repeatedly, like waves forming from the sea.

That is why the saints speak of Masters as waves, because they keep on coming. Waves will always go on forming from the ocean of Satnam, the true Name; emerging from the Word and Name, the Masters will always come to the world to continue revealing the Name.

∽

Says Nanak: O friend, the Lord has made this known:
Without a Guru, there is no salvation.

Kah naanak prabh ihai janaaee.
Bin gur mukat na paaeeai bhaaee.

In the end, Guru Sahib says that the Lord has guided and
taught us, and given us this understanding, that without a
Master, nobody can be liberated. Intellect and scholarship—
the power of the mind—will get us nowhere. Whatever we
are to attain will be attained through the Masters, through
our association with holy men and enlightened souls. As I
have already said, it is not that they somehow open people
up and place something in them. That wealth is already there
within us all. The Lord has kept it there within us for us to
use, and saints simply tell us how to find it. It is they who give
us the method. The fifth Padshahi says:

> He whose home has been locked,
> the key is with the Guru.
> Despite many attempts, the key cannot be obtained
> without surrender to the Satguru.
> *Jis kaa grih tin deeaa taalaa kunjee gur saopaaee.*
> *Anik upaav kare nahee paavai bin satgur sarnaaee.*
>
> Adi Granth, M5, p. 205

The Lord who made us has kept the wealth of the Name
within us for our use, but he has entrusted its secret to the
saints. However much we may search within ourselves with
our mind and intellect, we will never succeed in finding it

until we do as the saints instruct us. Whatever we are to attain, will be attained through the practice of the Word, and we can only meditate on the Word with the help of a saint. Guru Sahib states beautifully:

> Through the true Word one finds true honour;
> without the Lord's Name, there is no salvation....
> *Sachai sabad sachee pat hoee.*
> *Bin naavai mukat na paavai koee.*
>
> Adi Granth, M3, p. 1045

Only by listening to the true Word can you experience your true worth, can you have the privilege of being united with the Lord. Without this meditational practice, he states most emphatically, no one can ever attain liberation.

> ... Without the True Guru, none finds the Name;
> the Lord has willed it thus.
> *Bin satgur ko naao na paae*
> *prabh aisee banat banaaee he.*
>
> Adi Granth, M3, p. 1045

Without the Masters, we can have no understanding or knowledge of the Name, and our consciousness cannot be linked to it. Why do we need the Masters? The Lord has made this his natural law. Guru Sahib affirms that you may devise any technique or engage in any practice, but you will never attain liberation, nor will you escape the painful cycle of death and rebirth. From his own experience of searching for the Lord, of worshipping Him and attaining union with Him, he has learned that without the Masters, the question of salvation simply does not arise—it is difficult for us to take even one step inwards. That is why we love our Master.

7

Come, My Friend, to Your True Home

Dhaam apne chalo bhaaee

Come, my friend, to your true home.
Why live in an alien land?
Attend now to your own work;
do not get caught up in others' tasks.
Remember the Master's Name as you proceed through life—
it is the only wealth worth securing.
All the colours of the world are sullied;
be cleansed of them, I implore you.
Worldly pleasures last but a day;
try to renounce them gradually.
Resolutely surrender yourself to the perfect Master—
remain steadfast and apply yourself to this task.
Still the soul and mind within the body,
catch hold of the Melody
and focus your attention on the inner sky.
You are totally enmeshed in a net;
without this method, you will never get free.
The Master speaks out of compassion.
Heed his words; engrave them in your heart.
Why waste your life in futile search?
You will find fulfilment nowhere.
Come, live at the eye centre;
experience oneness here through concentration.
Here duality is transcended;
fix your attention in the inner light.
Give up the dark path, take the path of light.
Let your inner ear listen to the sound of the Melody.
Pierce through the entrance to Bank Nal
so you may reach Trikuti.
Go upwards, my friend, pierce Sunn;
bathe your soul in Mansarovar.
From the pitchdark crossroads of Maha Sunn,
pass on to Bhanwar Gupha.
Adorned in glory, enter the fourth realm.

There listen to the enchanting sound of the veena.
Beyond the regions of Alakh and Agam,
you will behold a wondrous palace.
There you will meet Radha Soami.
Your heart is now drenched in bliss.

Soami Ji, Sar Bachan 19:18, p. 152

Dhaam apne chalo bhaaee,
paraaye desh kyo^n rahanaa.
Kaam apnaa karo jaaee,
paraaye kaam nahi^n pha^{n}snaa.
Naam guru kaa samhaale chal,
yahee hai daam ga^{n}th bandhanaa.
Jagat kaa rang sab mailaa,
dhulaa le maan yaha kahanaa.
Bhog sa^{n}saar koi din ke,
sahaj me^n tyaagte chalnaa.
Saran satguru gaho drirh kar,
karo yaha kaaj pil rahanaa.
Surat man thaam ab ghat me^n,
pakar dhun dhyaan dhar gaganaa.
Pha^{n}se tum jaal me^n bhaaree,
binaa is jukti nahi^n khulanaa.
Guru ab dayaa kar kahte,
maan yaha baat chit dharanaa.
Bhatak me^n kyo^n umar khote,
kahee^n nahi^n theek tum laganaa.
Baso tum aae nainan me^n,
simat kar ek yahaa^n honaa.
Duee yahaa^n door ho jaave,
drishti jot me^n dharanaa.
Shyaam taj set ko gahanaa,
surat ko taan dhun sunanaa.
Ba^{n}k ke dwaar dhas baitho,
trikutee jaae kar lenaa.
Sunn charh jaa dhaso bhaaee,
surat se maansar nhaanaa.
Mahaasunn chauk andhiyaaraa,
vaha^n se jaa guphaa basanaa.
Lok chauthe chalo saj ke,
gaho vaha^n jaaee dhun beenaa.

Alakh aur agam ke paaraa,
ajab ik mahal dikhalaanaa.
Vahee^n raadhaaswaamee se milanaa,
huaa man aaj ati maganaa.

Soami Ji, *Sar Bachan Radhaswami,*
Chhand Band (Beas: Radha Soami Satsang Beas),
p. 152:19:18

~

Come, my friend, to your true home.
Why live in an alien land?

Dhaam apne chalo bhaaee, paraaye desh kyo^n rahanaa.

Yesterday I took my text from the writings of the house[*] of Shri Guru Nanak Dev Ji Maharaj, and today I am taking my text from the writings of Shri Hazur Soami Ji Maharaj. My sole intention in using the writings of different mystics is to emphasize that all saints bring just one message or teaching, they all explain the same method of worshipping God.

Soami Ji Maharaj says that all of us are looking for peace and happiness, but in our search for happiness, where does our attention normally turn? It turns towards the images and phenomena of the creation. Through these, he says, none of us have ever attained lasting peace and happiness, nor will we ever do so.

He explains that these images and forms are transient and perishable, and therefore the pleasure and contentment derived from them is also temporary and short-lived. With the passage of time, whatever happiness we experience will inevitably be transformed into pain.

All these gifts that the Lord has bestowed upon us, that we believe to be the source of our happiness, carry with them the fear that they might slip from our hands or that the Lord might take them back. Anything that keeps our minds in a state of anxiety twenty-four hours of the day will for certain transform happiness into pain.

---

[*] *See* Glossary and Translators' Note for explanations of unusual usage, and technical or Indian-language terms, such as: the house of Shri Guru Nanak, the true Name.

For example, when we get married, just think how happy everyone is. Money and gifts are given and people celebrate with singing and dancing. At the same time, however, our minds experience fear—fear that our partners might prove unfaithful or take to gambling, become alcoholics, quarrel with the neighbours, waste money, fall ill, or be called back by the Lord. These fears that take hold of the mind gradually transform all our happiness into a hell.

Similarly, when children are born, we naturally feel very happy, but this event also brings its share of anxiety. We worry about how we will raise them, how we will get sufficient money to meet their expenses, and how to educate them. We are concerned that they might fall into bad company, become criminals or alcoholics, or turn out to be no good. We fear they might desert us, get hurt in an accident, or fall ill. So gradually, instead of being a source of joy and contentment, our offspring become a cause of pain.

Sometimes we seek happiness through the intoxication of power. When people garland us with flowers, hold processions in our honour, put us up on elephants and shout and cheer for us, we become swollen-headed with pride and self-importance. But then we read the lives of great leaders and start worrying that we might also suffer their fate: What if I have to stand before a firing squad, or become the subject of an official enquiry? What if my name is dragged through the mud by the press, or I am suddenly thrown into prison by my opponents? These fears and apprehensions ultimately convert all our prestige and power into a source of misery and wretchedness.

In the same way, we definitely experience happiness when wealth and good fortune come our way—but then the mind again fills with worries. There may be tax problems, our friends may go back on agreements, or our shares and investments may decline in value. Such fears lead to stress, heart attacks, blood pressure problems, diabetes, depression and so on, so that instead of bringing happiness, our wealth becomes a cause of misery.

Yet another way we may seek happiness is through the pleasures of food and drink, through meat and alcohol. We may well derive pleasure from them at the time. Later on, when we have to pay for them through the damage they have done to our bodies, when we have to put up with the unrelieved routine of prison life, when we have to bear the expenses of lawyers and court cases, then we really find out whether such things bring pleasure or pain.

Why is it that we cannot find happiness through these worldly phenomena? Soami Ji says:

> Mind, renounce this world of pain and pleasure!
> Rise above it and attach yourself to the true Name.
> *Tajo man yaha dukh sukh kaa dhaam,*
> *lago tum charh kar ab satnaam.*
>
> Soami Ji, *Sar Bachan* 15:9, p. 119

The Lord has fashioned this world from both pleasure and pain. You will never find a person who has only experienced pain and misery without the respite of at least a few moments of happiness. Similarly, no one only experiences happiness without ever having to face pain. For example, if you experience ten days of happiness, after that you are likely to suffer some pain; if you undergo ten days of suffering, a breathing space with some degree of happiness is sure to follow.

Whatever happiness we experience is the result of our good actions in previous lives; whatever suffering we go through is the result of our bad actions in previous lives. We are each given a human life according to the way our good and bad actions combine, and while living that life we must settle the accounts of both. The good actions account for our periods of happiness, the bad ones for our moments of misery. People who have more good than bad actions to their credit appear to be comparatively happier and to suffer less, whereas those whose bad actions outweigh the good, suffer more and are happy less. It is inevitable, however, that each person experiences suffering as well as joy.

Saints do not come into the world in order to make it a happy place. If they had meant the world to become perfect, it would most certainly have become perfect by now.

History tells us that many great saints have made their appearance in different races, religions, countries and eras— Buddha, Jesus, Muhammad Sahib, Kabir Sahib, Guru Nanak Sahib and many other great saints have lived and taught in the world. Since it has not yet become a place of happiness in spite of their coming to this earth, then why should we delude ourselves that we can make it so?

How many problems can we resolve? How many thorns can we pick up in this world? However much we may try, it is not possible to remove them all. But if we are resolute, if we wear strong shoes, the thorns will have no effect on our feet. No one has ever resolved the problem of pain and pleasure, nor will it ever be resolved, but saints give us a method or practice—a way to pass through this life, worshipping the Lord all the while. This enables us to raise our attention above the experience of pleasure and pain.

Soami Ji says, "Rise above it and attach yourself to the true Name." If you want happiness, look for the true Name— the Supreme Being. Until the soul searches for the supreme soul and merges with it, there is no question of ever attaining lasting happiness. Guru Nanak Sahib says:

By returning to one's true home,
happiness, my friend, is attained.
Jinee ghar jaataa aapnaa se sukhee-e bhaaee.

Adi Granth, M3, p. 425

Anyone who reaches there, say the saints, finds everlasting happiness. And where is our true home? It is where the Lord resides.

We do experience a degree of happiness in the world provided that we are connected to the Lord through love and devotion. I often give the example of a small child who goes to a fair holding onto his father's finger. He thinks everything in the fair is very, very beautiful: in some places children's toys are on display, in others lights flash on and off, elsewhere there are stalls selling sweets. The child thinks his happiness comes from the wonderful things in the fair. If, by mistake, he lets go of his father's finger, even though the entire show is exactly as it was, the child begins to howl and cry. He realizes he was happy in the fair only as long as he held onto his father's finger.

Who is our father? He is none other than the supreme Lord, the Supreme Being. We enjoy peace and happiness in the world as long as our soul remains devoted to Him and continues in his worship. If we forget Him, then the entire world, for us, assumes the semblance of pain.

Just think, for example, of people who have been given every conceivable gift by the Lord: good health, respect, wealth, prosperity and a good life partner. He has not withheld anything from them, yet when they sit quietly on their own, they still do not have peace of mind or feel content. They may not even know what they are lacking—that the restlessness they feel is the soul's innate pull or yearning to return to its origin.

And how can they know peace or happiness until the soul is allowed to return to its source?

> O Nanak, the whole creation is miserable.
> *Naanak dukheeaa sabh sansaar.*
>
> Adi Granth, M1, p. 954
>
> Only those sustained by the Name are happy.
> *So sukheeaa jo naam adhaar.*

All beings, wherever and in whatever form they may be, are weighed down by problems and suffering. True happiness and peace belong only to the lovers of God, who have taken refuge in their love and devotion for Him. Baba Farid says:

> I thought I was the only one in pain, O Farid,
> but the whole world is suffering.
> When I reached up high,
> I found the fire of suffering in every being.
> *Fareedaa mai jaaniaa dukh mujh koo*
> *dukh sabaa-i-ai jag.*
> *Ooche char kai dekhiaa taa ghar ghar ehaa ag.*
>
> Farid, Adi Granth, p. 1382

He says: I thought that only I was suffering, but when I went to higher regions I saw that the whole world is being roasted in the fire of desires and cravings. Sehjo Bai says:

> All those who possess wealth are unhappy;
> the poor are the very picture of suffering.
> *Dhanvante sabahee dukhee, nirdhan hai^n dukh roop.*
>
> Sehjo, *Sehjo Bai ki Bani*, Doha 39[41]

It goes without saying that those who do not have anything to eat or drink and who go to bed at night hungry will feel miserable. But even those who possess great wealth and big estates are unhappy. They are so wretched that they often depend on pills and drugs to sleep at night. Guru Nanak Sahib says:

> Those who appear to be rich, important men,
> they are afflicted by the malady of anxiety.
> *Vade vade jo deesah log, tin kao biaapai chintaa rog.*
>
> Adi Granth, M5, p. 188

Rulers, royalty and millionaires appear to be important, successful people; yet they are the very ones who suffer from the worst disease—the disease of mental depression.

Soami Ji is therefore saying that as long as we are separated from the Lord, we will never experience happiness. And that is why he urges us: "Come, my friend, to your true home. Why live in an alien land?"

If you wish to attain happiness, if you wish to find peace, you must return to your real home. This land is not your land, this race is not your race, this religion is not your religion. Your native land is Sach Khand, the true realm; your race is Satnam, the true Name; your religion is love for the Lord. You have come into this world as a foreigner, and now you are wandering around restlessly, never feeling quite at home.

Just imagine: if we go to a country where we have absolutely no friends or acquaintances, can we ever be happy or enjoy peace of mind? This entire world is a foreign land for each one of us, and our real home is the home of the Supreme Being where our real self resides. We take this creation, this alien country, to be our home; we take what does not belong to us to be ours. How then can we possibly attain peace and happiness in it?

Our relationships with it are motivated by self-interest: we are creditors and debtors in a karmic transaction, giving to some and taking from others. As soon as our accounts are settled, we all go our separate ways. People with whom we have a karmic relationship come as brothers, sisters, parents, husband, wife, children, friends. As and when the debts are settled, those involved go their own separate ways. Many have already left us and gone ahead; many we have already left behind.

Imagine the currents in a river. The movement of one brings several pieces of wood together, while the movement of another disperses them. Similarly, a wave of karma arises and within moments all our relationships are established: brothers, sisters, sons, daughters, friends and acquaintances. Another wave of karma comes and they all scatter, all in their own particular directions. Similarly, if we travel daily by train, we encounter many different passengers. They all get down when they reach their destinations, and when we reach our station we also disembark. Actually, we have no connection or relationship with any of them.

This world is a large stage on which some play the part of heroes, some of heroines and some of villains. All speak and act according to the parts allotted to them, and once they leave the stage, they cease to be heroes, heroines or villains. Saints explain that we are given roles on the stage of the world according to our karmas—as brothers, sisters, sons, daughters and other relatives or friends—but none of us in this world actually belong to one another.

It is only because we think our relatives belong to us that we suffer day and night, that we lament and complain. In fact, we cannot make them ours—they never have belonged to us and they never will, and that is why we go on suffering. Soami Ji explains that no one can belong to anyone else because all of us are drops of the ocean of the true Name, our souls are particles of the Lord, the supreme soul. Having become separated from the Lord, we are enmeshed in the web of illusion and have to keep coming into the prison of chaurasi to undergo the consequences of actions performed in previous lives under the domination of our mind.

The world is a region of karmas, a field where we reap the harvest of actions we have sown.[42] Soami Ji says:

> For everything you do,
> you will have to experience the consequence.
> *Karam jo jo karengaa too, vahee phir bhognaa bharnaa.*
>
> Soami Ji, *Sar Bachan* 19:2, p. 143

If we do good deeds in this world, we come back to be rewarded; if we do bad deeds, we come back to suffer the painful results. We cannot escape from the imprisonment of the body by doing good deeds, nor can we find release from death and rebirth by doing bad deeds.

Good deeds may allow us to come back as rulers, royalty, religious leaders or people of great wealth. At most we will go to a paradise or a lower heaven, but even there we will be given a form of life with no free will *(bhog jooniaa^n)* and for a certain time only. Afterwards we will have to return once again to the prison of chaurasi, the endless cycle of life and death. If we do bad or criminal deeds, then hell and chaurasi stand ever ready to receive us.

Woman or man, king or subject, rich or poor, all come to the world to settle the accounts of their actions in previous lives. Where we are reborn is determined by those actions, and as we know from experience, we always suffer and face problems, irrespective of what form we take.

There is no physical form in which we can find peace or happiness. Consider the animals that humans eat—chickens,

cows, sheep—how they are butchered in the most terrible
ways, just to satisfy our stomachs! Have we ever thought how
we would feel if the situation were reversed? If, on account of
our karmas, our throats were being slit, and the knives and
hammers were in their hands? What suffering and terror we
would feel—we who only have to see an ordinary syringe being sterilized for an injection, to start trembling with nerves
and fear. But who cares what these animals undergo?

Look at the human form, considered to be the top of the
creation *(ashraf-ul-makhluqaat)*, and described by sages and
seers as the body in which God himself resides *(nar-naraayani
deh)*. What peace of mind or happiness can anyone experience while living in this form?

Some poor people are burdened by disease, others by
unemployment; some are miserable because they are child-
less, others because of their children; some have to repay
debts, others have to collect their dues. Go out into the streets
in the hot weather and notice the condition of the poor. Go
to the jails and listen to the stories of the prisoners. Go to the
hospitals and listen to the groans of the sick.

All around us we see nothing but suffering, misery and
trouble. Racial, religious and international hostilities follow
us wherever we go. How many poor people are slain, how
many women widowed, how many children orphaned!

In a world where people have to suffer and struggle simply to find food, clothing and shelter, how can anyone be
happy? We do not even know when, how or where death will
come. Soami Ji says:

> Listen to me, dear soul,
> your Husband lives in the regions above.
> *Surat sun baat ree, teraa dhanee base aakaash.*
> Soami Ji, *Sar Bachan* 19:6, p. 145

Soul, my friend—your husband is the Lord, the supreme soul. You are caught in this web of illusion, while He is there in the everlasting realm, Sach Khand. Until you return to your true home, you will never know fulfilment—you will always feel incomplete—and you will not be released from the painful cycle of death and rebirth.

Soami Ji is saying that we will attain happiness only when we go back to the lap of the Lord and merge ourselves with Him. Separate from Him, we will never be truly happy or at peace. That is why he arouses a yearning within us, a longing to meet the Lord, and reminds us that our true religion is nothing but love and devotion for the Lord. In other words, the relationship between the individual being and the Supreme Being is not a relationship of external observances; every saint has clearly stated that it is exclusively a relationship of devotion and love.

The religions we have made, and by which we live our lives, have masked this love and devotion; they have concealed it with their codes of conduct. It is these external practices and rituals that make some of us Sikhs, some Hindus, some Muslims and some Christians. Take off the coverings, and inside there is devotion and more devotion, love and more love, because that is the relationship between the soul and the Lord: devotion and love.

The spiritual essence of all religions is the same, but each has its own code of external practices. These fulfil the same function as a frame for a beautiful picture, a box to contain precious jewellery, or a scabbard to protect a sword. The value lies in the picture and the jewels, and it is the sword that achieves results; the frame, the box and the scabbard serve no useful purpose in themselves. Similarly, the code of external practices serves no purpose; it is devotion and love that work.

Soami Ji says: This is not your race, religion or country. Your race is Satnam, your religion is devotion to the Lord, your country is Sach Khand. That is why you need to detach your mind from this level and merge with the Lord through love and devotion for Him.

ᘖ

Attend now to your own work;
do not get caught up in others' tasks.

Kaam apnaa karo jaaee, paraaye kaam nahi^n pha^nsnaa.

Now Soami Ji Maharaj explains that whatever we see in this world is nothing but the vast prison of chaurasi. The Lord has provided just one way for us to escape. What is that? It is the human form. He has blessed us with the opportunity of a human life so that we can use it to search for Him, worship Him and become one with Him. In this way we can be freed forever from the ties of the body. Soami Ji says:

> Now you have this human body,
> do something for yourself.
> Don't toil vainly in this world—
> it is only a passing dream.
> Both body and home are unreal;
> why exhaust yourself over an illusion?
> *Milee nar deh yaha tumko, banaao kaaj kuchh apanaa.*
> *Pacho mat aai is jag me^n, jaaniyo rain kaa supanaa.*
> *Deh aur greh sab jhoothaa,*
> *bharm me^n kahe ko khapanaa.*

Soami Ji, *Sar Bachan* 15:13, p. 121

The Lord has blessed us with a human life so that we can accomplish our real task. Soami Ji says that while we are in this form, we should give some consideration to our own best interests. We should not be misled by the luxuries, pleasures, laughter and fun of the world; we should not believe it to be a place of great happiness. It is like a passing dream. Our bodies will perish, our homes will become dust. Everything is illusory, nothing in this world is real.

He urges us to keep our ultimate aim before our eyes, pursue our destination and make progress on the spiritual journey while living, so that the reason for coming into this human form is fulfilled. He tells us to do our own work: to keep in mind the purpose for which the Lord has sent us into this creation; to do the work that will liberate us from the imprisonment of the body; to avoid wasting our entire lives in activities that drag us back, time after time, into this prison.

What work will enable us to become one with the Lord? Love and devotion for Him. Everything else is cause and effect, karmic giving and taking, love with a motive. If we are constantly involved in activities connected with negative aspects of the mind, such as the pleasures of the senses, eating meat, drinking alcohol, and the endless issues of race, religion and nation, then these seeds that we are busily sowing will bring us back again and again. Guru Nanak Sahib cautions us:

> Like vermin in filth
> sustaining themselves on filth,
> we grow in filth, and ourselves become filth.
> *Bistaa ke keere bistaa kamaavah*
> *fir bistaa maahe pachaavaniaa.*
> Adi Granth, M3, p. 116

We human beings are like maggots. We are born in dirt, we live in dirt, we love dirt, we eat dirt, we die in dirt and then again we are reborn in dirt. Everything we see in this physical creation is dirt—it is transient and will perish—and yet we are attached to it. Sometimes this transient reality comes to us in the form of a mother or father, sometimes it is we who come as a brother or sister, as a mother or father, and in this way we never escape from the dirt.

For this reason, Soami Ji says we must do the work that will break the shackles of our karmas. We must not be burdened all our life with activities and involvements that bind us even further, repeatedly bringing us back to the world in one body or another. Guru Nanak Sahib says:

> Everyone is caught up in worldly activities;
> no thought is given to finding a solution.
> Man remains oblivious to the cycle of birth
>   and death,
> being foolish and ignorant under the sway
>   of his mind.
> *Dhandhai dhaavat jag baadhiaa*
> *naa boojhai weechaar.*
> *Jamman maran wisaariaa*
> *manmukh mugadh gavaar.*
>
>   Adi Granth, M1, p. 1010

How obsessed and foolish we are! We are so completely dominated by the mind that we do not even by chance think about the purpose for which the Lord sent us here. We are constantly running around to satisfy our basic needs, and we are forever restless, dissatisfied and unhappy because of our attachment to the images and forms of the creation. Our own house is being robbed and we are busy guarding other people's. We cannot lift our own load and we have made ourselves into beasts of burden for others. We deceive ourselves and we deceive the world.

Saints warn us not to take for granted that we will be given another human life after death. Who knows whether we will or not, or whether we might be born in a situation where our thoughts never turn towards devotion for God, even inadvertently. It is vital therefore that everyone take advantage of this opportunity. Soami Ji says:

> From this house, go to that house.
> *Is ghar se us ghar jaavo.*
> Soami Ji, *Sar Bachan* 20:10, p. 161

As long as the Lord grants us the opportunity of being in a human body, we must maintain our quest for that home which is real.

This body is a rented house—it is not ours. We are given it for fifty or sixty years, seventy or eighty years, and once we have exhausted the number of breaths allotted to us by the Lord, each of us must vacate it and move on. When we leave, it is consigned to fire or buried in the earth. Long before that time, we should search for our real home. That home, once found, will never again have to be left for a temporary one.

Soami Ji advises us: Do not remain entangled all your life in irrelevant activities. While you are in this body, make sure you do something for yourself.

~

Remember the Master's Name as you proceed through life— it is the only wealth worth securing.
Naam guru kaa samhaale chal, yahee hai daam gan th bandhanaa.

Whatever you acquire and accumulate during this life—
money, property, name and fame—none of it, Soami Ji says,
will go with you. When you leave, you will have to let go of
everything. The only thing that will accompany you is what
you have earned from the practice of the Name. Guru Nanak
Sahib says:

> Except Nam, you have no friend or companion.
> You will attain salvation
> only through the practice of Nam.
> *Bin naavai ko sang na saathee mukte naam dhiaavaniaa.*
>
> Adi Granth, M1, p. 109

Engrave this fact firmly on your mind: without the practice of the Name, the Word, you will neither attain salvation,
nor acquire anything that you can take with you into the next
life. The fifth Padshahi says:

> Friends, keep the company of saints
> and cherish the true Name;
> equip yourself with sustenance
> for this life and the next.
> *Sant janhu mil bhaaeeho sachaa naam samaal.*
> *Tosaa bandhahu jeea kaa aithai othai naal.*
>
> Adi Granth, M5, p. 49

Seek the company of saints, of Masters, and engage in the
practice of the Word, in the work of listening to the Sound.
This is your real 'sustenance'. If you practise the Name during this lifetime, it will enable you to pass your days happily
in this world, and moreover you can take it with you when
you leave.

As for the rest, you may accumulate whatever you wish, but you collect it here, and here you will leave it when you die. If we could take these things with us into the next life, there would be no such thing as legacies. People would make bookings and dispatch their possessions well in advance.

Saints tell us repeatedly that the only thing that stays with us is our practice of the Name. As we heard yesterday, in the writings of Guru Nanak Sahib:

> Here and hereafter, Nam is the only companion.
> *Aithai agai harnaam sakhaaee.*
>
> Adi Granth, M3, p. 230

The wealth of the Word remains with us both now and forever. In this world it brings us peace and happiness, and in the next it will take us to the inner sanctum of the Lord. The only thing that stays with us right to the Lord is the Name; everything else is left behind here. Saints say that if we want to earn this wealth, we must keep the company of the Masters and attend to the practice of the Name through them.

If you examine the writings of any saint, you will find they all praise the Name in verse after verse and page after page. What Name are they referring to? That which we cannot see with our eyes, describe with our tongue or hear with our ears. Hazur Maharaj Ji[*] used to call it 'the unwritten law, the unspoken language', and Christ refers to it when he says:

> Having eyes ye see not, having ears ye hear not.
>
> Mark 8:18

---

[*] The terms 'Hazur' and 'Hazur Maharaj Ji' are used by the speaker to refer to his Master, Maharaj Sawan Singh (1858–1948). *See also* Translators' Note and Glossary.

This is the same Name that is praised by the house of Guru Nanak Sahib:

> Seeing without eyes, hearing without ears,
> walking without feet, working without hands,
> speaking without tongue, thus dying while living,
> O Nanak, comprehending this divine Law
> shalt thou be able to merge in the Lord.
>
> *Akhee baajhah vekhnaa vin kan-naa sun-naa.*
> *Pairaa baajhah chalanaa vin hathaa karnaa.*
> *Jeebhai baajhah bolnaa io jeevat marnaa.*
> *Naanak hukam pachhaan kai tao khasmai milnaa.*
>
> Adi Granth, M2, p. 139

You will realize the Lord by listening to that Word which your physical eyes can never see, your ears can never hear, which the tongue cannot describe, hands cannot grasp, and feet cannot reach. This Word has no connection whatsoever with writing, reading or speaking. You can attain it only by "dying while living"—which means that you have to withdraw the attention from the nine doors of the body and bring it to a single focus behind the eyes.

Mystics describe this focusing of the attention within as 'dying while living' because, when someone dies, first the feet go cold and numb, then the attention rises up through the body towards the head, and the rest of the body becomes cold. When the attention or soul currents become one-pointed at the eye centre, the soul separates from the body, leaving it aside. Guru Sahib explains, as we will see, that through the process of simran and dhyan we are to do the same thing, to die while living, if we wish to merge with the Word or Name.

This Word, this Name, that is praised by the saints, is constantly reverberating behind the eyes in every living being. Guru Nanak Sahib says:

> Closing the nine doors
> and restraining the wandering mind,
> in the tenth, one finds one's true abode.
> There the unending music of the Word plays
>   day and night.
> Through the Guru's guidance, the celestial Word
>   is heard.
>
> *Nao dar thaake dhaavat rahaae.*
> *Dasvai nijghar vaasaa paae.*
> *Othai anahad sabad vajah din raatee*
> *gurmatee sabad sunaavaniaa.*
>
> Adi Granth, M3, p. 124

When you withdraw your attention from the nine doors or openings of the body and concentrate it behind the eyes, you will arrive at the door of your home. This entrance has one distinctive feature that is important to remember—the unending music of the Word that reverberates there all the time. Until we reach that door and hear the inner music reverberating within us, how can we accomplish our spiritual journey?

This resounding Melody is present within everyone— thieves, swindlers, holy men and saints—regardless of race, religion or country. Those who are blessed with the good fortune of concentrating their attention at the eye centre, whether they are Hindu, Sikh, Christian, or of any other faith, will hear the sound inside and see the light—the flame of the Word within themselves. Guru Sahib says:

> Just as fire is latent in wood
> and can be produced with skill,
> so is the flame of God's Name latent in everyone
> and can be revealed through the Guru's wisdom.
> *Kaasat mah jio hai baisantar*
> *math sanjam kaadh kadheejai.*
> *Raamnaam hai jot sabaaee*
> *tat gurmat kaadh laeejai.*
>
> Adi Granth, M4, p. 1323

Fire is latent in wood, but we cannot perceive it or make use of it. If we know the technique of rubbing one stick against another to produce it, then we will be able to see it, feel it and make use of it. In the same way, Guru Nanak Sahib says, the flame of God's Name is burning at the eye centre within each one of us, but it can only be revealed through the path of the saints, by turning inwards and searching within ourselves. What path do they teach?

> Nine are the doors, but all nine are insipid;
> the divine ambrosia flows from the tenth.
> *Nao darvaaj nave dar feeke ras amrit dasve chu-eejai.*
>
> Adi Granth, M4, p. 1323

They explain that sensual desires, negative tendencies, and the indulgences of eating and drinking, all lie below the eye centre. If we want to enjoy the ambrosia that is sweetness itself, it is to be found flowing at the eye centre. Unless we bring our attention to the point where the Lord bestows it, where He showers his grace and where the ambrosia of the Name can be tasted, how will we ever experience his gift?

Light is present behind our eyes and sound is continuously reverberating there as well, but we have been exiled—

a veil has been placed between us and the eye centre. That is why we live in the darkness of ignorance. The ambrosia that Guru Sahib praises in this verse is the true Word, the Shabd. The words and names we use in our daily lives are attributive *(varnaatmak)* words. They can be written, read and spoken. Out of their love, people have given countless names to the Lord. Countless saints have come into the world and they too have remembered the Lord with countless names. Many saints are yet to come and they will remember the Lord with still more names. We go on forgetting the names given by saints in earlier times, and out of our love, we keep on giving Him more and more new names.

These attributive names are just a means, but it is that other Name which is our ultimate aim and objective.

A mother uses many different terms of endearment for her child when she is moved by love, but this does not mean the relationship between the mother and her child is one of words. The relationship is one of devotion and love—the words just express it. Likewise, the relationship of the soul with the supreme soul is not one of words, but one of devotion and love. The words simply express that love. It makes absolutely no difference what words or names we use to remember the Lord.

Saints always sing the praises of the true Word, the everlasting Name. Scriptures and sacred texts are filled with its praise. By reading them we can discover how to contact and worship the Word. But as I said yesterday, reading itself does not bring liberation; only if we put into practice what we read will we be free. Soami Ji Maharaj lovingly reinforces this point when he says: Go to a saint and connect your attention to the Shabd, attach it to the Word, the Name. The third Padshahi says:

Friends, when you find a perfect Gurmukh,
he will teach you the true way to practise Nam.
Santah gurmukh pooraa paaee. Naamo pooj karaaee.

Adi Granth, M3, p. 910

When you go to a true devotee and lover of God, he will
show you the way to practise meditation and only then will
you be able to worship the Supreme Being. It is through the
practice of listening to the Shabd, the Name, that we truly
worship God. Soami Ji says:

The Master speaks out in clear terms:
Attach yourself to the unending music of the Word.
Other than the Word there is no way
to break from this mortal clay pot.
Guru kahe khol kar bhaaee
lag shabd anaahad jaaee,
bin shabd upao na doojaa
kaayaa kaa chhute na koozaa.

Soami Ji, Sar Bachan 20:10, p. 161

Soami Ji makes it clear there is no practice other than listening to the unending or limitless Word *(anahad shabd)*
through which we can be liberated from the prison of the
body. Guru Sahib says:

By merging into the Shabd,
one dies to the self
and gains everlasting life.
Sabad marai so mar rahai fir marai na doojee waar.

Adi Granth, M1, p. 58

If you keep your attention in the Shabd all day long, whatever

.you are doing, wherever you are, you will die forever; you will not have to die again and again, lifetime after lifetime. Guru Sahib says:

> One who dies while living, through God's holy
> Word,
> becomes whole and perfect;
> this is what Satguru, the brave warrior, proclaims.
> *Sabad marai soee jan pooraa.*
> *Satguru aakh sunaae sooraa.*
>
> Adi Granth, M3, p. 1046

Once you are absorbed in the Shabd and merged in it, once you annihilate your individual identity, you become whole and worthy of meeting the whole, perfect Lord. This is the method that our Master has explained for worshipping the Lord.

Saints say that whatever we are to receive will come through our practice. Their role is to explain to us this technique or practice. They do not open us up and place something within us that is not already there. The Lord has already placed everything we need within us, for us to use.

∽

> *All the colours of the world are sullied;*
> *be cleansed of them, I implore you.*
>
> *Jagat kaa rang sab mailaa, dhulaa le maan yaha kahanaa.*

Soami Ji lovingly explains that all worldly attachments, "the colours of the world", are impermanent. The love of sons and daughters, our involvement in worldly affairs, our physical appetites, are all unreal. They deceive us endlessly, they confuse and cloud our minds.

Now, Soami Ji says, go to a perfect Master and take your mind off these things. You have already wasted so much of your life in the luxuries and pleasures of the world. You should apply yourself to finding the Lord and worshipping Him.

ᕽᕽ

Worldly pleasures last but a day;
try to renounce them gradually.

Bhog sa^{n}saar koi din ke, sahaj me^n tyaagte chalnaa.

If we have not yet found lasting peace of mind and happiness through the senses, what makes us believe that they will ever make us happy? They bring nothing but suffering and more suffering, trouble and more trouble, sickness and more sickness. Soami Ji says we must stop thinking about them, we must withdraw our attention from them.

How can we withdraw our attention? He goes on to explain how this can be done.

ᕽᕽ

Resolutely surrender yourself to the perfect Master—
remain steadfast and apply yourself to this task.

Saran satguru gaho drirh kar, karo yaha kaaj pil rahanaa.

Soami Ji says that if we wish to detach ourselves from family ties, worldly affairs and the cravings of our senses, then we must find a perfect Master, keep his company and take refuge with him.

Our minds are very quickly influenced by the company we keep. If we associate with drinkers, we soon get into the habit of drinking; if we associate with gamblers, we acquire the habit of gambling. In the same way, if we associate with devotees and lovers of the Lord, their company inevitably awakens within us a desire to meet the Lord and a yearning for Him. Guru Sahib says:

> The worldly man with a confused mind
> is like a tangled skein of thread
> that cannot be woven into cloth.
> Nothing of value will come from this skein;
> we should avoid the company of such people.
> *Saakat soot bahu gurjhee bhariaa*
> *kiokar taan taneejai.*
> *Tant soot kichh niksai naahee*
> *saakat sang na keejai.*
>
> Adi Granth, M4, p. 1324

Cloth cannot be woven from yarn that is tangled. By keeping the company of people who are only interested in the material world, we will never be able to worship the Lord. So whose company should we keep? He says:

> O beloved Lord!
> Grant us the company of the true ones,
> that we may contemplate on God.
> *Gobind jeeo sat sangat mel har dhiaaeeai.*
>
> Adi Granth, M4, p. 1179

O Lord, please give us the company of saints and holy people. Give us satsang, so that we may worship you and love you. After being asleep for countless lifetimes, it is when we come into the presence of a saint that we wake up and understand. We understand the true nature of the relationship between the individual and the Supreme Being, the nature of the obstacle between them, and how to get rid of that obstacle. Realization and understanding of each and every thing comes by keeping the company of the Masters and associating with them.

When the mystics use the term 'satsang', it does not mean a gathering where one group abuses another, where the followers of one religion slander those of another, or where stories and legends about ancient kings and princes are narrated. In the satsang of the Masters no one is maligned or criticized. In their satsang, they speak of nothing but the glory of the Word. Guru Sahib says:

> Know that as true satsang
> where the doctrine of the one Name is explained.
> *Satsangat kaisee jaaneeai.*
> *Jithai eko naam vakhaaneeai.*
>
> Adi Granth, M1, p. 72

Satsang is where the teachings of the Word are preached, where the path of the Name is explained.

It is wrong of us to abuse and threaten people who do not worship God according to our way of thinking. We can lovingly explain to them: My friend, by following this path I have received these benefits. If it makes sense to you and suits you, you too are welcome to follow the same path and enjoy the same benefits. The fifth Padshahi says:

When the Satguru wishes to shatter the chains of
   attachment,
he places those souls in the company of saints
and immerses them in his love....
Jin ke bandhan kaate satgur
tin saadh sangat liv laaee.

Adi Granth, M5, p. 205

If a saint is to guide someone to God-realization, he first
attracts them to his satsang. He clears up their doubts and
misconceptions, detaches them from external forms of worship and attaches them to the Word, the Name. Then what
does he say?

... The five in unison sing the joyous song;
between them and the Lord, now no difference
   remains.
Panch janaa mil mangal gaaiaa
har naanak bhed na bhaaee.

Adi Granth, M5, p. 205

Once we come into the presence of a perfect Master and "sing
the joyous song", once we meditate on the Word, all distinctions between us and the Lord disappear. Through devotion
and love, the soul takes on the form of the Lord.

That is why Soami Ji praises satsang. We receive nothing
but benefit and blessings in the satsang of the Masters; there
is no question of loss. If a blind man goes into a flower garden,
he will not enjoy the beauty of the flowers but he will certainly
enjoy the beauty of their fragrance. If a stone is immersed in
water, it is not likely to dissolve but it will, at least, be spared
the burning heat of the sun. Even if we do not meditate on
the Name, at least we will be spared from doing bad deeds.

Soami Ji lovingly explains that if we wish to understand what is real in the world, if we wish to worship the Lord, we must associate with the lovers of the Lord and keep their company.

∽

Still the soul and mind within the body,
catch hold of the sound of the Melody
and focus your attention on the inner sky.

Surat man thaam ab ghat me^n,
pakar dhun dhyaan dhar gaganaa.

Soami Ji points out how, by attending the satsang of a Master, we are to detach ourselves from the pleasures of the senses.

He explains that our spiritual journey begins at the soles of the feet and ends at the crown of the head. There are two stages in the journey: the first is up to the eyes, the second is above the eyes. In the body, the seat of the soul and the mind is at a place behind the eyes. Known as the eye centre or third eye, the gateway to liberation *(mukti daa darvaazaa),* it is also called the eye of Shiva *(shiv netra),* the divine eye *(divya chakshu),* the door to our home *(ghar dar),* and the black point *(nuqtaa-e-savaidaa).*

From the eye centre our attention goes down and spreads out into the whole world through the nine doors or openings of the body. How does it spread out? Although we are sitting here, we are thinking sometimes of our children, sometimes of our homes, our businesses, friends, associates. The mind is never still. It is always busy with some thought or other.

This mental habit of thinking all day is described by saints as doing *simran*. Simran is natural to each one of us, it is inborn in us. Even if we completely isolate ourselves in pitch darkness in the innermost room of a house, our attention will not be there—our thoughts will have spread out into the whole world. Whatever we are thinking of, we automatically visualize its form in our mind's eye. If we do simran of our children, we see them in our imagination. If we do simran of any work connected with our home, we visualize that too. This tendency of the mind to visualize whatever is being remembered is known by the saints as *dhyan*.

So, whatever we constantly recall, we also visualize, and inevitably we become attached to it and start loving it. We become so attached to these images and forms that they even come to us in our dreams at night. At the time of death it is they that appear before our eyes as though on a cinema screen. "Where our desires are, there we dwell."[43] In this world, the direction in which our attention goes in our last moments determines the course of our next life.

So what brings us again and again into the imprisonment of the body? It is our attachment to the world and our love for it. What causes this attachment? Our habit of doing simran and dhyan, of thinking and visualizing. But the things we remember and visualize are all temporary and perishable. Indeed, everything we see in the world is transient and perishable.

Saints say: Since the mind is always occupied in simran and dhyan, take advantage of this natural habit. Only simran can replace simran, only dhyan can replace dhyan—but do simran and dhyan of that which is everlasting and imperishable. And who is that? The Supreme Being, the supreme Lord alone.

Mystics teach us how to do simran of the Lord's Name to bring our scattered attention back to the eye centre and make it one-pointed. Once there, the attention does not stay, because since time immemorial it has developed the habit of running out, of coming down into the world. Until we give it some form or other on which to contemplate, it will not develop the habit of staying still.

What form should we contemplate on, since we do not know what God looks like? We should contemplate on the perfect Masters, because the Masters' real form is the Word, the Name. They have emerged from the Word, they teach us about the Word, they go back and merge with the Word—and we too want to become one with the Word. Since our Master has already connected us to the Word or Name, it is his form we are to contemplate on. Guru Nanak Sahib says:

> Hold fast your mind
> in contemplation of the Guru's form.
> *Gur kee moorat man mah dhiaan.*
>
> Adi Granth, M5, p. 864

And Soami Ji says:

> Beloved, contemplate on the form of the Master!
> Without this there is no liberation.
> *Guru kaa dhyaan kar pyaare,*
> *binaa is ke nahee*^{n} *chhutanaa.*
>
> Soami Ji, *Sar Bachan* 19:2, p. 143

By contemplating on the Master's form, our attention develops the habit of staying still at the eye centre. Once it remains still and no longer goes out, it automatically starts listening to the sound of the Word inside. The more we develop a taste for the sweetness of the Word inside, the more our attachment to the things of the world decreases.

The fact is, the mind is a lover of pleasure. Until it is given a pleasure that is higher and better than any available in the world, it will never be prepared to give up its love for the things of the world. Guru Nanak Sahib says:

> The Word of the Guru is sweet beyond measure;
> that sweetness cannot be known unless you taste it.
> *Gur kaa sabad mahaa ras meethaa*
> *bin chaakhe saad na jaapai.*

Adi Granth, M3, p. 753

The Word to which we are connected by the Master is "sweet beyond measure"—its sweetness cannot be expressed in words. When it is a question of tasting and experiencing something, words serve no purpose.

Once we are given a taste of the Word, the mind automatically gives up its negative tendencies and cravings for the pleasures of the senses. Why should someone who has been given diamonds and precious jewels put up with being driven from door to door, begging for worthless trinkets? Little girls play with dolls only until they grow up and become mature.

Attachment to the Word automatically detaches us from the world forever. Soami Ji says that if we want our mind to be freed from its negative habits and physical appetites, we must listen to the Shabd through the practice of simran and dhyan.

✧

> *You are totally enmeshed in a net;*
> *without this method, you will never get free.*
> *Phanse tum jaal men bhaaree, binaa is jukti nahin khulanaa.*

Soami Ji says that all of us are caught in Kal's net in the most terrible way. The suffering we are undergoing now—our tears and anguish—is the result of our actions of previous lives. In our ignorance, we continue to commit the same dark and evil deeds, for which we will again have to return to the world and face more suffering. Apart from the practice of the Word, he says, there is no way to escape from the prison of the body.

We can only be taken beyond the influence of mind and the illusion of matter by a power that is itself beyond their orbit. The Word originates from the everlasting realm of Sach Khand. When we focus our attention at the eye centre and attach ourselves to the Shabd, it will pull us there too, merging us into itself and drawing us back to Sach Khand. Guru Sahib says:

> Through the grace of the Guru
> we rise above Trikuti
> and become absorbed in the fourth realm.
> *Gur parsaadee trikutee chhootai*
> *chaothai pad liv laaee.*
>
> Adi Granth, M3, p. 909

"Through the grace of the Guru" means that when we follow the teachings given to us by the Masters and apply ourselves to the practice of the Word, we leave Trikuti, the domain of Kal, and return to the fourth realm, Sach Khand. It is only the practice of listening to the Shabd that takes us out of the orbit of Kal and reunites us with the Lord. This is why the first Padshahi says:

> O father, the world is caught in the great net.
> By Guru's grace, contemplating the true Name, one
> is emancipated.

Baabaa jag phaathaa mahaa jaal.
Gur parsaadee ubare sachaa naam samaal.

Adi Granth, M1, p. 1009

We are alarmingly trapped in Kal's net. The Lord has provided just one means of escape, and that is to go to a perfect Master and meditate on the Word, do the practice of the Name. Guru Nanak Sahib says:

Without the Name, there can be no other worship
of God;
in vain, the world strays in doubt.
Bin naavai hor pooj na hovee bharam bhulee lokaaee.

Adi Granth, M3, p. 910

Apart from the practice of the Name, there is no other form of worship, no method or technique, through which you can be united with the Lord. To escape from this net in which everyone is caught, Soami Ji says there is one method only: attach yourself to the Name.

ᕫ

The Master speaks out of compassion.
Heed his words; engrave them in your heart.

Guru ab dayaa kar kahate, maan yaha baat chit dharanaa.

Soami Ji says that saints have no personal motive in their mission. They do not come to create sects, start religions, rule countries, or acquire property and accumulate wealth. They come out of compassion. They shower us with grace and mercy, knowing how long we have suffered in the cycle of chaurasi and with what difficulty we have attained the human form. They come to explain the way out of here—how to escape from this region. Moved by compassion, they have mercy on us.

It is in this context that Guru Nanak Sahib speaks of the Master's blessing *(gur parshaad)*—that which is given freely. Parshad is always given from the heart, freely. This parshad, the blessing of initiation, the gift of the Name *(naam-daan)*, is called parshad for the very reason that it is given freely. Just as no value can be put on a gift, so parshad cannot be bought at any price. Soami Ji explains that it is their grace that saints show us the way to escape from this prison; they do not have any ulterior motive or self-interest. They serve their disciples and, at the same time, they support themselves through their own hard work.

Guru Nanak Sahib, for example, tilled the land on his farm at Kartarpur with his own hands. He provided for himself and his family, and he served the sangat throughout his life without ever taking anything for himself. And what advice did he give the sangat?

> Never bow down before one
> who calls himself a Guru and a spiritual preceptor
> and goes begging.
> He who eats what he earns by his earnest labour
> and from his hand gives something in charity,
> Nanak says, he alone knows the true way.
> *Gur peer sadaa-e mangan jaa-e.*
> *Taa kai mool na lageeai paa-e.*
> *Ghaal khaa-e kichh hathah deh.*
> *Naanak raah pachhaanah se-e.*
>
> Adi Granth, M1, p. 1245

We should never bow in reverence before anyone who calls himself a Guru or Master and yet accepts donations from disciples. What sort of saint should we seek? One who not only earns his own living, but also serves his followers.

Consider the example of Kabir Sahib, who spent his whole life working hard weaving cloth at a loom, although he had disciples like the Shah of Balkh-Bokhara who could have kept him in the lap of luxury. Kabir Sahib says:

> I would rather die than beg for myself,
> but for spiritual work I feel no shame.
> *Mari jaau^n maangoo^n nahee^n apne tan ke kaaj,*
> *parmaarath ke kaarane mohi^n na aavai laaj.*
>
> Kabir, *Kabir Sakhi Sangreh*

Saints encourage philanthropy among their disciples, but they never ask for anything for themselves. They say:

> It is for the disciple to give everything to
>   the Master;
> it is for the Master to accept nothing from
>   the disciple.
> *Shishya ko aisaa chaahiye, guru ko sarbas dey,*
> *guru ko aisaa chaahiye, shishya kaa kachhu na ley.*
>
> Kabir, *Kabir Sakhi Sangreh*

It is a basic principle for disciples that they should look upon everything they have as belonging to the Master. But true Masters will not accept even a pin from their disciples. If they do, they are not true Masters.

Take the example of Saint Ravidas: he earned his own livelihood as a cobbler, making shoes all his life, yet Mira Bai, the princess of Chittor, and Raja Pipa, a Rajput warrior-king, were among his disciples. Baba Namdev earned his living printing cloth by hand. Dadu Sahib worked as a carder, processing raw cotton. Paltu Sahib supported himself by running a grocery shop. The lives of the Masters here in Beas are there for you to see.

By making their own lives examples for us, saints teach us how to serve the sangat while fulfilling our responsibilities in the world. They have no self-interest in what they do.

~

Why waste your life in futile search?
You will find fulfilment nowhere.

Bhatak me^n kyo^n umar khote, kahee^n nahi^n theek tum laganaa.

Soami Ji warns us of the danger that lies in turning outwards, trying one thing after another, since nothing is to be gained from such practices.

He says you may bow before the relics and tombs of different saints, pray to pictures and idols, bathe in holy waters, go on pilgrimages, pierce your ears, grow long hair, smear ash on your body, give in charity, do good deeds, chant sacred names, practise austerities, perform penances—you may do whatever you want, but any progress you are to make will come only through the practice of Shabd, through listening to its sound. Soami Ji says:

> Engage in the practice of listening to the Shabd.
> Put all other efforts aside.
> *Surt shabd kamaaee karnaa,*
> *sab jatan door ab dharnaa.*
>
> Soami Ji, *Sar Bachan* 20:10, p. 161

You need only attend to the practice of uniting the soul with the Name. There *is* no other method. Anything else would be a waste of time. Guru Nanak Sahib says:

> The whole world is engaged in the worship of
>   the Lord,
> but worldly people do not find their bearings.
> *Poojaa karai sabh lok santah*
> *manmukh thaae na paaee.*
>
> Adi Granth, M3, p. 910

All of us worship the Lord in our own various ways because our souls yearn to return to their origin. Under our soul's influence, we all experience the longing to unite with Him, but, as Guru Sahib says, in our search for God we are led by the mind. The mind drives us outwards, pushing us towards external rituals and ceremonies, and that is why "worldly people do not find their bearings." Worship that is directed by the mind is not true worship and will never take us to our destination.

> Friends, the mind becomes pure
> when it merges in the Word.
> This worship alone takes us home.
> *Sabad marai man nirmal santah,*
> *eh poojaa thaae paaee.*
>
> Adi Granth, M3, p. 910

When you listen to the Shabd, when you meditate on the Name, you cleanse the mind, you purify it. This is real worship. This is the devotion that will take you to your destination. The only form of worship acceptable to the Supreme Being is the practice of Shabd. Guru Nanak Sahib says:

By forsaking the Name
and following other paths,
you will be filled with regret at the time of death.
Naam visaar chalah an maarag
ant kaal pachhutaahee.

Adi Granth, M1, p. 1153

If you abandon the practice of the Name, then no matter what other path you follow, you will regret it at the time of death, realizing too late that you have wasted your precious time.

Soami Ji cautions us: Why go on running around after all these external rituals and practices, uselessly trying this and that? You will gain nothing from these things. Whatever you are to achieve will be through your practice of joining the soul with the Word *(surat shabd abhyaas)*, through meditation on the Name.

ॐ

Come, live at the eye centre;
experience oneness here through concentration.
Baso tum aai nainan me^n, simat kar ek yaha^n honaa.

Here duality is transcended;
fix your attention in the inner light.
Duee yaha^n door ho jaave, drishti jot me^n dharanaa.

In the end, Soami Ji tells us something of the inner spiritual journey. We know that this homeward journey starts behind the eyes, because the eye centre is the door to our home.

Below this point, there is nothing but the pleasures of the senses, the destructive tendencies of the mind and the indulgences of the flesh. He says that as long as our attention spreads downwards and outwards from the eye centre, we are trapped in duality.

Once we withdraw our attention from the outer world and focus it behind the eyes with the help of simran and dhyan, we transcend duality and become one. When that happens, we will see a light, a light that shines within everyone—thieves and swindlers, holy men and saints—regardless of race, religion or country. Anyone who is blessed with the good fortune of becoming one-pointed at the eye centre will see that light within. This is the light of which Kabir Sahib says:

> The lamp of Agam
> burns without wick, without oil.
> *Deepak jarai agamm kaa, bin baatee bin tel.*
>> Kabir, *Kabir Sakhi Sangreh*

To light an oil lamp, we need both wick and oil, and if one or the other is used up, the light goes out. But the lamp of Agam, the inaccessible region, needs neither wick nor oil. Similarly, Christ says:

> If therefore thine eye be single,
> thy whole body shall be full of light.
>> Matthew 6:22

If you close the nine doors of the body and open the third eye, you will see nothing but radiant light within. This is the light of which the saints say:

Within me is the light of the Word
from which music arises continuously;
it is through this that I am attached in love
to the true Lord.
Antar jot nirantar baanee saache saahib sio liv laaee.

Adi Granth, M1, p. 634

The light is within each one of us behind the eyes, and a
sweet melodious music emanates from within it. Whoever
sees that light and listens to that sound escapes from the attachments of the world and develops love for the Supreme
Being instead. That is the light we must see. Paltu Sahib says:

From within the lamp's light emanates a sound;
it is heard by one in deep meditation—no one else
can hear it.
Niksai ek aavaaz chiraag kee jyotihi^n maahee^n.
Gyaan samaadhee sunai aur kou suntaa naahee^n.

Paltu, *Paltu Sahib ki Bani*, Kundli 169

When we are absorbed in meditation, when, under the
guidance of a Master, we withdraw our attention to the eye
centre through the practice of simran and dhyan, we see a
lamp burning there. From within its light comes the melodious resonance of the sweetest of sounds. It is by listening to
this sound that we find the direction of our home, and we
travel the inner journey guided by the light, so that stage by
stage we reach our destination.

Think for a moment of the various places of worship
where people pray to the Lord according to their particular
ideas and beliefs. In temples, whether Hindu, Buddhist or
Jain, the first thing we notice is a bell hanging in the entrance
for people to ring as they go in, and we see lamps burning

inside. In a gurdwara, lamps are lit, bells rung and the conch is blown. In churches, bells are rung before the service and candles are lit inside. In a mosque the priest chants to call the faithful to prayer, and lamps are lit at night.

We never pause to think or ask ourselves why lamps are lit in all these places, why bells are rung and different sounds are made. All sages and seers, saints and enlightened beings, devotees and lovers of the Lord, have explained that the real temple, the real mosque, the real gurdwara, the real church, is this human body. Turn inwards and search within yourself, you will hear the sound of a conch and bell, and experience that light. This is why Guru Nanak Sahib refers to the body as God's temple *(hari mandar)*. In the Bible it is called the temple of the living God.[44] Hindu sages and seers speak of it as the human form divine *(nar-naraayani deh)*.

. But we make no attempt to go within. We just build edifices of brick and stone, ring bells and light candles. These things are there to help us understand; they are only symbols, whereas the reality lies within us, inside our body.

That is why Soami Ji Maharaj directs us inwards, explaining that we can only make our spiritual journey if we first come to the eye centre.

೧

Give up the dark path, take the path of light.
Let your inner ear listen to the sound of the Melody.

Shyaam taj set ko gahanaa, surat ko taan dhun sunanaa.

Pierce through the entrance to Bank Nal
so you may reach Trikuti.

Bank ke dwaar dhas baitho, trikutee jaae kar lenaa.

Go upwards, my friend, pierce Sunn;
bathe your soul in Mansarovar.

Sunn charh jaa dhaso bhaaee, surat se maansar nhaanaa.

From the pitchdark crossroads of Maha Sunn,
pass on to Bhanwar Gupha.

Mahaasunn chauk andhiyaaraa, vaha^n se jaa guphaa basanaa.

Adorned in glory, enter the fourth realm.
There listen to the enchanting sound of the veena.

Lok chauthe chalo saj ke, gaho vaha^n jaaee dhun beenaa.

Beyond the regions of Alakh and Agam,
you will behold a wondrous palace.

Alakh aur agam ke paaraa, ajab ik mahal dikhalaanaa.

There you will meet Radha Soami.
Your heart is now drenched in bliss.

Vahee^n raadhaaswaamee se milanaa, huaa man aaj ati maganaa.

8

He Is the True Creator, the Only Giver

Jagjeevan saachaa eko daataa

He is the true Creator, the only Giver,
revealed as the Word, through service of the Guru.
His is the sole kingdom, his Command is but one;
his law and governance prevail from age to age.

Pure are they who have realized the self;
the source of all joy Himself comes and meets them.
They who sing the Lord's praise, immersed in the Word,
are honoured in the court of the Eternal One.

Honoured is the Lord's lover, who is one with his Word;
dishonoured is the slanderer and the slave of the mind.
Imbued with the Name, the supreme swans remain detached;
they live in their own home, their devotion unbroken.

One who dies while living, through God's holy Word,
    becomes whole and perfect;
this is what Satguru, the brave warrior, proclaims.
Within the body lies the real pool of nectar;
the mind drinks from it with serene devotion.

The learned man reads and teaches others,
oblivious of the fires that burn his own home.
Without serving the Satguru, one is not blessed with the Name;
one may read till exhausted, yet will not find peace.

Hypocrites proclaim purity by smearing ash on themselves;
but who can kill the ego without the Lord's Word?
The fires of their senses rage day and night;
deluded, they wander, lost in outward forms.

Some remain detached, even in home and family;
they die through the Word and dwell in God's Name.
Steeped, day and night, in the colour of devotion,
their hearts are filled with fear, love and devotion.

Egocentric people waste their lives in slander;
within them barks the dog of greed.
They are never let free by the agents of Death;
they regret in vain at their final hour.

Through the true Word one finds true honour;
without the Lord's Name, there is no salvation.
Without the True Guru, none finds the Name;
the Lord has willed it thus.

While some seek enlightenment through yogic practices
    and some through the intellect,
there are some who remain immersed, day and night, in the Formless.
Those the Lord unites with himself, they alone realize Him.
Through devotion and love, all fears are dispelled.

Enlightenment is never gained through holy baths and works of charity,
but by vanquishing the mind alone, as though fighting a great battle.
Dyed in the unifying colour of the true Word,
they leave duality and are merged with the true Word.

He himself creates beings, He himself bestows honour,
He himself brings union through his divine Will.
Through his own grace He abides in the mind;
my Lord has ordained it so.

Know them to be true who serve the Satguru;
false are the self-willed, who know not how to serve him.
The Lord himself creates, and watches his creation;
He makes it act according to his Will.

In every age He is the Truth, the one benevolent Lord.
When one's destiny is perfect, He is realized through the Guru's Word.
Those united to Him through the holy Word are never separated;
His glance of grace bestows bliss on them.

Through ego one gathers the dirt of illusion;
caught in duality, one suffers in the circle of birth and death.
Without serving the Satguru, there is no salvation;
with this realization, will the mind become absorbed.

That alone comes to pass as is willed by the Lord;
of itself nothing has ever happened, nor ever shall.
Through the Lord's Name, O Nanak, come honour and glory,
and one is exalted at the gate of the true Lord.

Adi Granth, Guru Amardas, p. 1045

Jagjeevan saachaa eko daataa. Gur sevaa te sabad pachhaataa.
Eko amar ekaa paatisaahee jug jug sir kaar banaaee he.

So jan nirmal jin aap pachhaataa. Aape aae miliaa sukhdaataa.
Rasnaa sabad ratee gun gaavai dar saachai pat paaee he.

Gurmukh naam milai wadiaaee. Manmukh nindak pat gavaaee.
Naam rate paramhans bairaagee nijghar taaree laaee he.

Sabad marai soee jan pooraa. Satguru aakh sunaae sooraa.
Kaa-i-aa andar amritsar saachaa man peeve bhaae subhaaee he.

Par pandit avaraa samjhaae. Ghar jalte kee khabar na paae.
Bin satgur seve naam na paaeeai par thaake saant na aaee he.

Ik bhasam lagaae phirah bhekhdhaaree. Bin sabdai haomai kin maaree.
Andin jalat rahah din raatee bharam bhekh bharmaaee he.

Ik grih kutamb mah sadaa udaasee. Sabad mue harinaam nivaasee.
Andin sadaa rahah rang raate bhai bhaae bhagat chit laaee he.

Manmukh nindaa kar kar wigutaa. Antar lobh bhaokai jis kutaa.
Jamkaal tis kade na chhodai ant ga-i-aa pachhutaaee he.

Sachai sabad sachee pat hoee. Bin naavai mukat na paavai koee.
Bin satgur ko naao na paae prabh aisee banat banaaee he.

Ik sidh saadhik bahut weechaaree. Ik ahinis naam rate nirankaaree.
Jis no aap milaae so boojhai bhagat bhaae bhao jaaee he.

Isnaan daan karah nahee boojhah. Ik manooaa maar maanai sio loojhah.
Saachai sabad rate ik rangee saachai sabad milaaee he.

Aape sirje de wadiaaee. Aape bhaane de-e milaaee.
Aape nadar kare man wasiaa merai prabh io furmaaee he.

Satguru sevah so jan saache. Manmukh sev na jaanan kaache.
Aape kartaa kar kar wekhai jio bhaavai tio laaee he.

Jug jug saachaa eko daataa. Poorai bhaag gur sabad pachhaataa.
Sabad mile se wichhure naahee nadree sahaj milaaee he.

Haomai maa-i-aa mail kamaa-i-aa. Mar mar jammah doojaa bhaa-i-aa.
Bin satgur seve mukat na hoee man dekhah liv laaee he.

Jo tis bhaavai soee karsee. Aapah hoaa naa kichh hosee.
Naanak naam milai wadiaaee dar saachai pat paaee he.

Shabdarath Sri Guru Granth Sahib Ji (Amritsar: Shromani
Gurdwara Prabandhak Committee), M3, p. 1045

He is the true Creator, the only Giver,
revealed as the Word, through service of the Guru.
Jagjeevan saachaa eko daataa. Gur sevaa te sabad pachhaataa.

Yesterday I took my text from the writings of Shri Hazur
Soami Ji Maharaj, and today I am taking it from the line of
Gurus[*] who said specifically that their teachings are for all
four castes, for all humanity, and not directed to any particular race, sect or group.[45] They made it clear that their message is the same for all, since they saw everyone as belonging
to one family. They wrote:

> With none have I enmity or ill will.
> None is alien to me; all are my own.
> *Naa ko bairee nahee bigaanaa*
> *sagal sang ham kao ban aa-ee.*
>
> Adi Granth, M5, p. 1299

Guru Sahib explains that since every living being, everyone
in the whole creation, has been made by the same one supreme
Lord, we have no enemies and consider no one a stranger—
we love everyone and everyone is dear to us. Again they say:

> All belong to you, O Lord; you belong to all.
> Whom shall we call bad, when there is none other
>   than you?

---

[*] *See* Glossary and Translators' Note for explanations of unusual usage, and technical or Indian-language terms, such as: line of Gurus, tattva.

Jeea jant sabh tis de sabhnaa kaa soee.
Mandaa kis no aakheeai je doojaa hoee.

Adi Granth, M3, p. 425

O Lord, you have created everyone in the universe and you yourself are present in everyone. I could only criticize or speak ill of people created by one other than you. See how the saints try to raise our awareness!

Notice also with what words they teach us to pray: "By thy Will, let all be blessed!"[46] Whenever we pray to the Lord, we are to pray with a sincere heart that He shower his blessings on the whole world. How can we speak ill of one another, be malicious, or consider anyone bad, when we invoke God's blessings on all humankind?

These verses by the third Padshahi, Shri Guru Amardas Ji Maharaj, explain every aspect of the teachings of the house of Guru Nanak Sahib. He says: "He is the true Creator, the only Giver." The Supreme Being is one. It is not that there is one God for Hindus, another for Sikhs or Christians, and another for Muslims; nor that people who live in India worship one God, while those who live in Africa or America worship another. Guru Nanak Sahib says:

> There is only one Bestower for all beings.
> May I never forget Him!
> *Sabhnaa jeeaa kaa iku daataa so mai wisar na jaaee.*

Adi Granth, M1, Japji, p. 2

Everything we see in the world was created by the one Supreme Being who is the benefactor and emperor of all, and takes care of everyone. Muslim faqirs describe Him as 'God of all the worlds' *(rab-ul-aalameen)*, not just 'God of the Muslims' *(rab-ul-musalmeen)*, since He is God of the entire universe. Hindu sages always describe Him as 'the One, the One alone' *(ek-ekaa)*. All saints point out that there is only one Supreme Being and it is He who is everpresent and everlasting. In the opening verse of the Japji, Guru Nanak Sahib explains:

> True in the beginning, True through the ages,
> True He is, and True He shall be.
> *Aad sach jugaad sach.*
> *Hai bhee sach naanak hosee bhee sach.*
>
> Adi Granth, M1, Japji, p. 1

Guru Sahib says that through his own personal experience he has realized the truth that has always been and will always be. By 'true' he means that which will never perish or pass away. This can be nothing other than the supreme Lord, the Supreme Being. In the beginning was the Lord alone and everything was created by Him. Whatever He created is subject to dissolution and will perish, but the One who created everything is everlasting and eternal. He was present in the beginning, present through all ages, is present now, and will be present forever. This is why it is written:

> Apart from the Lord, my friends, everything is
>   impure.
> *Har bin sabh kichh mailaa santah.*
>
> Adi Granth, M3, p. 910

Apart from the Lord, everything is false, everything is perishable. Guru Sahib explains in Asa di Var:

> The false are in love with the false
> and have forgotten their Creator;

whom to love and make one's friend
when the whole world is in a state of flux?
Koor koorai nehu lagaa wisariaa kartaar.
Kis naal keechai dostee sabh jag chalanhaar.

Adi Granth, M1, p. 468

Our bodies are like rented houses that do not belong to us. They have been given to us for our use for a certain period of time—possibly fifty, sixty or even seventy years. After that they are buried or consigned to fire, dust returning to dust and ashes to ashes. Guru Sahib explains that the loves and attachments we develop through our material association with the world are transitory and will also perish. We live out our lives in forgetfulness of the Supreme Being because this transient body is always entangled in its transient attachments and loves.

He urges us to consider carefully and deeply what there is in the creation that is really worthy of our love and devotion, since everything will leave us, and only the Lord remains. This is why He is described as 'true'—because He exists beyond the painful cycle of death and rebirth. He is called 'the true Creator' because He is the Almighty who created the entire universe, giving life to the whole world.

He is the One, the only Supreme Being. He does not belong to any specific race, religion or people. And our being is part of the Supreme Being, our soul is part of that supreme soul— a drop of the one ocean of the true Name. Guru Sahib says:

God abides in the soul, the soul in God;
this is what one learns from the Guru's teaching.
Aatam mah raam, raam mah aatam
cheenas gur beechaaraa.

Adi Granth, M1, p. 1153

The supreme soul exists within each soul, and all souls are contained within the supreme soul. However, we will only recognize and understand this truth when we become capable of recognizing our true self within, as we follow the directions of a lover of the Lord and advance on our spiritual journey.

Take the example of a banyan tree—how huge it is, and yet how small is its seed. If someone were to tell us that this very small seed contains such a huge tree, we would find it difficult to comprehend. But if we sow the seed and take good care of it, we will see it grow into a sapling and gradually attain its full size. We will then know for ourselves how such a huge tree can exist in such a small seed, how such a small seed can be said to contain such a great tree. In just the same way, saints say, our souls are part of the Almighty, drops of the divine ocean of the true Name.

> Says Kabir, the soul is a particle of the Lord.
> *Kahu kabeer ihu raam kee ans.*
> Kabir, Adi Granth, p. 871

Now when the Lord, the supreme soul, cannot be described in terms of race, religion or country, then how can our individual souls be thought of as belonging to any such group? Guru Sahib says:

> He has no colour, caste and mark.
> By his Command, He creates the whole world.
> *Varan jaat chihan nahee koee.*
> *Sabh hukame srisat upaa-idaa.*
> Adi Granth, M5, p. 1075

God Almighty, by whose Command the whole creation
was brought into existence, is neither dark nor fair, Hindu
nor Sikh, nor does He live in any particular country. Indian
tradition divides humanity into four different castes, but
Guru Sahib explains that the Supreme Being can never be
limited to such categories. When the Lord does not belong
to any particular category, how can our souls, which are part
of Him, be described in these terms? If the ocean has no race
or caste, can its drops be defined in such terms? If the sun
does not belong to a particular community or faith, can its
myriad small rays be thought of in this way?

The Supreme Being created human beings. It is we humans who have divided ourselves into castes and creeds, nations and religions. It is we who are always getting embroiled
in these differences and distinctions. If we search deeply in
the teachings of any saint, we find that they all seek to raise
our awareness high above the tensions that arise from such
distinctions. This is why Guru Sahib says:

Where you render account of your deeds,
there neither body nor caste go with you.
Jithai lekhaa mangeeai tithai deh jaat na jaa-e.
Adi Granth, M3, p. 1346

Listen, my friends! Your body will not go with you when
you have to account for your actions—no one there will be
interested in your caste or creed. This body is consigned to
fire or buried in the ground. For some, their race and religion come to an end in the cremation flames; for others, their
caste and social status are trampled into the earth. Only your
actions will be considered—what you did with your life; your
devotion and reverence; your love and longing for the Lord.
Kabir Sahib says:

No one will ask your caste or creed;
whoever contemplates on Him becomes His.
Jaat-paat poochhe nahi^n koy,
hari ko bhajai so hari kaa hoy.

Kabir

At that point no one will ask us about our religion or our status in this life. People who meditate on the Lord will assume the form of the Lord, whether they are Hindu, Sikh, Christian or Muslim. It is devotion to the Lord that brings union with Him. Let no one be under the impression that we must convert from Hinduism to Sikhism, from Sikhism to Christianity, or from Christianity to Islam, in order to find God. Kabir Sahib says that we should cast out such thoughts from our minds forever. Bulleh Shah says:

You will be judged by your actions alone;
your caste and creed will go unnoticed.
Amalaa^n utte hon nibere,
khareeaa^n rahingeeaa^n jaataa^n.

Bulleh Shah, Kafian Bulleh Shah

Those who are mindful of their actions during their lifetime will be able to close their karmic accounts, whereas pride in family status or caste will count for nothing. Paltu Sahib, a well-known and outspoken saint of Uttar Pradesh, says this in one of his compositions:

Paltu says, because of high birth, let no one
    feel proud;
in the court of the Lord, devotion and love
    alone count.

Paltoo oo^nchee jaati kau jani kou karai ha^nkaar.
Saahib ke darbaar me^n keval bhakti piyaar.

Paltu, Paltu Sahib ki Bani, Kundli 218

Let no one think that being born into a priest's family, for example, gives a special right to union with the Lord. Nor should one ever think that being born in some other family makes one inferior and unworthy of worshipping Him. Paltu says that we should never think such thoughts, since only love and devotion are needed to reach the home of the Supreme Being. Guru Nanak Sahib says:

> All those bereft of Nam are of low birth;
> they exist like vermin in filth.
> *Bin naavai sabh neech jaat hai bistaa kaa keeraa hoe.*

Adi Granth, M3, p. 426

Who could possibly be inferior to those who do not worship the Lord? After death they will go on to become miserable insects living out their lives in filth and dung. And who are the true nobility?

> With the Name in the heart, one is revered
>   amongst all.
> With the Name in the heart, one is the Creator
>   incarnate.
> With the Name in the heart, one is exalted
>   above all.
> *Jis naam ridai so sabh mah jaataa.*
> *Jis naam ridai so purakh bidhaataa.*
> *Jis naam ridai so sabh te oochaa.*

Adi Granth, M5, p. 1156

It is those who have love for the Lord, and for his Word enshrined in their hearts, who are the noblest of the noble and the purest of the pure. It is they who will return to their home and become one with the true Lord. Guru Nanak Sahib says:

> With the Name in one's heart, there is only one
> great big family.
> *Jis naam ridai tis wad parvaaraa.*
> Adi Granth, M5, p. 1156

When a person's heart is filled with the love of the Lord, the whole world becomes his family and he sees everyone as his. Saints lovingly explain that no one will be assessed on the basis of birth and status—it is our actions that count.

Love and devotion is the very nature of the relationship between the individual and the Supreme Being. Saints generally explain it in terms of a human ideal, using the example of the relationship of a wife and her husband; Guru Nanak Sahib, Soami Ji Maharaj, Kabir Sahib and Dariya Sahib all make this comparison. Followers of the Rama Krishna Mission compare the relationship to that of a mother and son. Christ uses the metaphor of a father's love for his son. The common factor in all these relationships is love, and the saints' sole purpose in making such comparisons is to emphasize that the relationship between the individual being and the Supreme Being is one of love alone. Paltu Sahib says:

> In the court of the Lord, devotion and love
> alone count.
> *Saahib ke darbaar me[n] keval bhakti piyaar.*
> Paltu, *Paltu Sahib ki Bani,* Kundli 218

If you wish to reach the Lord's home, you need nothing but love and devotion. Guru Nanak Sahib says:

> Only those who have loved, have found the Lord.
> *Jin prem kiyo tin hee prabh paayo.*
>
> Dassam Granth, Akal Ustat, M10, p. 14:9:29

Restlessness for the Lord, intense love and longing for Him in our heart, gives us the privilege of returning to our true home and finding the Supreme Being. Dadu Sahib says:

> Love is the Lord's essence, love is his nature;
> love is his form, love is his colour.
> *Ishq alah kee zaati hai, ishq alah kaa ang,*
> *ishq alah aujood hai, ishq alah kaa rang.*
>
> Dadu, *Dadu Dayal*

If you ask what the Lord's name is, the answer is love. If you ask for details of his birth and faith, they are all love. In the New Testament we read:

> God is love.
>
> 1 John 4:8

The Lord's true identity is love and nothing but love. In the Gospel of Saint Matthew, it is written:

> Blessed are they that mourn:
> for they shall be comforted.
>
> Matthew 5:4

Most blessed and fortunate are they who have love, longing and an intense desire in their hearts to meet the Lord. Their birth in human form is cause for celebration, because it is they who will ultimately find rest and peace in the lap of the Lord. Guru Nanak Sahib gives a beautiful example when he says:

> The virtuous bride finds union with her Lord,
> for she adorns herself with love and fear.
> *Kaaman gunwantee har paae.*
> *Bhai bhaae seegaar banaae.*
>
> Adi Granth, M3, p. 123

A wife always pleases her husband when she has two particular qualities: one is intense love for him and the other is fear—fear in her heart lest she should displease him by something she might say or do. She is always careful to say and do only those things that will please him and make him happy. Such a wife is cherished by her husband. Similarly, says Guru Nanak Sahib, a soul filled with love and longing for the Lord and with awe and fear of the Lord, will have the privilege of finding its way back to merge with the Lord. This awe that Guru Nanak Sahib is speaking about is fear lest the soul might do some wrong or sinful deed displeasing to its benefactor, God Almighty, the Supreme Being.

Saints urge us therefore, if we want to find the Lord, to detach ourselves from racial, religious and political issues and concentrate on developing love and devotion for Him within ourselves.

The problem that now arises is how to develop such love, since we can only love someone we have seen. How can we love someone we have never had the opportunity to meet, whose face and features we do not know?

We grow to love the faces and objects of the world because we see them and interact with them. We love our parents because they gave birth to us, our children because we gave them birth, our wife because she is the mother of our children, and our friends because we have associated with them since childhood. We love our wealth because we have acquired it with our sweat and blood, and our properties because we have inherited them. We love our community and religion because we have been part of them since birth.

How can we engender love for the Lord when we have only heard stories about Him, when we have never even seen Him and know nothing of his face or features? Is there someone whom we can love who will instil this love in us, who will create in us love and devotion for the Lord? To consider this question properly it is necessary to look carefully at the whole of creation. Only then will we discover whose company and love will engender such love in us.

When we look at the creation, we see that everything is made from five vital elements *(tattva):* earth, air, fire, water and ether. In every form of life there is at least one element active. Only the human form has all five active and is therefore described by saints as the five-element form, and is at the top of the creation.

In the first class of living beings, only the water element is active. This class consists of grasses, vegetables, trees, fruits, flowers and suchlike. If we, who have all five tattvas active, worship trees or anything in the vegetable kingdom, then we will descend into a lower form of life in our next birth, because "Where our desires are, there we dwell".[47] When we are reborn after the death of our present body, we assume the form of whatever we have loved and worshipped in this life. That is why nothing in the plant kingdom is worthy of our love.

In the second class of beings are earthbound creatures, such as scorpions, snakes, insects and so on. In them, two tattvas are active, so they are also lower than the human level.

In the third class are all the feathered species: doves, sparrows, parakeets and other birds. If we, the five-element form, worship such creatures, we can imagine what will happen—we will ourselves return to the creation as doves, sparrows, parakeets and so on. We were wanting to love and worship a form that would draw us above the human level, but this achieves the opposite—we go down to these lower forms.

The fourth class of beings is that of four-legged creatures. They have four tattvas or vital elements active but lack the fifth, ether, which gives the power of discrimination—so they too are not worthy of our worship.

The fifth class is the human race itself. Since all five tattvas are active in everyone, why should one human worship another, particularly in present times when there is so much emphasis on everybody being equal?

Thus we have a situation where one human does not wish to worship another, we do not speak the language of animals, we have never seen any gods and goddesses, and we have no experience of the form and appearance of the Lord. What, then, we must ask ourselves, is worthy of our love? Who in this creation can we love, who can we worship who will engender love and devotion for the Lord in our hearts?

Hazur[*] used to give an excellent analogy. He would explain that we may put as many radios in a room as we like, but as long as they are not connected to a source of power, we will never be able to hear the news from any country. As soon as we connect them to a battery or a power point, however, we will be able to hear broadcasts from anywhere we want.

---

[*] The terms 'Hazur' and 'Hazur Maharaj Ji' are used by the speaker to refer to his Master, Maharaj Sawan Singh (1858–1948). See also Translators' Note and Glossary.

We must seek a devotee and lover of the Lord, a true
Master, who is connected by an all-consuming love to the
Supreme Being. We must keep his company and associate
with him so that through him our thoughts and love may also
be attuned to love and devotion for the Lord. This can be
done through him because his real form is Shabd, the Word,
and the essence of the Supreme Being is also Shabd, the creative power, the Name of God. Guru Nanak Sahib explains
most eloquently:

> The whole world, the netherworlds, the islands,
>   the spheres,
> have all been put under Kal; such is the Lord's
>   design....
> *Khand pataal deep sabh loaa.*
> *Sabh kaalai was aap prabh keeaa.*
>
> Adi Granth, M5, p. 1076

The Supreme Being himself created the whole universe
in all its complexity. He has entrusted responsibility for its
administration to Kal, whose authority extends to the top of
the three worlds, Triloki, the domain of Brahm. Whatever
falls within Kal's jurisdiction is trapped in the cycle of death
and rebirth. However, as Guru Sahib says:

> ... The only immutable one is the eternal God;
> those who contemplate on Him become immutable
>   too....
> *Nihchal ek aap abinaasee*
> *so nihchal jo tisah dhiaa-idaa.*
>
> Adi Granth, M5, p. 1076

The One who created everything is beyond change. The suffering of death and rebirth does not apply to Him, for He lives in Sach Khand, the true realm. Anyone who loves this one Lord, who worships Him, also becomes changeless and escapes from the cycle of transmigration forever.

So again the question arises as to how we can love and worship the Lord when He exists in Sach Khand. Guru Nanak Sahib explains:

> ... The Lord's servant is like unto the Lord;
> do not think him to be different because of his
>   human frame ...
> *Har kaa sevak so har jehaa.*
> *Bhed na jaanah maanas dehaa.*
>   Adi Granth, M5, p. 1076

The lovers of the Lord, those who are beloved of Him, take on the form of the Lord by worshipping Him. There is no difference, no distinction, between them and the Supreme Being. And what is their relationship to the Supreme Being?

> ... just as a myriad waves rise from the ocean,
> and then subside, merging back into its depths.
> *Jio jal tarang uthah bahu bhaatee*
> *phir salalai salal samaa-idaa.*
>   Adi Granth, M5, p. 1076

Waves rise from the surface of the ocean for a matter of minutes and then merge back into it. The Masters, the lovers of the Lord, are related to the Supreme Being in a similar way. Waves never become separate from the ocean; however high they rise, they always remain part of the ocean. In the same way, the Masters are waves of the ocean of the true Name. They come into the world to proclaim the existence of the Shabd, they bear witness to the Shabd, and then they merge back into the Shabd, taking us with them into that ocean of the Name. Guru Nanak Sahib says:

> Know thou, Guru and God are one.
> *Guru parmesar eko jaan.*
>
> Adi Granth, M5, p. 864

There is no difference at all between the Supreme Being and the lovers of the Lord. Bulleh Shah says:

> The Lord has transformed himself
> and come as a man.
> *Maulaa aadmee ban aaiaa.*
>
> Bulleh Shah, *Kulyat Bulleh Shah*[48]

God himself has come into this world as a human being. Christ says:

> I and my Father are one.
>
> John 10:30

God the Father, the Almighty Lord, and I are one and the same. Soami Ji says:

> Radha Soami has assumed the human form in
> this world;
> He comes as a Master and awakens souls.
> *Raadhaaswaamee dharaa nar roop jagat meⁿ,*
> *guru hoy jeev chitaaye.*
>
> Soami Ji, *Sar Bachan* 1:2, p. 6

Radha Soami is the name given to the absolute Lord. He comes in the guise of a human being in order to engender within us love for God and the desire to meet and merge with Him. This is why saints tell us that we must seek the company of the Masters and associate with them. Guru Sahib says:

> The Word is the Guru,
> the soul attuned to the Word is the disciple.
> *Sabad guroo surat dhun chelaa.*
>
> Adi Granth, M1, p. 943

Our real Master is the Word; the real disciple is the soul. The physical body will be left here in the physical creation by both the disciple and the Master. But the soul will be accompanied forever by the Word if the disciple gets attached to the Word within, through the Master. We must understand that the real Master is the Word and the real disciple is the soul. Kabir Sahib says:

> The soul merges into the Word,
> the body does not merge.
> *Shabd milaavaa hvai rahaa, deh milaavaa naahi^n.*
>
> Kabir, *Kabir Sakhi Sangreh*

It is the soul, not the body, that will reach Sach Khand, the abode of the Supreme Being, and it will be attracted and carried there by the Word. We must associate with saints and keep their company in order to attach our soul to the Word. Guru Nanak Sahib says:

> Revealed as the Word, through service of the Guru.

We must search for a lover of the Lord and be with him because it is they who attach our attention to the Word, the Name. When we understand their teachings and meditate on the Word according to their instructions, we are freed from our worldly attachments, and we develop love for the Lord and become attached to Him. That is why Guru Sahib says:

> Through the Guru's Word,
> one is immersed in Truth.
> *Gursabdee sachee liv laae.*
> Adi Granth, M3, p. 115

Until we come into the presence of an enlightened being, a Master, we remain caught in a web of delusion, entangled by illusory attachments in an illusory world. Once we find a Master and are guided by him to the practice of the Word, we are able to worship the true Lord, and our worship and love themselves become true.

The bliss we experience through listening to the sound of the Name is so elevating and pure that once we taste it, all worldly love and attachments leave us automatically. Guru Nanak Sahib says:

> The Word of the Guru is sweet beyond measure;
> that sweetness cannot be known unless you taste it.
> *Gur kaa sabad mahaa ras meethaa*
> *bin chaakhe saad na jaapai.*
> Adi Granth, M3, p. 753

The Word to which God's lovers attach us is sweet beyond description. Why do we refer to it in this way? Because everything we relish—the pleasures of children and family, the satisfaction of eating and drinking, and our taste for issues of race, faith and nation—all these seem bland by comparison with the sweetness of the Word. A person who owns precious jewels will not put up with being driven from door to door in search of worthless trinkets. Little girls play with dolls only while they are young and immature.

It is our attachment to the Word, the Name, that detaches us from our worldly ties forever. If we study the teachings of any saint carefully, we will find them praising the Word in verse after verse and page after page.

I often submit that every religion has its particular rituals and ceremonies, and advocates different rules and modes of living, whereas the spirituality, the reality, the essential truth or spiritual basis is the same in each one of them. Saints come into the world only to spread this spirituality. Until we are steeped in its colour, we will never be liberated from the prison of the body—whatever our religious background.

The same essential truth has been explained in different terms by different saints from different races, countries and religious traditions. Generally speaking, Muslim saints refer to this spiritual essence as the Call from the skies *(baang-e-aasmaanee)*, the Word of God *(kalaam-e-ilaahee)*, the imperial Sound *(nidaa-e-sultaanee)*, the Word *(kalmaa)*, and the Command *(kun)*. Hindu sages call it the Voice from the skies *(aakaash vaanee)*, the Name of God *(raam naam)*, the Melody of God *(raam dhun)*, the pure Sound *(nirmal naad)*, the divine Melody *(divya dhuni)*, and various other names.

Christ refers to it as the Holy Ghost, the Spirit, the Name, the Word, and the Logos. Many saints describe this power as the Word *(shabd)* and the Name *(naam)*. In the house of Guru Nanak Sahib, it is referred to as the Guru's Voice *(gur kee baanee)*, the Voice from the highest *(dhur kee baanee)*, the true Voice *(sachee baanee)*, the Order *(amar)*, the Command *(hukam)*, the unutterable Lore *(akath kathaa)*, and God's Song of praise *(hari keertan)*. The Chinese refer to it as the Way, or Tao *(daao)*. Until our mind gets a taste of this spirituality, there is absolutely no way we will escape from the ties of a physical body.

The relationship between this spirituality and the external practices of a religion is like that of an especially beautiful photograph and its frame. The frame is there to protect the photograph; on its own it has no value. In the same way, everyone understands that it is jewels that are precious, not the box containing them. It is a sword that does the work, not its scabbard—the scabbard exists only to hold the sword. Similarly, it is the spiritual essence within a religion that is real, whereas the rituals and external practices provide a framework to protect and spread that spiritual truth.

This framework or code of conduct should not be so rigid as to destroy the fragrance of spirituality forever. Religious customs and rituals are like covers that are placed over the essential truth. The spirituality gets lost, leaving only the empty cover of the religion, and we lose sight of the truth. However, someone who has intense love and longing for the Lord is able to shatter the chains of rituals and ceremonies and strip off the enveloping cloak of formal religion. Such people transcend their religious conditioning—they go beyond mosque, church and temple.

We all know how a needle is intrinsically attracted to a magnet, but if we place a stone on the needle it becomes powerless—immobilized by the weight of the stone. The moment we remove the stone, the needle automatically goes straight to the magnet. Similarly, the soul is filled with true love for the Lord and a real desire to unite with Him, but we have weighed it down with religion, with external observances, with the heavy burden of karma on our mind. As we remove

this load, love is awakened within the soul. It is then automatically attracted to the Lord and merges with Him.

Saints explain that if we wish to find the Supreme Being,
we must develop true love and longing within ourselves. And
how do we develop such love? Through the practice of the
Word, through listening to the Shabd. Because the mind loves
pleasure, it will never be ready to give up its love and attachment for the world until it is given something better, higher
and purer than the worldly pleasures it craves. That is why
saints attach our minds to the Word, the Shabd, the Name.

∾

His is the sole kingdom, his Command is but one;
his law and governance prevail from age to age.

Eko amar ekaa paatisaahee jug jug sir kaar banaaee he.

Guru Nanak Sahib explains most beautifully that since there
is only one Supreme Being for everyone, his divine Command, his Order, his Cosmic Law, will of necessity be one and
the same for every being in the whole world. Saints are sent
into this world to administer the divine Law on his behalf.
They come into the world in every age; they come by his
Command *(hukam);* they come to reveal and teach us his
Command; and they merge back into the Command, which
is the Word of God.

The meaning of Guru Sahib's words is that in the natural
order of the creation, the Lord has provided only one way for
us to reach Him—and that is by listening to the Word, by
uniting ourselves with the Name. This practice is only possible once our mind has been connected to the Word, and
this only happens through a saint, an enlightened being, a

true Master. He says such saints are always present in the
world. We read in the scriptures:

> Through all the ages shall run the Satguru's lineage.
> *Jug jug peeree chalai satgur kee.*
>
> Adi Granth, M4, p. 79

Saints, the lovers of the Lord, keep coming into the world in
every age. Tulsi Sahib of Hathras explains:

> But for the presence of saints on earth,
> the world would burn to death.
> *Sant na hote jagat me^n jal martaa sa^{n}saar.*
>
> Tulsi Sahib, *Shabdavali*[49]

It is only by going to a saint and engaging in the spiritual
practice of the Word that we will know God.

This Word the saints praise is no ordinary word, but the
creative power that brought the whole universe into being
with all its regions and divisions. Guru Sahib says:

> All creation emanates from the Word,
> by the Word it is dissolved,
> and through the Word it is created again.
> *Utpat parlao sabde hovai. Sabde hee fir opate hovai.*
>
> Adi Granth, M3, p. 117

The universe came into being through the power of the
Word. When the Lord chooses to withdraw this power, dissolution or grand dissolution takes place. Hazur used to explain this as the dissolution of the five vital elements: earth is
dissolved in water, water is dried up by fire, fire is blown away

by air, ether consumes air, and then the whole world is obscured in a thick dark fog.

We must search, therefore, for this Word that created the universe. And where is it to be found?

> In this body is a multitude of precious treasures,
> but one is able to realize them within
> only when one meets a true Gurmukh.
> *Is kaa-i-aa andar vast asankhaa.*
> *Gurmukh saach milai taa vekhaa.*
>
> Adi Granth, M3, p. 110

This body of ours is not just a bundle of flesh, blood and bones. It is not just a clay puppet five or six feet tall. The Almighty has kept many things in it, countless treasures. Even He is here within it, as is the path we need to follow in order to reach Him. When will we realize this? "Only when one meets a true Gurmukh". We have to meet a lover of the Lord who can explain the method to us, and then we can find the Lord within. And what do they explain?

> Closing the nine doors,
> one finds liberation at the tenth;
> there ever resonates the limitless melody
>   of the Word.
> *Nao darvaaje dasvai muktaa*
> *anahad sabad vajaavaniaa.*
>
> Adi Granth, M1, p. 110

Saints tell us that our spiritual journey starts from the soles of the feet and ends at the crown of the head. In this journey there are two stages: the first goes as far as the eyes, the second is above the eyes. In the body, the natural seat of the soul and mind is the same for everyone—a point between the two eyes known as the eye centre. Muslim faqirs refer to it as the black point *(nuqtaa-e-savaidaa)*. Christ describes it as the single eye. In the Adi Granth it is referred to as the door to our home *(ghar dar)*, the tenth *(dasvaan)*. Hindu sages refer to it as the eye of Shiva *(shiv netra)*, the divine eye *(divya chakshu)*. Some saints call it the third eye, the infinitesimal point or grain of sesame *(til)*, the gateway to liberation *(mukti daa darvaazaa)*.

From this place our attention descends and spreads out into the entire world through the nine doors of the body. We have to bring back our scattered attention by reversing its outward journey and bringing it to a single focus at the eye centre.

Guru Sahib explains that the cravings for physical pleasures and all the negative tendencies of the mind lie below the eyes, whereas the door to our true home is at the eye centre. What distinguishes this door? It is the place where "ever resonates the limitless melody of the Word", the door where the unending Shabd is playing as audible, reverberating sound.

This sound resonates in everyone—in thieves and swindlers, saints and sages. The question of race, religion or nation does not arise. Whether Hindu, Sikh, Christian or of any other faith, those who are blessed with the good fortune of being able to concentrate their attention at the eye centre will hear within themselves the resounding music of the Word. They will hear its sound and see its light and brilliance.

The sound leads us in the direction of our inner home, the light guides us on our inner spiritual journey, so that, passing from one stage to the next, we eventually reach our true home. This sound and light are what saints describe as the true Name.

The scriptures and holy books of every religion are filled with praise of the true Word, the Name. By reading them, we get an indication of how we can conduct our spiritual practice, but the Word itself cannot be found in them, nor can it be found in temples, mosques, gurdwaras or churches. It can be found only within the body, within the human frame. Through the scriptures we come to know about the technique for worshipping the Word, but salvation can be attained only through putting into practice what we read—not by mere study.

Medical books may well describe the remedy, but the actual medicine can be given only by the doctor himself. Reading medical books day and night will never cure a sick man. He will be cured only when he takes medicine according to the doctor's prescription. It is one thing to read, but another to practise what one has read. By purchasing a recipe book and reading it all day, you will not taste any food, nor will your hunger be satisfied. But if you go out, buy the ingredients and cook them according to the recipe, then you will enjoy the food and satisfy your hunger.

We get misled by insignificant and trivial details and we think that by endless reading, liberation will automatically be achieved. The saints make it clear that the living Word is nowhere outside; on the contrary, it vibrates at the eye centre within everyone.

> Closing the nine doors
> and restraining the wandering mind,
> in the tenth, one finds one's true abode.
> There the unending music of the Word plays
>   day and night.
> Through the Guru's guidance, the celestial Word
>   is heard.

Nao dar thaake dhaavat rahaae.
Dasvai nijghar vaasaa paae.
Othai anahad sabad vajah din raatee
gurmatee sabad sunaavaniaa.

Adi Granth, M3, p. 124

We can reach the entrance to our real home only by with-drawing our attention from the nine doors that lead out into the world and by making it one-pointed at the eye centre. We will recognize this entrance by the unending music of the Word that resounds at this very spot. This music, as Guru Sahib explains, never ceases, but keeps on reverberating within us day and night, even while we sleep.

> Without the Word, there is utter darkness within;
> one neither finds the precious treasure of Nam
> nor escapes the cycle of birth and death.
> *Bin sabdai antar aaneraa.*
> *Na vast lahai na chookai feraa.*

Adi Granth, M3, p. 124

We can never remove the darkness of ignorance from within, or meet the Supreme Being, without practising the Word, without meditating on the Name. Whatever we are to attain will be through the practice of the Word. The Word contains the melody, the pure sound, the call, and has within itself light, refulgence and brilliance. That Word is within each one of us, and Guru Sahib explains that saints come into the world in order to bear witness to this power and proclaim its truth.

∽

Pure are they who have realized the self;
the source of all joy Himself comes and meets them.

So jan nirmal jin aap pachhaataa. Aape aae miliaa sukhdaataa.

Guru Nanak Sahib explains that we become pure—cleansed of the dirt of the mind—when we are able to recognize the self, to know who we are. And when are we capable of knowing ourselves? When we go beyond the orbit of mind and illusion, when all the soiled coverings of the soul are removed, and the knot that ties the soul to the mind has been untied.

I have already submitted to you that our soul itself is absolutely pure, because it is a particle of the Lord, the supreme soul. It has become entangled in a web of illusion and taken the company of the mind. Mind is a slave to its negative tendencies and the pleasures of the senses, and because the soul is at the command of the mind, it too has to undergo the consequences of all actions, along with the mind. Until the soul leaves the company of the mind, it cannot know itself or discover its true identity. Socrates said, "Know thyself." Above all else, achieve self-realization.

Consider how a brilliant light can be totally concealed when wrapped in twenty or so black cloths. As long as the light is covered, we can neither see it nor make use of it, but this does not mean that its brilliance has diminished. If we remove the covers, the light will become apparent; we will both see it and be able to benefit from it.

The condition of every soul is like that of clean pure water when manifest as clouds in the sky. When it falls as rain on the earth, it gathers so much dirt and so many impurities that it not only stagnates and begins to smell, but it also begins to identify itself with the dirt. Only when it separates from the dirt, when it is exposed to the heat and warmth of the sun and is transformed into vapour, does it see that the water is one thing and the dirt something else. Out of ignorance, it has confused its identity with that of the dirt. Once it is in a position to know its own nature, once it realizes it is the same as the clouds in the sky, it immediately leaves the dirt and rises back to merge with the clouds. This is the condition of every soul.

Guru Sahib lovingly explains that it is not possible for us to know the Supreme Being until we know ourselves. How will we know ourselves? Through our meditation on the Shabd. He says:

> Only he who tastes of the Word
> can understand the self.
> *Sabdai saad jaanah taa aap pachhaanah.*
> Adi Granth, M3, p. 115

Anyone who has personally experienced the bliss of the Shabd is able to know the self.

So what is it that keeps attracting the mind towards the physical pleasures? It is our craving for physical gratification that keeps dragging the mind outwards and makes us slaves of our senses. The mind will never let us leave the senses until it has enjoyed a sweeter and higher pleasure than any offered by the senses. What brings us such pleasure, what love is so great, that by merely tasting it, we are detached from worldly pleasures? It is the enjoyment of the Word, the bliss of God's Name. Guru Sahib explains:

The Lord God's Name is an immortalizing
    sweet ambrosia.
Har har naam amrit ras meethaa.
Adi Granth, M4, p. 1323

The Word of God is nectar, it is sweetness itself. We call
it sweet because the pleasures of the world, which are usually
thought of as sweet, appear insipid by comparison. Someone
given delicious food loses all interest in food that is tasteless.

They who hear the Word within, realize themselves;
    they alone attain the Truth....
Jin antar sabad aap pachhaanah gat mit tin hee paaee.
Adi Granth, M3, p. 910

The saints, the lovers of the Lord, attain supreme realization by listening to the Word within and realizing themselves.
It is they who attain the highest state and have qualified to
unite with the Lord.

... Then the mind enters the state of deep
    meditation;
the soul's flame merges with the all-pervading
    divine light.
*Eh manooaa sunn samaadh lagaavai
jotee jot milaaee.*
Adi Granth, M3, p. 910

They are the ones whose minds merge back into Brahm; their
light dissolves into the supreme light.

The knot that ties the soul to the mind is released by
meditation on the Word. The mind can then stay in its own
natural abode, while the soul becomes free to return to its

own home. Once the soiled coverings are removed from the soul, it will automatically merge back into the Lord, just as a needle is drawn to a magnet when the weight is lifted from it.

Guru Sahib once again explains that it is just not possible to realize the Lord so long as we do not realize ourselves.

༈

They who sing the Lord's praise, immersed in the Word,
are honoured in the court of the Eternal One.

Rasnaa sabad ratee gun gaavai dar saachai pat paaee he.

It is the lovers of God, self-realized beings, always absorbed in the worship of God, who can awaken love for Him within us.

> They who merge with the Word
> become pure beings and Truth-realized.
> *Pavit paavan se jan saache ek sabad liv laaee.*
> Adi Granth, M3, p. 910

People who are detached from all worldly ties and are attached only to the Word become absolutely pure. They then transform others by attaching them also to the Word, so that they too become pure beings like themselves.

> By serving the emancipated, one becomes
>   emancipated.
> Through the Word, one is rid of ego and
>   selfish love.
> *Mukte seve muktaa hovai.*
> *Haomai mamtaa sabde khovai.*
> Adi Granth, M3, p. 116

Freeing themselves from all attachments, from all ego, they attain liberation by listening to the Shabd. If we keep the company of such people, they attach us to the Word so we also become free. That is why he says that the Masters, because they are devoted to the Lord, awaken within us love for Him, and so we too long for union.

∽

Honoured is the Lord's lover, who is one with his Word;
dishonoured is the slanderer and the slave of the mind.

> *Gurmukh naam milai wadiaaee.*
> *Manmukh nindak pat gavaaee.*

Guru Sahib explains that there are two kinds of people in the world: the lovers and devotees of the Lord *(gurmukh)*, and the lovers of the world *(manmukh)*. Both have been made by the Lord. Whomsoever He wants, He makes his devotees. It is in his hands.

Who are the devotees of the Lord? Those who keep the company of the saints and practise meditation on the Word. They are able to realize their true self, return to their true home, and realize the Lord. And why are they honoured? Because they meditate on the Word.

The rest, the worldly minded, pass their time criticizing and slandering other people, pandering to the senses, or indulging in racial, religious and national disputes. Guru Sahib says:

> Blind and foolish are they who do not serve
>   the Satguru;
> how can they reach the gate of salvation?

They die to be born, they are born to die;
they suffer repeated blows at the hands of Death.
Satgur na sevahi moorakh andh gavaaraa.
Phir o-i kithahu paa-in mokhduaaraa.
Mar mar jammahi phir phir aavahi,
jam dar chotaa khaavaniaa.

Adi Granth, M3, p. 115

How can people who do not keep the company of God's lovers attain liberation, when they spend all their time indulging in their senses and satisfying their physical cravings? They
will be born again and again, and will die again and again.
They will have to keep on coming to the prison of chaurasi.
The third Padshahi says:

> Like vermin in filth
> sustaining themselves on filth,
> we grow in filth and ourselves become filth.
> *Bistaa ke keere bistaa kamaavah*
> *fir bistaa maahe pachaavaniaa.*

Adi Granth, M3, p. 116

Worldly people are like maggots. They are born into dirt,
they love it, they go on living in it, they consume it, they die
in it, and then they are born into it again. The saints refer to
the whole creation as dirt because it is perishable and transient. Guru Sahib compassionately explains that such people
are not to be blamed, because everything is in the hands of
the Supreme Being and all that happens in the creation happens by his will. Our attention can never turn towards the
Lord until He showers his grace and mercy on us.

The counterfeit and the genuine,
you yourself have created.
You yourself are the judge of all.
Having judged, you put the true in your treasury
and the false are lost in delusion.

Khote khare tudh aap upaae.
Tudh aape parkhe lok sabaae.
Khare parkh khajaanai paa-i-h
khote bharm bhulaavaniaa.

Adi Granth, M3, p. 119

O Lord, it is you who have made both the genuine and the counterfeit, the pure and the impure. You live in both, and you are the final judge. As well as being the judge, you are also present in the one who is judged. All will come to judgement when they leave their human form. Those whom you have made fit to be chosen will be admitted to your treasury; those who are not fit will come back into the wheel of chaurasi.

Those blessed with divine grace find a Guru;
they alone are true who live in the Lord's will.

Jin kao nadar bha-ee gur mele
prabh bhaanaa sach so-ee.

Adi Granth, M1, p. 1153

Lord, how do you make us worthy of admission into your treasury? You bring us into the company of a saint. Once we live in your will and engage in the practice of meditation on the Word, we become worthy of being chosen and are given admission to your treasury. Guru Sahib says:

The Lord himself is both the doer and the cause,
and He himself enshrines the Guru's Word in
    the heart.

Aape kartaa kare karaae.
Aape sabad gur man vasaae.

Adi Granth, M3, p. 125

Everything that happens, it is the Supreme Being alone who makes it happen. Those souls He wants to extricate from the world, He attaches to the Shabd through the perfect Master.

∽

**Imbued with the Name, the supreme swans remain detached;
they live in their home, their devotion unbroken.**

Naam rate paramhans bairaagee nijghar taaree laaee he.

*M*any people are under the impression that it is necessary to renounce their families and retreat to some forest or remote place in order to worship the Lord. Guru Nanak Sahib says that we can shed our attachments and realize the purity of our soul even while living in our homes and in the world. We must be brave and valiant warriors, living in the world but not contaminated by its dirt.

When will we become 'supreme swans'? When, through meditation, we become dyed in the love and worship of God; when, while living in the world, we become detached. The supreme swans are they who have transcended the realm of mind and illusion—in whom the knot binding the soul to the mind has been released.

He explains that self-realization cannot be had by running away from the world, by wearing special clothes, or by isolating ourselves. If we sincerely wish to attain a state of supreme detachment, then we must attend to our worldly responsibilities and meditate on the Word. True love and longing for union with the Lord will be awakened within us through meditation.

❧

One who dies while living, through God's holy Word,
becomes whole and perfect;
this is what Satguru, the brave warrior, proclaims.

Sabad marai soee jan pooraa. Satguru aakh sunaae sooraa.

𝐻e says that our valiant Satguru teaches us that we will become whole, will become worthy of meeting the Lord, and will come to know our true selves, only when we steadfastly keep our attention in the Shabd, wherever we are and whatever we are doing, day or night. There is no need to renounce the world or change our religion or country. We must live in the world bravely and valiantly, and not let ourselves be affected by its dirt.

> Just as the lotus lives detached in water
> and the duck swims on the surface yet remains dry,
> attached to the Word, the soul crosses the ocean of
>   phenomena
> through the practice of the Name, O Nanak.
> *Jaise jal mah kamal niraalam murgaaee naisaane.*
> *Surat sabad bhav saagar tareeai*
> *naanak naam wakhaane.*
>
> Adi Granth, M1, p. 938

Guru Sahib points out that a duck lives on water, but when it flies away, its wings are dry. The lotus flower remains above the water, although it has its roots beneath the surface. Similarly, we must settle and close our karmic accounts while attending to the practice of our meditation, so that ultimately we can fly from this world unaffected by them. We must settle the debits and credits of our karmic account and, while we are here, we must also do something for ourselves.

Hazur used to say that if a bee sips honey while sitting on the rim of the pot, it can fly away with dry wings after enjoying the honey. If it sinks into the honey, however, it cannot enjoy it, its wings get stuck, it struggles in vain and loses its life. Like the bee, we must remain sufficiently detached, so that we can work for the well-being of our soul while living in this human form.

❧

> *Within the body is the real pool of nectar;*
> *the mind drinks from it with serene devotion.*
>
> *Kaa-i-aa andar amritsar saachaa man peeve bhaae subhaaee he.*

Saints say that the pool of true nectar (*amritsar saachaa*) is within our body. There the soul, black like a crow, immerses itself and emerges pure and white like a swan. This pool is where worldly people are transformed into lovers of God. There is no such pool anywhere outside where a crow can be transformed into a swan by immersing itself in water. No matter how pure it is, water can only cleanse the dirt of our body. As for our mind, Guru Sahib says,

When the mind is polluted with sin,
it can only be cleansed with love of the Name.
Bhareeai mat paapaa kai sang.
Oh dhopai naavai kai rang.

Adi Granth, Japji, M1, p. 4

It is through the practice of Shabd, the practice of the Word, that we are cleansed.

We respect the city of Amritsar because its foundation was laid by the fourth Padshahi and it was completed by the fifth Padshahi.* But this stanza, in which the word *amritsar* (pool of nectar) is mentioned, was written by the third Padshahi, before the city was built. The first Padshahi also uses the term *amritsar* in his writings. Guru Sahib explains:

O friends, this body is a pool;
bathe in it and attach yourself through love
to the Lord.
They who bathe in the pool of the Name
are purified;
through the Word all dirt is cleansed.
Eh sareer sarvar hai santah
isnaan kare liv laaee.
Naam isnaan karah se jan nirmal
sabade mail gavaa-ee.

Adi Granth, M3, p. 909

We will find no pool in the world greater or deeper than that of our body. We must turn within and bathe in it if we wish to be imbued with the love of God. What kind of

---

* *Padshahi* is an honorific commonly used in the Sikh community to refer to the Gurus in the line of Guru Nanak. *See also* Glossary.

bathing is this? It is immersing ourselves in the Name, in the waters of the Word. Ritual bathing can never wash away the dirt of our karmas or cleanse our soul; the real bathing is the practice of the Name.

That is why Guru Sahib says that the pool of true nectar where people like us, worldly people, bathe and are transformed into lovers of God, where our entire karmic debt comes to an end, lies within each one of us.

ᕦ

The learned man reads and teaches others,
oblivious of the fires that burn his own home.
Without serving the Satguru, one is not blessed with the Name;
one may read till exhausted, yet will not find peace.

Par pandit avaraa samjhaae. Ghar jalte kee khabar na paae.
Bin satgur seve naam na paaeeai par thaake saant na aaee he.

Through his teachings, Guru Nanak Sahib wants to rid us of every possible doubt and misconception. Like a surgeon who disregards the cries of a patient when performing an operation, and skilfully scrapes and removes every trace of pus from the wound so that it does not get infected, Guru Nanak Sahib does not want any doubt or misconception to remain. He does not want us to remain entangled by any outward rituals and ceremonies in case we waste the valuable opportunity of human life on account of some illusion of the mind.

So he comes to the question of reading the scriptures. Many people have the idea that liberation can be attained through reading religious books and scriptures. He says:

The learned man reads and teaches others,
oblivious of the fires that burn his own home.

Priests and learned men explain the scriptures to the
world, but do nothing to extinguish the fires raging within
their own homes, nor are they even aware of them. Our hearts
are being consumed by the flames of lust, anger, greed, attachment and pride, yet we are busy guiding others. Our
houses are being robbed and we are acting as watchmen for
others. Hardly able to carry our own burdens, we act as beasts
of burden for the world. Guru Sahib says:

> Without serving the Satguru, one is not blessed
>   with the Name;
> one may read till exhausted, yet will not find peace.

We may exhaust ourselves reading, wear ourselves to a
thread by reading day and night, but we will never experience
contentment and peace of mind unless we worship the Name.
This is why Guru Sahib says:

> If one reads year after year, if one reads month
>   upon month,
> if one reads for a lifetime, breath upon breath,
> Nanak, only one thing is of value;
> all else is but prattling in pride.
> *Pareeah jete baras baras pareeah jete maas.*
> *Pareeah jetee aarjaa pareeah jete saas.*
> *Naanak lekhai ik gal hor haomai jhakhnaa jhaak.*
>   Adi Granth, M1, p. 467

However much we read, the only thing that will be recorded in our account is whether our soul has attached itself

to the Name. Everything else is just a waste of time. Butter cannot be made by churning water.

Let no one take me to mean that we should give up reading. We must read, but we should read with thoughtfulness and understanding, realizing that our duty does not end with reading. We must put into practice what we have read, because whatever we are to gain will come through practice, not through reading.

❧

Hypocrites proclaim purity by smearing ash on themselves;
but who can kill the ego without the Lord's Word?
The fires of their senses rage day and night;
deluded, they wander, lost in outward forms.

Ik bhasam lagaae phirah bhekhdhaaree.
Bin sabdai haomai kin maaree.
Andin jalat rahah din raatee bharam bhekh bharmaaee he.

Guru Sahib now draws a comparison. He has already said that those who lead a householder's life and settle their karmic accounts while always remembering the Lord and hearing his Word will be dyed in the colour of God's love. They are the realized souls, the supreme swans.

Now he describes various kinds of ascetics—people who renounce home and family. Some keep matted hair, some smear ash on their bodies, some wear special robes—they perform all sorts of rituals. Guru Sahib says: What is the point in all these things? Their minds are still filled with the same desires, still full of those cravings, they are still attached to the world and in love with the creation.

Who can kill the ego without the Lord's Word?

He challenges us: Try anything you want, you will never rid yourself of your attachment to this illusory world without the practice of the Name.

It is a popular misconception that retreating from the world engenders great love for the Lord. We forget that the basic needs of life accompany us wherever we go. What do we really need? Food for our body, clothes to cover us, and a roof over our head. These three basic necessities go with us everywhere. Wherever we choose to hide, they never leave us.

Even when we retreat from the world we still have to eat, so we satisfy our hunger by stretching our hand out to others and begging from them. We give up our honest jobs and the food provided by our family, and fill our stomach through begging. But our stomach has renounced nothing. We give up our normal clothes and put on saffron or blue robes, but we still need clothes of some sort to cover our body. We give up the comfort of our homes and live in a temple, ashram or gurdwara; we may even make a small hut or cave for ourselves—but we cannot do without a roof over our head. So what have we renounced? In fact, we have done the opposite—we have become a burden on society.

That is why Guru Nanak Sahib says there is no need to give up our homes. We must get rid of our love and attachment for this illusory world, and instead put our attention in the Word, the Name. The mind loves pleasure, and the more we enjoy listening to the Word inside, the more our love for the Lord will increase, while our love and attachment for the world will decrease.

೧೮

Some remain detached, even in home and family;
they die through the Word and dwell in God's Name.
Steeped, day and night, in the colour of devotion,
their hearts are filled with fear, love and devotion.

Ik grih kutamb mah sadaa udaasee.
Sabad mue harinaam nivaasee.
Andin sadaa rahah rang raate bhai bhaae bhagat chit laaee he.

Leading a householder's life, living in the midst of their families, the devotees' hearts are always filled with true love, longing, fear and reverence for the Lord. They are careful to see
that they do not displease the Lord by anything they do. They
serve humanity. They only do that which pleases the Lord;
they do not do anything that might lead them to incur his
displeasure. Guru Sahib says that they are dyed in the colour
of the Lord, steeped in his love.

೧೮

Egocentric people waste their lives in slander;
within them barks the dog of greed.
They are never let free by the agents of Death;
they regret in vain at their final hour.

Manmukh nindaa kar kar wigutaa. Antar lobh bhaokai jis kutaa.
Jamkaal tis kade na chhodai ant ga-i-aa pachhutaaee he.

Guru Nanak Sahib now looks at worldly people. He says
that they are opinionated and argumentative, considering

themselves to be very important, while looking on others as inferior. They are constantly deriding and speaking ill of others, and the dog of greed howls endlessly within them. In spite of the blessings that the supreme Lord showers on them, they are never satisfied, never content.

Their true condition becomes apparent when the agents of Death come to drag them bodily from this world and they have to take their next birth wherever the Lord sees fit. They are hardly set free, shrieking and crying, from the shackles of one body, than another is ready to receive them. No sooner do they enter the new body, than death again looms large before their eyes. Again, after death there is another body waiting to receive them. Like habitual criminals, they are always handcuffed and chained to this endless cycle of birth and death.

◦◦◦

Through the true Word one finds true honour;
without the Lord's Name, there is no salvation.
Without the True Guru, none finds the Name;
the Lord has willed it thus.

Sachai sabad sachee pat hoee. Bin naavai mukat na paavai koee.
Bin satgur ko naao na paae prabh aisee banat banaaee he.

Guru Nanak Sahib has conveyed beautifully the whole philosophy and message of every saint in this one stanza. He says: "Through the true Word one finds true honour." If we meditate on the Shabd, we will gain true honour and glory in the court of the Lord, and the privilege of meeting the Lord will be bestowed on us. Apart from this, he says, there is absolutely no way to escape from the imprisonment of the body.

He also says that this meditation will only be possible with the help of a saint, a lover of God. What is the need for a saint, a Master, when there are innumerable scriptures for us to read and so many enlightened souls giving discourses? Guru Sahib says: "The Lord has willed it thus." This is the natural law of God's creation, and until we are obedient to this law, until we find a Master and practise meditation on the Word under his guidance, we will never escape from the limitations of the body, we will never attain salvation. Guru Sahib says:

> The Lord himself is both the doer and the cause,
> and He himself enshrines the Guru's Word in
> the heart.
> *Aape kartaa kare karaae.*
> *Aape sabad gur man vasaae.*
>
> Adi Granth, M3, p. 125

Whatever the Lord does, He does through his own Will. If He wishes to take a soul out of the creation, He attaches that soul, through the grace of the Masters, to the Word of God. Guru Sahib lovingly explains that whatever we are to gain will be through the practice of the Name; that this practice can be learned only through the Masters; and that we will find a Master only through the mercy, grace, and benevolence of the Lord.

❧

While some seek enlightenment through yogic practices
and some through the intellect,
there are some who remain immersed, day and night,
in the Formless.

Those the Lord unites with himself, they alone realize Him.
Through devotion and love, all fears are dispelled.

Ik sidh saadhik bahut weechaaree.
Ik ahinis naam rate nirankaaree.
Jis no aap milaae so boojhai bhagat bhaae bhao jaaee he.

Enlightenment is never gained through holy baths
and works of charity,
but by vanquishing the mind alone,
as though fighting a great battle.
Dyed in the unifying colour of the true Word,
they leave duality and are merged with the true Word.

Isnaan daan karah nahee boojhah.
Ik manooaa maar maanai sio loojhah.
Saachai sabad rate ik rangee saachai sabad milaaee he.

He himself creates beings, He himself bestows honour,
He himself brings union through his divine Will.
Through his own grace He abides in the mind;
my Lord has ordained it so.

Aape sirje de wadiaaee. Aape bhaane de-e milaaee.
Aape nadar kare man wasiaa merai prabh io furmaaee he.

Know them to be true who serve the Satguru;
false are the self-willed, who know not how to serve him.
The Lord himself creates, and watches his creation;
He makes it act according to his Will.

Satguru sevah so jan saache. Manmukh sev na jaanan kaache.
Aape kartaa kar kar wekhai jio bhaavai tio laaee he.

In every age He is the Truth, the one benevolent Lord.
When one's destiny is perfect,
He is realized through the Guru's Word.
Those united to Him through the holy Word
are never separated;
His glance of grace bestows bliss on them.

Jug jug saachaa eko daataa. Poorai bhaag gur sabad pachhaataa.
Sabad mile se wichhure naahee nadree sahaj milaaee he.

Through ego one gathers the dirt of illusion;
caught in duality, one suffers in the circle of
birth and death.
Without serving the Satguru, there is no salvation;
with this realization, will the mind become absorbed.

Haomai maa-i-aa mail kamaa-i-aa. Mar mar jammah doojaa bhaa-i-aa.
Bin satgur seve mukat na hoee man dekhah liv laaee he.

That alone comes to pass as is willed by the Lord;
of itself nothing has ever happened, nor ever shall.
Through the Lord's Name,
O Nanak, come honour and glory,
and one is exalted at the gate of the true Lord.

Jo tis bhaavai soee karsee. Aapah hoaa naa kichh hosee.
Naanak naam milai wadiaaee dar saachai pat paaee he.

Endnotes

1. *Shabdarath Sri Guru Granth Sahib Ji*, 4 volumes (Amritsar: Shromani Gurdwara Prabandhak Committee), hereafter referred to as *Adi Granth*.

2. "Whatever we sow, it is that we shall reap—this life is **a field of actions**" *(Jehaa beejai so lunai karmaa sandraa khet)*. Adi Granth, M5, p. 134.

3. Soami Ji, *Sar Bachan Radhaswami, Chhand Band* (Beas: Radha Soami Satsang Beas), hereafter referred to as *Sar Bachan*.

4. Allahabad: Belvedere, 1967.

5. Allahabad: Belvedere, 1980 (hereafter referred to as *Kabir Sakhi Sangreh*).

6. Allahabad: Belvedere, 1967 (hereafter referred to as *Paltu Sahib ki Bani*).

7. Jesus says, "The kingdom of God is within you" (Luke 17:21). John the Baptist says, "Repent, for the kingdom of heaven is at hand" (Matthew 3:2).

8. *Jahaa[n] aasaa tahaa[n] baasaa* (Indian proverb).

9. Two proverbs that the speaker quoted regularly: *Eh jag mitthaa, aglaa kin ditthaa* (Indian proverb) and *Baabar ba-aish kosh ke aalam dobaaraa nest* (Persian proverb).

10. The speaker uses the Punjabi idiom, *"Saade man te safedee jitnaa asar nahee[n] hondaa"*—"It doesn't even have as much effect on our mind as whitewash."

11. *Haathee ke paao[n] me[n] sab kaa paao[n]* (Indian proverb). Literally: "All footprints fit into the elephant's footprint."

12. Edited by Parashuram Chaturvedi (Varanasi: Nagri Pracharni Sabha, 1966), hereafter referred to as *Dadu Dayal*.

13. *See* endnote 8.

14. "In the beginning was the Word, and the Word was with God, and the Word was God" (John 1:1).

[15] "And the Word was made flesh, and dwelt among us" (John 1:14).

[16] "I am in my Father, and ye in me, and I in you" (John 14:20). "He that hath seen me hath seen the Father.... Believest thou not that I am in the Father, and the Father in me?" (John 14:9-10). "I pray for them that they all may be one; as thou, Father, art in me, and I in thee, that they also may be one in us.... And the glory which thou gavest me I have given them; that they may be one, even as we are one. I in them, and thou in me, that they may be made perfect in one" (John 17:21-23).

[17] Allahabad: Belvedere.

[18] *See* endnote 7.

[19] "For we are a temple of the living God; even as God said, I will dwell in them, and walk in them; and I will be their God and they shall be my people" (2 Corinthians 6:16). "Know ye not that ye are a temple of God and that the Spirit of God dwelleth in you? If any man destroyeth the temple of God, him shall God destroy; for the temple of God is holy, which temple ye are" (1 Corinthians 3:16).

[20] *Tere bhaane sarbat kaa bhalaa.* Part of the traditional Sikh prayer (the Ardas), recited daily and at ceremonial functions.

[21] *See* endnote 8.

[22] *See* endnote 8.

[23] *See* endnote 14.

[24] "I am in my Father, and ye in me, and I in you" (John 14:20).

[25] *Aasaa^n parbat jediaa^n, maut tanaavaa^n heth* (Indian proverb).

[26] *See* endnote 7.

[27] *See* endnote 19.

[28] "True worshippers shall worship the Father in spirit and in truth: for the Father seeketh such to worship him. God is spirit: and they that worship him must worship him in spirit and in truth" (John 4:23-24).

[29] Kashi: Nagri Pracharni Sabha, 1959.

[30] Hadith, a collection of stories and sayings attributed to Prophet Muhammad.

[31] 1 Corinthians 15:31.

³² Beas: Radha Soami Satsang Beas, 1995, p. 299.
³³ *See* endnote 2.
³⁴ *See* endnote 25.
³⁵ A metaphor for a hypocritical devotee *(bhaglaa bhagat),* since the heron stands motionless on one leg with eyes half-closed like a yogi, when in fact it is about to catch a fish.
³⁶ *See* endnote 2.
³⁷ *See* endnote 8.
³⁸ "He knows the unutterable Lore, who has merged in the Satguru" *(Akath kathaaa veechaaree-ai je satgur maahe samaae).*
Adi Granth, M1, p. 62, context: *Raam naam man bedhiaa.*
"Our coming and going ceases when we merge in the true Name" *(Aavan jaanaa thaak rahaae, sachai naam samaavaniaa).*
Adi Granth, M1, p. 109.
"Blessed that place where God's praise is ever sung, where we are merged in the true Word" *(Bais suthaan sad hargun gaavai, sachai sabad samaavaniaa).*
Adi Granth, M3, p. 124, context: *Is gufaa mah akhut bhandaaraa.*
³⁹ The speaker is quoting here from the following stanza: "The five in unison sing the joyous song; between them and the Lord, now no difference remains" *(Panch janaa mil mangal gaaiaa har naanak bhed na bhaaee,* Adi Granth, M5, p. 205).
⁴⁰ Edited by Faqir Muhammad (Lahore: Punjabi Adabi Academy, 1970), Kuliyat 60, p. 119.
⁴¹ Allahabad: Belvedere, 1967.
⁴² *See* endnote 2.
⁴³ *See* endnote 8.
⁴⁴ *See* endnote 19.
⁴⁵ "Warrior, priest, merchant, artisan—my teachings are the same for all four castes" *(Khatree braahman sood vais updes chahu varnaa kau saanjhaa),* Adi Granth, M5, p. 747.
⁴⁶ *See* endndote 20.
⁴⁷ *See* endnote 8.
⁴⁸ Edited by Faqir Muhammad (Lahore: Punjabi Adabi Academy, 1970), Kuliyat 60, p. 119.
⁴⁹ Allahabad: Belvedere.

Glossary

Adi Granth   Primal *(aadi)*, scripture *(granth);* known also as 'Guru Granth Sahib' and 'Granth Sahib'. Sacred scripture of the Sikhs.

Agam   *See* **Sach Khand.**

ages   *See* **Kaliyug.**

Alakh   *See* **Sach Khand.**

Amritsar   Situated in Punjab, it is the most sacred city for the Sikhs.

Asa di Var   A section of the Adi Granth.

attributive names   Descriptive *(varnaatmak)* names *(naam);* always used in contradistinction to the melodious *(dhunaatmak)* Name, which refers to the creative power of God. Attributive names are words that can be written, spoken and read; names which describe (indicate the attributes of) that which they refer to. They are symbols of the reality they indicate, whereas the melodious Name is the divine power, the reality itself.

Ayodhya   A town in Uttar Pradesh, believed to be the birthplace of Lord Ram and held sacred by Hindus.

Babar   The founder of the Mughal dynasty, who conquered Delhi in 1526, in the days of Guru Nanak.

Balkh-Bokhara, king of   Ibrahim Adham, the king of Bokhara, a devoted disciple of Kabir, who, legend tells, did menial work for twelve years before Kabir saw fit to bestow upon him the precious gift of the Name, after which he lost interest in his kingdom.

Bank Nal   Crooked, curved or oblique *(ba^{n}k)* tunnel or passage *(naal)*, which leads from Sahansdal Kanwal to Trikuti.

Bhanwar Gupha   Revolving *(bha^nwar)* cave *(guphaa)*; refers to the fourth spiritual region. *See also* **Sach Khand.**

bhog jooniaan   Life forms *(jooniaa^n)* that undergo or suffer *(bhog)* actions, rather than initiate actions *(karam)*; they are simply reaping the harvest of actions of previous lives. Of all the life forms, human beings alone have the active power of discrimination, which gives them limited free will and the ability to choose a course of action that will lead them out of the cycle of transmigration. Thus, only humans are described as *karam jooniaa^n*. *See also* **chaurasi; vital elements.**

Brahm   The ruler of the three worlds, Triloki (the physical, astral and causal worlds); the universal mind, known also as Kal. Brahm's seat is Trikuti, the second of five regions above the physical plane. This is the home of the mind, the seedbank or source of all action (karma). Saints explain the universe by saying that all that is subject to change and death falls within the realm of Brahm. *See also* **Sach Khand; regions.**

Bulleh Shah (1680–1758)   Born into a high-class Muslim family (Sayyad), he was known as a scholar of theology; he lived in Kasur, near Lahore, and incurred the wrath of his community when he became the disciple of the mystic saint Inayat Shah of Lahore, a simple gardener. Bulleh Shah's poetry and songs of mystical love and longing are still recited and sung in India and Pakistan today.

caste   Four divisions of Hindu society: priests and scholars (brahmin), warriors (kshatriya), merchants and all professionals (vaishya), menial workers (shudra); a pattern of social organization that evolved from an early guild system and was formalized by Manu in *Manu Smriti,* the code of conduct which is central to Hindu society. Intended to define individual responsibility and patterns of social interdependence, it became a means of oppression by one section of society over another and even persuaded people that they had less or no rights to worship God.

chaurasi   Eighty-four; refers to the eighty-four lakh (8,400,000) species or life forms by which Indian philosophy describes the manifest creation. It is described as a cycle, a circle or a wheel—an endless round of life and death—due to the law of karma, whereby all life forms have to undergo the consequences of their own actions. The soul moves from one form to another, reaping the harvest of seeds it has sown in previous lives, and is thus trapped for aeons in separation from its source. Saints describe the soul's pain by speaking of chaurasi as a prison, an entangling web, a vast net, the fearful ocean of existence. *See also* **vital elements; karma.**

collyrium *(anjan)* Made of herbs and various substances, collyrium is imputed with magical properties and is used in the eyes to improve sight. The mystics of the East use it as a metaphor, conveying the power of the Word to bring sight to the spiritually blind.

cycle of transmigration, cycle of death and rebirth *See* **chaurasi.**

Dadu (1544–1603) A saint of Rajasthan, formerly Rajputana, a cotton carder from a Muslim family. Legend tells that Dadu made a deep impression on the Mughal emperor Akbar, who, known for his secular views, brought together at his court scholars, theologians and saints of all religions. It is said that Dadu's famous verse, defining God as love and quoted by Maharaj Charan Singh in the discourses, was spoken by him at Akbar's court. Known as Dadu Dayal, Dadu the Merciful, for his extremely compassionate nature.

darshan Beholding, seeing. The term is used to designate seeing at the physical level whenever there is inherent respect for the object or person whom one sees, including seeing the Master's physical form (outer darshan). True darshan (inner darshan) takes place at an inner level of consciousness and is the encounter between the disciple and the Radiant Form of the Master; it is the surrendering of the self and the absorption of the disciple into the Shabd, the Word, which is the Master's Radiant Form.

Dark Age *See* **Kaliyug.**

Dera   Habitation, tent, encampment; refers here to Dera Baba Jaimal Singh (near Amritsar, Punjab), a residential colony on the banks of the river Beas. Since the 1890s, when Baba Jaimal Singh (1839–1903) first settled at this spot, it has been a centre for spiritual activity, growing from a barren wilderness with a few mud houses to a small township with modern amenities, tree-lined roads, and different types of accommodation catering to the needs of the vast sangat. Much of the land has been reclaimed from the ravines that originally edged the river Beas.

dhyan   Attention, concentration, contemplation; the second aspect of the spiritual practice taught by the saints, in which the disciple contemplates on the form of the Master so as to hold the mind still at the eye centre. True contemplation is achieved naturally once the attention is focused and the mind becomes fully concentrated. *See also* **simran.**

dissolution, grand dissolution *(pralay, mahaa pralay)*   The process whereby the creative power, the Word, is withdrawn from the creation, the five vital elements disunite, and the manifest creation is dissolved. The same process takes place in the human body at the time of death. Dissolution *(pralay)* indicates the end of the creation up to the level of Daswan Dwar, the third region beyond the physical; grand dissolution *(mahaa pralay)* indicates the end of everything to the level of Bhanwar Gupha, the fourth region. *See also* **regions; Sach Khand.**

doors, nine *(nau darvaaze)*   Referred to also as the nine gateways or openings of the body: the two eyes, two ears, two nostrils, the mouth, and the openings of procreation and elimination, through which the attention, the soul current, disperses out into the world.

Draupadi   The wife of the five Pandav brothers, an important figure in the great Indian epic, the Mahabharat, which is deeply embedded in the psyche of the Indian people and recounts the war between the Pandavs and the Kauravs, presided over by Lord Krishna.

Duryodhan   The eldest of the Kaurav brothers, who fought their cousins, the Pandavs, in the great battle of the Mahabharat.

Duryodhan's lifelong jealousy and hatred of his cousins led to the war.

elements *See* **vital elements.**

eye centre Also referred to as the tenth door, the gateway to liberation, the third eye; a place between and slightly above the two eyes where the disciple focuses the attention in order to pass to a higher level of consciousness. Known in different cultures and religions by different terms, it marks the transition point of the two stages of the spiritual journey. Once the soul passes beyond the eye centre, the disciple is always conscious of the Word. As long as the attention remains below the eye centre, the Word cannot attract the soul of the disciple and the attention is dissipated through the mind and senses in the lower pleasures. *See also* **Word.**

Farid (1173–1265) Born near Multan in northwestern India, now Pakistan, Baba Farid was a disciple of Khwaja Qutabuddin Bakhtiar Kaki and an adept of the path of the Word. Baba Farid, or Sheikh Farid as he is also known, is the earliest recorded poet of the Punjabi language, his writings having been preserved in the Adi Granth.

five elements *See* **vital elements.**

five robbers, five passions *See* **passions.**

fourth realm *See* **realms.**

gateway to liberation *See* **eye centre.**

gayatri mantra A sacred incantation recited daily by all orthodox Hindus, which it is believed brings a degree of peace of mind to the devout practitioner.

Gurdas (1551–1636) Known always as Bhai Gurdas, he was the maternal uncle of Guru Arjan, the fifth Guru in the line of Guru Nanak; he served as scribe to Guru Arjan when he collated the writings of the saints and Gurus for the Adi Granth.

gurdwara Door *(dwaaraa)* to the Guru; the name given to the place of worship of the Sikh community.

gurmukh One whose face *(mukh)* is turned towards the Guru (the

Lord), as opposed to a *manmukh,* one whose face is turned towards the mind (the world). Defined in the discourses as a person who keeps the company of the saints and practises meditation on the Word, and used frequently to refer to the Masters. *See also* **Translators' Note.**

Guru Amardas (1479–1574)   Third Guru in the line of succession of Guru Nanak.

Guru Angad (1504–1552)   Second Guru in the line of succession of Guru Nanak.

Guru Arjan (1563–1606)   Fifth Guru in the line of succession of Guru Nanak.

Guru Gobind Singh (1666–1708)   Tenth Guru in the line of succession of Guru Nanak.

Guru Nanak (1469–1539)   Born near Lahore (now in Pakistan), Guru Nanak Sahib spent a large part of his life travelling to spread the doctrine of the Name. In days when there was no mechanized form of transport, legend says that he went as far as the south of India and to Mecca in the West. He was the first Guru in the line of the ten Gurus whose teachings are recorded in the Adi Granth and who are referred to in this book as 'the Gurus'. Like all true saints, Guru Nanak swept away the prejudices and superstitions of organized religious belief, emphasizing that ritualistic practices and external forms keep the seeker of God from the truth. *See also* **Translators' Note.**

Guru Ramdas (1534–1581)   Fourth Guru in the line of succession of Guru Nanak.

Guru Sahib   An honorific used to refer to any Guru, and used specifically in the Sikh community and culture to refer to the ten Gurus in the line of Guru Nanak.

the Gurus   *See* **Guru Nanak.**

habitual criminals *(das nambariyaa^n)*   Translates a reference to a commonly known aspect of the Indian police system, used for identifying habitual offenders. A metaphor depicting the condition of the soul perpetually caught up in the wheel of chaurasi by the karmic law.

Hathras A town near Agra in Uttar Pradesh, where Tulsi Sahib settled and taught.

Hazur Maharaj Ji *See* Maharaj **Sawan Singh.**

house of Shri Guru Nanak Refers to the writings of the Gurus in the line of Guru Nanak.

householder's life A familiar concept in Indian thought, where human life is traditionally divided into four phases; the householder phase is when the individual faces his or her responsibilities towards the family as a provider and carer. Saints continually point out that it is not necessary to renounce the world, but that it is necessary to integrate spiritual practice into one's daily life.

hypocrite Used to translate the term *'bhekhdhaaree'*, a sect of yogis or ascetics recognizable by their appearance *(bhekh)*. The word also has the connotation of disguise and a misleading exterior.

Japji Recite *(jap)*. The name of the opening section of the Adi Granth, written by Guru Nanak and recited daily by devout Sikhs.

Ka'aba The focal point of the Islamic world; a sacred building in Mecca containing the sacred black stone. Devout Muslims always face Mecca, the birthplace of Prophet Muhammad, when praying, and aspire to make a pilgrimage *(haj)* to Mecca at least once during their lifetime.

Kabir (1398–1518) One of the best-known saints of India. Part of his writings were incorporated into the Adi Granth in 1604. Kabir Sahib was a contemporary of Guru Nanak and lived hardly half a century after the great flowering of mysticism in Europe and Britain (Richard Rolle, Mother Julian of Norwich, Meister Eckhart, Thomas a Kempis, and others). His writings are still widely quoted in daily life throughout India and have been incorporated into folk music and culture. Legend surrounds his birth and background, and both Hindus and Muslims claim him as theirs. He travelled extensively and taught the practice of the Word, speaking out against external forms of worship and all institutionalized centres of power that keep people from the truth.

Kal *(kaal)* Time or Death; the negative power, known as Dharam Rai (the lord of judgement) and Yama (the lord of death). Kal is the personification of the negative force in the creation, in contradistinction to Dayal (the Merciful), the eternal positive power, the Supreme Being. Dependent for all power on the Supreme Being, Kal is the universal mind, known also as Brahm, the ruler of the three worlds (physical, astral, causal). *See also* **Sach Khand.**

Kaliyug The Dark Age, the Iron Age. Hindu mythology divides time into four great ages *(yug)*, following each other in endless recurring cycles: Satyug, Tretayug, Dwaparyug, Kaliyug. Saints use this mythology to portray the ever-changing nature of the universe.

karma Action; the law of action and reaction, of cause and effect, whereby the soul has to face the consequences of all its actions. It is the law of karma that keeps the soul imprisoned in the creation, as it has to endlessly take birth in different forms to keep settling its accounts. There are three types of karma: pralabdh (or *praarabdh)* karma, the fate or destiny the soul experiences in the present life—the karmic account arising from a portion of its previous actions; kriyaman karma, the debits and credits created by actions in the present life that are to be settled in future lives; sinchit (or *sanchit)* karma, the balance or store of unsettled karmas. The soul cannot escape from the cycle of death and rebirth and reunite with its source until its karmic account is fully settled. *See also* **chaurasi.**

Kashmir Valley Referred to by Maharaj Charan Singh because it has long been thought of as one of the most beautiful scenic places on earth.

Krishna An incarnation of Vishnu, the sustainer, one of the three gods of the Hindu triad (Brahma, the creator; Vishnu; and Shiv, the destroyer). Lord Krishna is much loved and worshipped across India.

kun   An Islamic term designating 'Be!', the divine command or power, synonymous with the Word, the Shabd, the Command *(hukam)*.

line of Gurus   Refers specifically to the ten Gurus in the line of Guru Nanak.

lotus feet   A translation of the term *charan*, which literally means 'revered feet', having a connotation of love and respect. When used in reference to a spiritual Master, it designates the Master's Radiant Form.

Maha Sunn   The great void; an inner spiritual region that is devoid of matter in any form; part of the third spiritual region (Daswan Dwar), a level of impenetrable darkness that can be crossed only with the help of and in the company of a perfect Master.

Mansur (870–923)   Persian mystic, known also as Hazrat Mansur-al-Hallaj. For proclaiming in a state of mystic ecstasy that he was God, he was stoned, dismembered and put to death by the orthodoxy.

manmukh   One whose face *(mukh)* is turned towards the mind *(man)*, the world. A lover of the world, a self-willed person dominated by the ego, as opposed to the *gurmukh*, who lives in the will of the Lord.

maya   Illusion; often described as the web of illusion; denotes everything that comes and goes, that is transient; the entire creation, the three worlds, ruled by Brahm. It is described as illusory and false because it is impermanent, in contrast to Satnam, the true Name, the Supreme Being, which alone is permanent, eternal and true.

Mira Bai (1498–1563)   A Rajput princess, she was married into the princely state of Chittorgarh. She was a devotee of Lord Krishna until she met her Master, Sant Ravidas. Her poetry is still sung throughout the villages of Rajasthan.

Namdev (1270–1350)   Born in Maharashtra, he was a disciple of

Visoba Khechar. He spent the latter part of his life in Punjab and died in the village of Ghuman, the birthplace of Baba Jaimal Singh. Some of Baba Namdev's writings are included in the Adi Granth, and others have been preserved in *Namdev Gatha*.

Name *(naam)*   Known in the different religions under a multitude of names, it designates the dynamic power of God, which creates, enlivens and sustains the universe, and through which the soul returns to its source. The central reality of the teachings of the saints. *See also* **Word; attributive names.**

nine gateways, nine doors   *See* **doors.**

ocean of existence *(bhav saagar)*   Also described as the fearful ocean, the ocean of phenomena. It is used as a metaphor for the three worlds (the physical, astral and causal), where the soul 'drowns' under the weight of its karma. *See also* **chaurasi.**

Padshahi   Lit., 'Your Highness', from *paadshaah*, 'emperor' (Persian). Commonly used by the Sikh people when referring to the ten Gurus. *See also* **Translators' Note.**

Paltu (1710–1780)   Referred to as Paltu Sahib, he was a disciple of Govind Sahib and lived in Ayodhya, Uttar Pradesh, a town sacred to the Hindus. He spoke out fearlessly against the prejudices and superstitions of organized religion and was consequently burned to death.

Pandavs   The five sons of King Pandu, who fought their cousins, the Kauravs, in the great war of the Mahabharat to regain their kingdom.

parshad   A blessing, grace; generally used to refer to something blessed by the Master, whether food or anything else. In the context of this book, parshad refers to the gift of initiation.

passions   Five modes of destructive mental action, perversions of the intrinsic nature of the mind. The five passions are: lust *(kaam)*, anger *(krodh)*, greed *(lobh)*, attachment *(moh)* and ego *(ahankaar)*. Referred to as the five robbers, they deprive the soul of its rightful inheritance, which is union with the

Lord. Acting as agents of Kal, in cahoots with the senses, they keep the mind enmeshed below the eye centre, involved in the outer world.

pralabdh   *See* **karma.**

prison of chaurasi   *See* **chaurasi.**

Radha Soami   Lord (swami) of the soul (radha); refers to the absolute Supreme Being, known also as the Nameless One.

Ramchandra   Also known as Lord Ram, said to be the seventh incarnation of the god Vishnu, the sustainer; the hero of the Ramayan, the oldest Sanskrit epic poem. The festival of Diwali, celebrated every year in India, commemorates Ram's victory over Ravan, when he rescued his wife, Sita, from Ravan's kingdom and returned victorious to Ayodhya.

Ravan   Ravan was the legendary king of Lanka when Ramchandra was king of Ayodhya. Ravan's effigy is burnt every year ten days before the festival of Diwali, to celebrate the victory of good over evil. In spite of having the four Vedas at his fingertips and being renowned as a scholar without parallel, Ravan became a victim of his passions when, out of revenge, he abducted Ramchandra's wife, Sita, as recounted in the great epic of the Ramayan.

Ravidas   Lived in the fifteenth and early sixteenth centuries in Kashi (now Varanasi, Uttar Pradesh) and in Rajasthan; a contemporary of Kabir, Guru Ravidas was a cobbler by trade and travelled widely, teaching the path of devotion to the Word. Some of his compositions are included in the Adi Granth. Among his disciples were the princess of Merta, Mira Bai, and Raja Pipa, a Rajput warrior-saint.

realms   The four great realms or divisions of the universe: *Sach Khand,* the spiritual (the ocean of the true Name, the home and source of the soul). Its reflection, *Brahmand,* the causal (the home of the universal mind from which all individual minds are derived); its reflection, *And,* the astral (including all the heavens and paradises); its reflection, *Pind,* the physical. Sach Khand is the positive pole of the creation, pure spirit;

Pind is the negative pole, gross matter, with just enough mental and spiritual substance present to give it life and motion; And and Brahmand partake of the properties of both, growing more positive from below upwards.

regions   Refers to five regions or spheres of consciousness, which the soul crosses or experiences on its journey to perfection, to God-realization: Sahansdal Kanwal (the thousand-petal lotus, the astral region); Trikuti (the three prominences, the causal region); Daswan Dwar (the tenth door, the first level of the spiritual realm), also referred to as Sunn; Bhanwar Gupha (the revolving cave, the second level of the spiritual realm where the soul first recognizes God but still retains consciousness of its separate existence); and Sach Khand (the realm of truth, the region of pure spirit where the soul merges into its source).

Sach Khand   True, eternal, immutable *(sach)* realm or region *(khand);* the realm of pure spirit, unalloyed by even the most subtle forms of matter, by change, transience or death. This realm or level of being is sometimes further divided into three: the invisible realm, Alakh; the inaccessible realm, Agam; the nameless realm, Anami, Radha Soami. The entire universe is described either in terms of four grand divisions or realms: the physical, astral, causal and spiritual (Pind, And, Brahmand and Sach Khand, also known as Satlok); or in terms of five regions above the physical: Sahansdal Kanwal, Trikuti, Daswan Dwar, Bhanwar Gupha, Sach Khand. Sach Khand is also known as the ocean of Satnam (the true Name), through which the nameless, formless reality of God (Anami) is made manifest. It is the home of the soul. The divine power at this supreme level is referred to in the discourses as *parmaatmaa,* the Supreme Being, Almighty God, the supreme soul, and *maalik,* the Lord.

saint   This word is used in the book, not to designate a canonized person as is commonly understood in the Christian world, but to designate a liberated being who has escaped from the circle of transmigration, who has travelled beyond the three lower worlds and expanded his/her consciousness to the level of the fifth spiritual region, Sach Khand. It has been used in the book mostly to translate the word *gurmukh*. *See also* **Translators' Note.**

sangat Community or fellowship of disciples.

Sarmad (1618–1661) A Jewish trader from Kashan in Persia, Hazrat Sarmad settled in Delhi in his later years and taught the practice of devotion to the Word. He had a large following and antagonized the establishment of his day. He was beheaded under the orders of Emperor Aurangzeb in front of the Jamma Masjid in Old Delhi, where his tomb now stands. Legend tells that when he was beheaded, every drop of his blood called out "Ana-ul-haq" ('I am God!').

Satguru True *(sat)* Master *(guru)*.

Satnam True *(sat)* Name *(naam)*. *See also* **Name; Sach Khand.**

satsang Association *(sang)* with the true *(sat)*; commonly used to denote a spiritual discourse. Inner satsang, the highest form of satsang, is the conscious encounter of the soul with the Word (truth) on the inner planes of being.

Sawan Singh (1858–1948) Affectionately known as the Great Master, Maharaj Sawan Singh was the spiritual Master of Maharaj Charan Singh, who refers to him in the discourses as 'Hazur' and 'Hazur Maharaj Ji'. He was appointed by Baba Jaimal Singh as Satguru of the Radha Soami line at Beas in 1903; he was a scholar of Persian, wrote numerous books, and spread the teachings of the Word in India and abroad for almost fifty years.

seasons, six The Indian lunar calendar divides the year into six distinct seasons: the hot weather (April to June), monsoon (July, August), late summer (September, early October), autumn (late October, November), winter (December, January), spring (February, March).

Sehjo Bai A woman saint of Rajasthan, then Rajputana, who lived in the eighteenth century. A disciple of Saint Charandas. Her poems, simple and direct in expression, are full of devotion and love for the Master.

Shastras   Hindu scriptures; books of philosophy and moral code.
simran   Repetition, remembrance (from the Hindi *smaran*).
Simran is the first part of the spiritual practice taught by the
saints; its technique is given to the disciple at the time of initiation. Taking advantage of the mind's natural habit of unceasing activity, simran is the process whereby the attention is
withdrawn from the outer world and concentrated at the eye
centre. Once the mind is focused, dhyan (contemplation) automatically takes place. *See also* **dhyan.**
sinchit   *See* **karma.**
Soami Ji (1818–1878)   Born Shiv Dayal Singh in Agra, Uttar
Pradesh. As a child, he was raised on the scriptures of the Adi
Granth; he was a disciple of Tulsi Sahib of Hathras; he started
preaching the way of the Word after spending the greater part
of seventeen years meditating. Soami Ji (as he was called by
his disciples) gave out the universal teachings of the saints in
unveiled, simple language through his two books, *Sar Bachan
Poetry* and *Sar Bachan Prose*. His disciple and successor, Baba
Jaimal Singh, was the first Master to settle at the place now
known as the Radha Soami colony or Dera Baba Jaimal Singh,
in Punjab.
spiritual sky   Used to translate *gagan* (sky), and sometimes used
by mystics to refer to the highest reaches of Trikuti, the second region.
stages   *See* **realms; regions.**
suhaag   The married state of a woman, fulfilment, in contradistinction to the state of desolation *(duhaag)*, which describes
widowhood. A word specific to traditional Indian culture,
arising from the respect and recognized position in society
of a married woman *(suhaagan)*, it acquires its meaning in a
social context where the woman's aspirations are fulfilled in
marriage.
Sunn   *See* **regions.**
supreme soul   The literal rendering of *parmaatmaa*, the Supreme
Being. *See also* **Translators' Note.**
sustenance   Traditionally, in many parts of India, when a person

left home to go on a journey, special food was prepared to tide them over until they reached their destination or to sustain them in case of emergency, and it would be tied into a cloth bundle *(tosaa)* to protect it from the dust. The *tosaa* is often used by saints as a metaphor for the practice of the Name, as in: "Cherish the true Name; equip yourself with sustenance *(tosaa)* for this life and the next" *(Sant janhu mil bhaaeeho sachaa naam samaal. Tosaa bandhahu jeea kaa aithai othai naal.* Adi Granth, p. 49).

swindler, cheat Used to translate the Hindi word *thug*. In nineteenth-century India, bands of 'thugs' roamed the countryside with the intention of waylaying travellers. Their method was to win the confidence of the travellers, make friends with them and then rob them. They would often kill their victims. The word thug came into the English language from this period.

tattva *See* **vital elements.**
tenth door *See* **eye centre.**
third eye *See* **eye centre.**
thug *See* **swindler.**
Trikuti *See* **Brahm; regions.**
Tulsi Sahib (1764–1845) From the ruling family of the Peshwas in Maharashtra, he settled in Hathras, Uttar Pradesh. He was the Master of Soami Ji Maharaj and is known for his two books, *Ghat Ramayan* and *Ratan Sagar,* through which he expressed the teachings of the Word.

Vedas Knowledge; four early Indian scriptures (Rig Ved, Sama Ved, Yajur Ved, Atharva Ved); also refers to Vedic literature in general (including the Upanishads and various interpretive texts).

vital elements *(tattva)* Indian philosophy describes all life forms in terms of five tattvas or life-giving (vital) elements: earth *(prithvi)*, water *(jal)*, fire *(agni)*, air *(vaayu)* and ether *(aakaash)*. Only humans have all five active, so they are considered to be the highest form of life. The greater the number

of active tattvas, the greater the responsibility involved in kill-
ing that form, and the greater the burden of karma assumed.
This understanding motivates people to choose to lead a life
of non-violence, including a vegetarian diet, so the karmic
burden they incur is less. *See also* **karma; chaurasi.**

Word *(shabd)*   Known in the different religions under a multitude
of names, it designates the dynamic power of God which created, enlivens and sustains the universe, and through which
the soul returns to its source. The central reality of the teachings of the saints. *See also* **Name; attributive names.**

Yudhishtra   The eldest of the Pandav brothers in the great epic,
the Mahabharat.

Index

Addresses for Information and Books

INDIAN SUB-CONTINENT

INDIA
The Secretary
Radha Soami Satsang Beas
P.O. Dera Baba Jaimal Singh 143204
District Amritsar, Punjab

BAV Distribution Centre
Radha Soami Satsang Beas
5, Guru Ravi Dass Marg
Pusa Road, New Delhi 110 005

NEPAL
Mr. Prakash Gauchan
RSS(B)—Nepal
P.O. Box 1646
Sundarighat, Kirtipur, Kathmandu

SRI LANKA
Mr. D. H. Jiwat
c/o Geekay Ltd.
33 Bankshall Street, Colombo 11

SOUTHEAST ASIA

INDONESIA
Mr. Gope L. Nanwani
Jl. Kelinci Raya No. 32A
Jakarta Pusat 10710

MALAYSIA
Dr. Narjit Singh Dhaliwal
Kumpulan Perubatan SMP
18 Lorong Sempadan, Jalan 16/7
(or P.O. Box 7081)
Shah Alam 40702

SINGAPORE
Mr. Sajan Shankardas Nanwani
Beas Enterprises
111 North Bridge Road
#04-40 Peninsula Plaza
Singapore 0617

THAILAND
Mr. Harmahinder Singh Sethi
ASA International Ltd., Part.
43/17/-18, SOI Sawasdee,
Sukhumvit SOI 31, Bangkok 10110

ASIA PACIFIC

AUSTRALIA
Mrs. Janet Bland
P.O. Box 3, Oaklands Park
Adelaide, S. Australia 5046

HONG KONG
Mrs. Cami Moss
T.S.T., P.O. Box 97739, Kowloon

JAPAN
Mr. Jani Mohinani
1-1-10 Akamatsu-cho, Nada-ku
Kobe 657

NEW ZEALAND
Mr. Tony Waddicor
10 Maxine Place, Tauranga

PHILIPPINES
Mr. Kay Sham
P.O. Box 2346
MCC Makati, Metro Manila

385

TAIWAN R.O.C.
Mr. Larry T. Nanwani
No. 57 Tun Hwa South Road Sec. 1
Room 808, Choo Woo House
(*or* P.O. Box 68-1414), Taipei

NORTH AMERICA

CANADA
Mr. John W. Abel
701-1012 Beach Ave.
Vancouver, B.C. V6E 1T7

Dr. Peter Grayson
177 Division Street South
Kingsville, Ontario N9Y 1R1

UNITED STATES
Dr. Eugene Ivash
4701 Shadow Lane
Austin, TX 78731

Dr. Vincent P. Savarese
3507 Saint Elizabeth Road
Glendale, CA 91206

Dr. John Templer
114 Verdier Road
Beaufort, SC 29902

Dr. Frank Vogel
7 Pelham Terrace
Arlington, MA 02174

Science of the Soul Study Center
Route 24, Box 79
Fayetteville, NC 28306

CARIBBEAN ISLANDS

CARIBBEAN ISLANDS
Mr. Sean Finnigan
Villa Rosa, Canape Vert
(*or* P.O. Box 2314)
Port-au-Prince, Haiti

BARBADOS
Mr. Bhagwandas Kessaram Gopwani
c/o Kiddies Corner, 43 Swan Street
(*or* P.O. Box 603)
Bridgetown

TRINIDAD (WEST INDIES)
Mr. Thakurdas Chatlani
8A Saddle Road, Maraval

CENTRAL AMERICA

MEXICO
Mr. Jorge Angel Santana
Cometa 2821, Jardines del Bosque
Guadalajara, JAL 44520

For the following countries, contact:
Mr. Jorge Angel Santana, MEXICO

> **BELIZE**
> **COSTA RICA**
> **GUATEMALA**
> **HONDURAS**
> **NICARAGUA**
> **PANAMA**
> **SAN SALVADOR**

SOUTH AMERICA

BRAZIL
Mr. Alberto Cancio Ferreira
See PORTUGAL.

COLOMBIA
Mr. Alberto Garcia Botero
Calle 147 #23-21, Bogota

ECUADOR
Mr. Gonzalo Vargas Noriega
Calle Montalvo No. 200, Oficina 201
Edificio Ponce Larrea
(or P.O. Box 17-21-1477)
Quito

GUYANA
Mrs. Rajni B. Manglani
c/o Bhagwan's Store
18 Water Street, Georgetown

PERU
Mr. Gonzalo Vargas Noriega
See ECUADOR.

VENEZUELA
Mr. Jose Antonio Penaherrera
Calle Mohedano Con Sucre
Edif. Don Jose, Local 2
Apartado Postal 63-436
Chacaito, Caracas 1.016

EUROPE

AUSTRIA
Mr. Hansjorg Hammerer
Sezenweingasse 10
Salzburg A-5020

BELGIUM
Mr. Jacob Hofstra
See NETHERLANDS.

BULGARIA
Mr. Emil Saev
P.O. Box 342, Sofia 1000

CYPRUS
Mr. Heraclis Achilleos
18 Kyriacou Matsi, Flat 101
(or P.O. Box 9077)
Pallouriotissa, Nicosia 116

CZECH REPUBLIC
Mr. Vladimir Skalsky
Maratkova 916, Prague 4, 142 00

DENMARK
Mr. Rudolf Walberg
See GERMANY.

FRANCE
Mr. Pierre de Proyart
7 Quai Voltaire
Paris 75007

GERMANY
Mr. Rudolf Walberg
P.O. Box 1544
D-65800 Bad Soden/Taunus

GIBRALTAR
Mr. Sunder T. Mahtani
Radha Soami Satsang Beas
401 Ocean Heights

GREECE
Mr. Dimitrios Sotiriou
Moschoula 4, Penteli
Athens 152-36

ITALY
Mrs. Wilma Salvatori Torri
Via Bacchiglione 3-00199
Rome

NETHERLANDS, THE (HOLLAND)

Mr. Jacob Hofstra
Geulwijk 6, Leusden 3831 LM

NORWAY

Mr. Rudolf Walberg
See GERMANY.

PORTUGAL

Mr. Alberto Cancio Ferreira
Urb. do Buzano
Av. Comandante Gilberto
Duarte e Duarte, Lote 2, 3° Esq.
S. Domingos de Rana 2775

SLOVENIA

Mr. Marko Bedina
Brezje PRI, Trzicu 68, 4290 Trzic

SPAIN

Mr. Hiro W. Balani
Radha Soami Satsang Beas
Loma Del Valle, Cruce del Pinar
Alhaurin de la Torre
(or P.O. Box 486)
Malaga 29012

SWEDEN

Mr. Lennart Zachen
Norra Sonnarpsvagen 29
S-286 72 Asljunga

SWITZERLAND

Mr. Olivier de Coulon
Rue du Centre
Tolochenaz (VD) CH-1131

UNITED KINGDOM

Mrs. Flora E. Wood
Haynes Park
Haynes, Bedford MK45 3BL

AFRICA

BENIN

Mrs. Priya J. Vaswani
c/o Mr. Jaikumar Vaswani
B.P. 951, Cotonou

KENYA

Mr. Surinder Singh Ghir
P.O. Box 39993, Nairobi

MAURITIUS

Mrs. Doolaree Nuckcheddy
17 Leconte de Lisle Ave.
Quatre Bornes

MOROCCO

Mr. Hiro W. Balani
See SPAIN.

NIGERIA

Mr. Nanik N. Balani
120 Awolowo Road
(or G.P.O. Box 10407)
Ikoyi, Lagos

SOUTH AFRICA

Mr. Sam Busa
P.O. Box 41355, Craighall 2024

TANZANIA

Mr. Diljeet Nath Pandit
83 Lugalo Rd., East Upanga
(or P.O. Box 1963), Dar-es-Salaam

UGANDA

Mr. Sylvester Kakooza
Alanda Ltd., Plot 64, William Street
(or P.O. Box 31381), Kampala

ZIMBABWE

Mrs. Dorothy Roodt
102 Suffolk Rd., Strathaven
(or P.O. Box 7095), Harare

MIDDLE EAST

BAHRAIN, U.A.E.
Mrs. Shiela Chand
P.O. Box 3079

DUBAI, U.A.E
Mr. Chander Bhatia
Shabnam Trading Co.
P.O. Box 2296

ISRAEL
Mrs. H. Mandelbaum
P.O. Box 22121, Tel Aviv 61221

Radha Soami Satsang Beas®

BOOKS ON THIS SCIENCE

SOAMI JI MAHARAJ
Sar Bachan

BABA JAIMAL SINGH
Spiritual Letters (to Hazur Maharaj Sawan Singh: 1896-1903)

MAHARAJ SAWAN SINGH
The Dawn of Light (letters to Western disciples: 1911-1934)
Discourses on Sant Mat
My Submission (introduction to Philosophy of the Masters)
Philosophy of the Masters (Gurmat Sidhant), 5 vols.
  (an encyclopedia on the teachings of the Saints)
Philosophy of the Masters (abridged)
Spiritual Gems (letters to Western disciples: 1919-1948)
Tales of the Mystic East (as narrated in satsangs)

MAHARAJ JAGAT SINGH
The Science of the Soul (discourses and letters: 1948-1951)

MAHARAJ CHARAN SINGH
Die to Live (answers to questions on meditation)
Divine Light (discourses and letters: 1959-1964)
Light on Saint John
Light on Saint Matthew
Light on Sant Mat (discourses and letters: 1952-1958)
The Master Answers (to audiences in America: 1964)
The Path (first part of Divine Light)
Quest for Light (letters: 1965-1971)
Spiritual Discourses
Spiritual Heritage (from tape-recorded talks)
Teachings of the Saints (first chapter of Die to Live)
Thus Saith the Master (to audiences in America: 1970)
Truth Eternal (a discourse)

BOOKS ABOUT THE MASTERS
Call of the Great Master—Diwan Daryai Lal Kapur
Heaven on Earth—Diwan Daryai Lal Kapur
Treasure Beyond Measure—Shanti Sethi
With a Great Master in India—Julian P. Johnson
With the Three Masters, 3 volumes—from the diary of Rai Sahib
    Munshi Ram

BOOKS ON SANT MAT IN GENERAL
The Holy Name—Miriam Bokser Caravella
In Search of the Way—Flora E. Wood
The Inner Voice—Colonel C. W. Sanders
Liberation of the Soul—J. Stanley White
Message Divine—Shanti Sethi
Mystic Bible—Randolph Stone
The Mystic Philosophy of Sant Mat—Peter Fripp
Mysticism, The Spiritual Path, 2 volumes—Lekh Raj Puri
The Path of the Masters—Julian P. Johnson
Radha Soami Teachings— Lekh Raj Puri
A Soul's Safari—Netta Pfeifer
Teachings of the Gurus— Lekh Raj Puri
Yoga and the Bible—Joseph Leeming

MYSTICS OF THE EAST SERIES
Bulleh Shah—J. R. Puri and T.R. Shangari
Dadu, The Compassionate Mystic—K. N. Upadhyaya
Dariya Sahib, Saint of Bihar—K. N. Upadhyaya
Guru Nanak, His Mystic Teachings—J. R. Puri
Guru Ravidas, Life and Teachings—K. N. Upadhyaya
Kabir, The Great Mystic—Isaac A. Ezekiel
Kabir, The Weaver of God's Name—V. K. Sethi
Mira, The Divine Lover—V. K. Sethi
Saint Namdev, His Life and Teachings—J. R. Puri and V. K. Sethi
Saint Paltu—Isaac A. Ezekiel
Sant Charan Das—T. R. Shangari
Sarmad, Jewish Saint of India—Isaac A. Ezekiel
Sultan Bahu—J. R. Puri
Tukaram, Saint of Maharashtra—C. Rajwade
Tulsi Sahib, Saint of Hathras—J. R. Puri and V. K. Sethi